A Theory of African American Offending

A little more than a century ago, the famous social scientist W.E.B. Du Bois asserted that a true understanding of African American offending must be grounded in the "real conditions" of what it means to be black living in a racially stratified society. Today and according to official statistics, African American men—about 6 percent of the population of the United States—account for nearly 60 percent of the robbery arrests in the United States. To the authors of this book, this and many other glaring racial disparities in offending centered on African Americans is clearly related to their unique history and to their past and present racial subordination. Inexplicably, however, no criminological theory exists that fully articulates the nuances of the African American experience and how they relate to their offending. In readable fashion for undergraduate students, the general public, and criminologists alike, this book for the first time presents a theory of African American offending.

James D. Unnever is an Associate Professor of Criminology at the University of South Florida Sarasota-Manatee. Dr. Unnever was the recipient of the Donal A.J. MacNamara Award by the Academy of Criminal Justice Sciences in 2009. The author of over 40 publications appearing in such journals as *Social Forces, Criminology, Social Problems, Journal of Research in Crime and Delinquency*, and *Justice Quarterly*, Dr. Unnever was ranked as the fifth most innovative author in criminology from 2000–2010. His areas of expertise include race and crime, public opinion about crime-related issues including the death penalty, the testing of theories of crime, and school bullying. Professor Unnever can be contacted at unnever@sar.usf.edu.

Shaun L. Gabbidon is Distinguished Professor of Criminal Justice in the School of Public Affairs at Penn State Harrisburg. Dr. Gabbidon has served as a fellow at Harvard University's W.E.B. Du Bois Institute for Afro-American Research, and as an adjunct faculty member in the Center for Africana Studies at the University of Pennsylvania. The author of more than 100 scholarly publications including 50 peer-reviewed articles and 12 books, his most recent books include *Race, Ethnicity, Crime and Justice: An International Dilemma* and *Criminological Perspectives on Race and Crime* (2nd edition). Dr. Gabbidon currently serves as the editor of the new SAGE journal, *Race and Justice: An International Journal*. The recipient of numerous awards, Dr. Gabbidon was most recently awarded the 2009 W.E.B. Du Bois Award from the Western Society of Criminology for his outstanding contributions in the area of race, ethnicity, and justice. Dr. Gabbidon can be contacted at slg13@psu.edu.

Criminology and Justice Studies Series

Edited by **Chester Britt**, *Northeastern University*, **Shaun L. Gabbidon**, *Penn State Harrisburg*, and **Nancy Rodriguez**, *Arizona State University*

Criminology and Justice Studies offers works that make both intellectual and stylistic innovations in the study of crime and criminal justice. The goal of the series is to publish works that model the best scholarship and thinking in the criminology and criminal justice field today, but in a style that connects that scholarship to a wider audience including advanced undergraduates, graduate students, and the general public. The works in this series help fill the gap between academic monographs and encyclopedic textbooks by making innovative scholarship accessible to a large audience without the superficiality of many texts.

Books in the Series
Published:
Biosocial Criminology: New Directions in Theory and Research edited by Anthony Walsh and Kevin M. Beaver
Community Policing in America by Jeremy M. Wilson
Criminal Justice Theory: Explaining the Nature and Behavior of Criminal Justice edited by David E. Duffee and Edward R. Maguire
Lifers: Seeking Redemption in Prison by John Irwin
Race, Law and American Society: 1607 to Present by Gloria J. Browne-Marshall
Today's White Collar Crime by Hank J. Brightman
White Collar Crime: Opportunity Perspectives by Michael Benson and Sally Simpson
The New Criminal Justice: American Communities and the Changing World of Crime Control by John Klofas, Natalie Hipple, and Edmund McGarrell
The Policing of Terrorism: Organizational and Global Perspectives by Mathieu Deflem
Criminological Perspectives on Race and Crime, 2/e by Shaun Gabbidon
Corrections by Jeanne Stinchcomb
Community Policing by Michael Palmiotto

Forthcoming:
Crime and the Lifecourse by Michael Benson
Structural Equations Modeling for Criminology and Criminal Justice by George Higgins
Crime Emergence: Reducing Uncertainty in Theory and Research by Christopher Sullivan, Jean McGloin, and Les Kennedy
Criminal Justice Research by Brian Withrow
Experiencing Criminal Justice: Practitioners' and Outsiders' Perspectives of Policing, Courts, and Corrections edited by Heith Copes and Mark Pogrebin
Program Evaluation for Criminal and Juvenile Justice by J. Mitchell Miller and Holly Ventura Miller
Causes of Delinquency Revisited by Chester Britt and Barbara Costello

A Theory of African American Offending
Race, Racism, and Crime

James D. Unnever
University of South Florida Sarasota-Manatee

Shaun L. Gabbidon
Penn State Harrisburg

NEW YORK AND LONDON

First published 2011
by Routledge
711 Third Avenue, New York, NY 10017

Simultaneously published in the UK
by Routledge
2 Park Square, Milton Park, Abingdon, Oxon OX14 4RN

Routledge is an imprint of the Taylor & Francis Group, an informa business

Library of Congress Cataloging-in-Publication Data
Unnever, James D.
Race, Racism, and Crime: A Theory of African American Offending/
James D. Unnever, Shaun L. Gabbidon.
p. cm.—(Criminology and Justice Studies Series)
1. Crime and race—United States. 2. Discrimination in criminal justice administration—United States. 3. African Americans. 4. African American criminals. I. Gabbidon, Shaun L., 1967– II. Title.
HV6197.U5U56 2011
364.3´496073—dc22
2010039487

ISBN: 978–0–415–88357–3 (hbk)
ISBN: 978–0–415–88358–0 (pbk)
ISBN: 978–0–203–82856–4 (ebk)

Typeset in Caslon by RefineCatch Limited, Bungay, Suffolk
Printed and bound in the United States of America on acid-free paper by Walsworth Publishing Company, Marceline, MO

SUSTAINABLE FORESTRY INITIATIVE

Certified Sourcing

www.sfiprogram.org

The SFI label applies to the text stock.

Dedication

This book is for my parents, who I have recently lost. Its foundation is built upon their honesty and concern for others.
J.D.U.

This book is dedicated to the many teachers, students, and scholars who have stimulated my intellectual curiosity.
S.L.G.

Brief Table of Contents

PREFACE   XV

1 AFRICAN AMERICAN OFFENDING   1
2 AN AFRICAN AMERICAN WORLDVIEW   25
3 PERCEPTIONS OF CRIMINAL JUSTICE INJUSTICES AND
   AFRICAN AMERICAN OFFENDING   52
4 RACIAL DISCRIMINATION, NEGATIVE STEREOTYPES,
   STEREOTYPE THREATS, AND AFRICAN AMERICAN
   OFFENDING   73
5 RACIAL SOCIALIZATION AND AFRICAN AMERICAN
   OFFENDING   113
6 A THEORETICAL MODEL OF AFRICAN AMERICAN
   OFFENDING   167
EPILOGUE: ENVIRONMENTAL RACISM AND AFRICAN
   AMERICAN OFFENDING   207

NOTES   225
REFERENCES   233
INDEX   263

TABLE OF CONTENTS

PREFACE   XV

1 AFRICAN AMERICAN OFFENDING   1
  Introduction   1
  African Americans and the Criminal Justice System   1
  The Uniqueness of Being Black in America: The Need
  for a Black Criminology   4
    The African American Heritage   *4*
    A Black Criminology   *7*
  General Theories on African American Offending   10
    Social Disorganization Theory   *11*
    Hirschi's Social Control Theory   *13*
    Gottfredson and Hirschi's General Theory of Crime   *14*
    Strain Theories   *15*
      Merton's Strain Theory   *15*
      Agnew's General Strain Theory   *16*
    Aker's Social Learning Theory   *19*
    Afrocentricity   *21*
  Conclusion   24

2 AN AFRICAN AMERICAN WORLDVIEW   25
   The Basic Premise of Our Theory
   of African American Offending   26
   The Racial Divide   29
     Evidence of a General Racial Divide   29
     Hurricane Katrina   30
     Does Race Matter?   30
     Success of the Civil Rights Movement   31
     Reparations and Race Relations   31
   The Racial Divide in Perceptions of the Criminal
   Justice System   32
     The Racial Divide in Support for the Death Penalty   32
     The Racial Divide in Perceptions of Injustice in the
     Criminal Justice System   34
     The Racial Divide in Support for the "War on Drugs"   37
     A Worldview that is Shared Among all African Americans   39
     Why African Americans Share this Perception of the
     Criminal Justice System   41
     The Election of Barack Obama   46
   Perceived Racial Discrimination   47
     Would Employers Rather Hire Whites than African
     Americans?   48
     Perceptions of Racial Discrimination   49
   Conclusions   51

3 PERCEPTIONS OF CRIMINAL JUSTICE INJUSTICES AND
   AFRICAN AMERICAN OFFENDING   52
   Perceptions of Criminal Justice Injustices   52
     Why People Obey the Law   52
     Procedural Justice   53
     Legal Socialization   55
   Perceptions of Criminal Justice Injustices and Defiance   57
     Shame, Anger, and Defiance   57
   Hirschi's Control Theory and the Bond of Belief   62
   Variations in African American Offending   65

*Variations in the Degree to which African Americans
Perceive Criminal Justice Injustices*   65
Variations in Place   66
Variations in Defiance   70
Variations by Gender   70

4 RACIAL DISCRIMINATION, NEGATIVE STEREOTYPES,
   STEREOTYPE THREATS, AND AFRICAN AMERICAN
   OFFENDING   73
   Racial Discrimination and the General Well-Being of
   African Americans   76
   Racial Discrimination and African American
   Offending   78
   Racial Discrimination and Weak School Bonds   80
   Stereotypes of African Americans   88
   Prevailing Racial Stereotypes   88
   The Impact that Negative Stereotypes Have on
   African Americans   92
   Stereotypes and Offending   93
   Stereotype Threat and Weak Social Bonds   94
   Stereotype Threats   94
   *Stereotype Threat, Weak Bonds, and African American
   Offending*   96
   Pejorative Stereotypes and Offending   98
   Summary   101
   White Collar Crime   102
   Gender and Crime   103
   The Significance of Place   106
   Conclusions   111

5 RACIAL SOCIALIZATION AND AFRICAN AMERICAN
   OFFENDING   113
   Introduction   113
   The Different Dimensions of Racial Socialization   119

Cultural Socialization   120
Preparation for Racial Bias   121
Promotion of Mistrust   122
Egalitarian Values   124
Racial Socialization and Racial Identity   125
Racial Identity and Offending   128
Racial Socialization and Gender   129
Racial Socialization and Social Bonds   133
Racial Socialization and the Black Church   137
Racial Socialization, Racial Discrimination, Hostility,
Depression, and Offending   138
Coping with Racism   140
Our Theory on Racial Socialization and Offending   144
Racial Socialization and Weak Bonds   151
Gender and African American Offending   152
Drugs, Gender, and Crime   158
Racial Socialization, Place, and Offending   160
Why Place Matters   161

6 A THEORETICAL MODEL OF AFRICAN AMERICAN

OFFENDING   ꜱ   167
The Unique Worldview of African Americans   167
African American Offending and Criminal Justice
Injustices   169
Criminal Justice Injustices and Weakening the Restraints of
the Rule of Law   171
African American Offending and Racial Discrimination   173
Negative Stereotypes   177
Individual Offending   182
Variations in Experiences with Racial Injustices   182
Variations in Racial Socialization   183
Our Theoretical Model of African American
Offending   186
Gender and African American Offending   190
Place Matters   195

Ethnic Differences in African American Offending 201
Ethnicity and Immigration Status 201
Colorism 203
Conclusion 204

EPILOGUE: ENVIRONMENTAL RACISM AND AFRICAN

AMERICAN OFFENDING 207
Introduction 207
Environmental Racism 208
The Empirical Research on Environmental Racism 210
Race and Proximity to Environmental Toxins 210
The Health Effects of Environmental Racism 211
The Deleterious Consequences of Exposure to Lead 212
Lead Exposure and Cognitive Impairment 213
Lead Exposure and Education 214
Lead Exposure and Crime 215
Lead Exposure and African American Offending 218
Our Theory of African American Offending 219
Environmental Racism and African American Offending 220

NOTES 225
REFERENCES 233
INDEX 263

PREFACE

According to official statistics, African American men—about 6 percent of the population of the United States—account for nearly 60 percent of the robbery arrests in the U.S. It is obvious to us that this incredible racial disparity in offending must be related to the past and present racial subordination of African Americans. However, inexplicably, no criminological theory exists that fully articulates the nuances of the African American experience and how they relate to their offending.

While eating dinner at the 2009 ASC conference, we looked at each other and lamented about the lack of a definitive work that integrates the best of existing criminological theories with a new theory that examines the profound and nuanced ways that the African American experience causes their offending. One by one we discussed the many theories that have been applied to African American offending and noted where they fall short. But unlike so many conversations in the discipline on race and offending, ours covered the pioneering criminological ideas presented by early black social scientists who offered an array of criminological ideas that have largely been neglected in the discipline (Gabbidon, Greene, and Young, 2002; Greene and Gabbidon, 2000). Our dinner lasted for hours given the complexities of the topic and the richness of the discussion! Soon afterward, we came to the conclusion that our combined passion for the topic, the body of scholarly work we have each produced, distinctive personal experiences and racial backgrounds, and the mutual sense of urgency, *required* us to tackle this project. In short, we both felt that criminology had matured enough to accept a distinct theory of African American offending.

We moved forward with several mutually agreed notions. First, we agreed that any theory that addresses African American offending must consider their unique worldview that has emerged from centuries of racial oppression in the United States. Second, we agreed that we needed to incorporate the keen insights that black scholars have long presented on African American offending. For example, we agreed that Du Bois's seminal work, *The Philadelphia Negro* (1899), should be the starting point for scholarship on African American offending. Thus, the foundation of our book is built upon Du Bois's century-old assertion that a true understanding of African American offending must be grounded in the "real conditions" of what it means to be black living in a racially stratified society. Third, we had to synthesize the literature across vast domains including criminology, psychology, Afrocentricity, biology, the environmental sciences, and sociology to construct a holistic understanding of African American offending. Fourth, we recognized that our theory had to explain within differences (e.g., gender disparities) in African American offending. Fifth, we decided that our theory needed to explain both African American offending and the reasons why the majority of blacks refute their racial subordination and live healthy and productive crime-free lives. Finally, we agreed that the basic assumption of our book is that the African American experience does not generalize to other races (e.g., whites, Asians, Native Americans) or to other ethnicities (e.g., Hispanics). That is, we stipulate that the African American experience is peerless and that it can only explain black offending.

Our book targets multiple audiences including students, scholars, activists, practitioners, researchers, and those who are just interested in why people choose to engage in crime. We include innumerable hypotheses that potentially will generate a vast volume of research on African American offending. The research generated from tests of our theory will allow concerned individuals, whether they are police agencies or community activists, to generate sound evidence-based policies designed to both reduce African American offending and their mass incarceration of African Americans.

Our volume includes six chapters and an epilogue. In the first chapter, we outline why our theory is necessary. We present data that show that African Americans are disproportionately arrested for the offenses that define the "index crimes" including both property (e.g., burglary) and violent crimes (e.g., homicide). We argue that the general theories of crime, such as Hirschi's social bond, Gottfredson and Hirschi's low self-control theory, and social disorganization, do not fully capture the dynamics of why African Americans offend. In the second chapter, we present substantial evidence that shows that African Americans have a unique worldview that emerged from centuries of racial subordination. We argue that this peerless worldview—one that is not shared by other races or ethnicities—is continually being reaffirmed and shaped as African Americans confront everyday racism. We conclude that this worldview informs the decisions of individual African Americans to offend.

In Chapter 3 we argue that a core feature of the worldview shared by African Americans is their experiences with criminal justice injustices (e.g., the beating of Rodney King). We contend that perceptions of these injustices undermine the legitimacy of the law. In addition, we stipulate that perceptions of criminal justice injustices increase the likelihood that African Americans will become defiant and angry. Thus, we hypothesize that the more African Americans perceive criminal justice injustices the more likely they are to defiantly offend. Chapter 4 explains how African American offending is related to racial discrimination, pejorative stereotypes, and stereotype threats. We assert that these multilayered forms of racism have two profound consequences related to black offending. First, they undermine the ability of African Americans to build strong bonds with white-dominated institutions. Second, we state that perceptions of racial injustices deplete the emotional capital of African Americans. That is, perceptions of racial injustices increase the likelihood that African Americans will experience anger-defiance-depression, which in turn increases their probability of impulsively offending.

Chapter 5 presents an extended review of the literature on racial socialization. We contend that racial socialization is a key to explaining why some but not other African Americans offend even though they share the same worldview. We assert that African Americans who offend had parents who ill prepared them to cope with their experiences with racial injustices. Chapter 6 provides a comprehensive overview of the entirety of our theory of African American offending. It also presents a formal model of our theory that articulates the reasons why some African Americans offend. We conclude with an Epilogue. It asserts that an additional cause of African American offending, which is extraneous to our model, is the deleterious consequences of environmental racism. We contend that African Americans are disproportionately exposed to environmental toxins, such as lead, that inhibit their ability to bond to white-dominated institutions and to fend off the injurious consequences of experiencing racial injustices.

In closing, the authors acknowledge Steve Rutter, Editor at Routledge, for recognizing the need for our book and quickly signing the project. We also thank our universities for the continuing support of our research. At the University of South Florida Sarasota-Manatee, Jane Rose, Dean of the College of Arts and Sciences, and at Penn State Harrisburg, Steven Peterson, Director of the School of Public Affairs, is thanked for his longstanding commitment to helping faculty achieve their scholarly potential. We also thank Ron Simons and Chet Britt for their reviews. The first author additionally extends a thank you to Frank Cullen for his continued support and keen insights.

1

AFRICAN AMERICAN OFFENDING

Introduction

In this book, we present a theory of African American offending. Our basic assumption is that a theory of African American offending must be derived from the lived experiences of blacks as they negotiate living within a conflicted racially stratified society. We further assume that the past and present lived experiences of African Americans have created a shared worldview that is unlike those that inform whites or other minorities. Put most simply, this book presents a theory of offending grounded in the lived experiences of African Americans that enriches our understanding of why, for example, approximately 6 percent of the United States population—black men—account for 56 percent of the official arrests for robbery.[1]

African Americans and the Criminal Justice System

For more than a century, there has been concern about the nature and extent of crime in the African American community (Du Bois, 1898). This concern has generated numerous media stories, community and state-level commissions/panels, and various grassroots efforts to ameliorate the problem. Despite these notable efforts, recent figures from a variety of data sources paint a grim portrait of the state of crime and victimization in the African American community. For example, the

Center for Disease Control (CDC) annually provides figures on the leading causes of death among Americans. Disturbingly, these data show that homicide is a leading cause of death among young African Americans (Heron, 2010). Data from the National Crime Victimization Survey (NCVS) also point to the acute victimization trends among African Americans. In 2008, African Americans experienced higher rates of victimization than whites for every violent crime measured by the NCVS, except simple assault. In addition, the NCVS data reveal that African Americans had higher rates of overall violence than other minorities, including Hispanics (Rand, 2009).

Arrest statistics tallied by the FBI's Uniform Crime Reports (UCR) program and reported in their annual *Crime in the United States* publication provide another barometer of the offending levels among African Americans. We present these statistics with caution, recognizing that they reflect possible racial bias in laws and the arrest patterns of the police (Donzinger, 1996; Miller, 1997; Russell-Brown, 2009; Schlesinger, 2011; Tonry, 1995).[2] Nonetheless, these statistics reveal that African Americans account for 28 percent of all arrests, yet, blacks make up only 13 percent of the American population (U.S. Census Bureau, 2009; *Crime in the United States*, 2008). Even more striking, blacks were over-represented in every UCR arrest category (there are 29) except driving under the influence (*Crime in the United States*, 2008). The most alarming numbers are for arrests for robbery and homicide. In 2008, blacks represented 56.7 percent of those arrested for robbery and 50.1 percent of those arrested for murder and non-negligent manslaughter (*Crime in the United States*, 2008). Thus, these data indicate that African Americans are four times more likely to be arrested for murder and robbery than they should be based on their proportion of the U.S. population. But these data do not paint the true picture of violent crime. Both robbery and homicide are overwhelmingly committed by men. Therefore, the data reveal that 6 percent of the population—black men—are arrested for approximately half of the robberies and homicides committed each year in the U.S.

While some scholars have made a strong argument against using UCR data to estimate rates of offending (see Young, 1994)—especially since stereotypes that pathologize African Americans might emerge from such an analysis (Young, 2006; Russell-Brown, 2009)—the fact remains that, by any metric used, African Americans are disproportionately more likely to engage in street-related crimes, especially violent crimes. Alarmingly, this quagmire of over-representation extends to black youth. Here, the picture is even bleaker, although black youth are 16 percent of the youth population ages 10–17, in 2008 they accounted for 52 percent of the juvenile violent crime index arrests and 33 percent of the juvenile property crime index arrests. Moreover, statistics reveal that blacks accounted for 58.5 percent of the youth-related arrests for homicide and *67 percent* of the arrests for robbery (Puzzanchera, 2009). This over-representation continues across all UCR offense arrest categories except three (i.e., driving under the influence, liquor laws, and drunkenness).[3] The problem, however, is not limited to black men or African American youth; it also extends to black women. For example, black women represent approximately *7 percent* of the United States population (U.S. Census Bureau, 2009; *Crime in the United States*, 2008), yet, in 2008, they were arrested for approximately *40 percent* of the homicides committed by women.

These racial disparities are reflected throughout the criminal justice system. Incarceration figures for 2008 show that there were more than 1.4 million inmates in state and federal prisons. Of these, 528,200, or 37 percent, were black. The gender split reveals that black males represented 37 percent of the male inmates and African American women were 52 percent of the female inmates. These figures translate into pronounced imprisonment rates among African Americans. For example, the incarceration rate was six and a half times higher for black males than white males (3,161 per 100,000 residents versus 487 per 100,000). Though the incarceration rate for black females was lower than that of African American men, it was still nearly three times higher than the rate for white women (Sabol, West, and Cooper, 2009).

Given these indisputable racial disparities, we are perplexed why so few scholars have devoted time to pursuing theoretical formulations exclusively devoted to African American offending (Hawkins, 1990, 1995). We are not alone. Scholars for the last 20 years have been calling for a "black criminology" that centers the explanation of African American offending in their unique lived experiences—similar to how feminist criminologists center their explanation of female offending in the unique lived experiences of women in a gender stratified society (Belknap, 2007; Chesney-Lind and Pasko, 2004; Daly and Chesney-Lind, 1988). Until now, this clarion call has largely fallen on deaf ears. It is our contention that, because of their unique American experience, there are salient reasons why African Americans offend that are not shared by whites and other minority groups (e.g., Hispanics, Asians). Below, we discuss why a theory of African American offending is warranted and then review how prevailing general theories of crime attempt to explain black offending.

The Uniqueness of Being Black in America: The Need for a Black Criminology

The African American Heritage

Blacks in America have had and continue to have unique lived experiences that are not shared by whites or by other minorities. After being forcefully brought to the United States, they suffered through chattel slavery for more than 200 years (Franklin and Higginbotham, 2010). The brutal slave system was followed by a Jim Crow system—based on white supremacy—that reduced blacks to second class citizens. Faced with pervasive systemic discrimination that was legally condoned, blacks were largely restricted to a segregated existence in American society. This unprecedented isolated and segregated existence continues to this day despite extensive civil rights victories including the landmark 1954 Brown decision.

Scholars have documented the painful specifics of the inimitable peerless racial oppression of African Americans within the U.S.[4] King (1997), for example, states the obvious; that is, no other racial or ethnic group (i.e., whites, Hispanics) experienced centuries of being brutally forcefully enslaved. Treated no better than and often times worse than farm animals, black slaves were only valued for their potential to increase the wealth of whites. The torturous treatment of black male slaves is also unparalleled. This included "unmerciful beatings, lynchings, and the mutilation of various body parts, particularly the male genitalia, were all routine disciplinary measures used to punish enslaved African males" (King, 1997:83). Black females, too, were also targeted for brutal treatment. Their treatment, however, came not only in the form of beatings and mutilations but also in the form of repeated rapes by white masters who did not view such acts as criminal since slaves were considered property not citizens (Russell-Brown, 2009).

The brutal and violent subordination of African Americans continued after the abolition of slavery.[5] The Reconstruction period saw resentful whites brutalizing African Americans through collective acts of domestic terrorism that resulted in countless deaths—lynchings—in the late 1800s (e.g., carried out by white terrorist groups such as the Ku Klux Klan) (Gabbidon and Greene, 2009). Most notably, from the very beginning law enforcement officials were either directly involved in or turned a blind eye to these terrorist activities carried out against innocent African Americans (King, 1997). The first half of the 20th century proved to be no different than previous centuries with police brutality against blacks remaining commonplace and the use of capital punishment in rape cases being almost exclusively reserved for blacks who were *alleged* to have raped white women.[6] In short, the criminal justice system has a long documented history of being violently involved in the racial oppression of blacks.

The brutal oppression of African Americans was not limited to the south—that is, states that legally condoned slavery and enacted Jim Crow laws. African Americans encountered vile overt racial hatred that was systemic as they fled the Jim Crow south and migrated north "to the promised land." Northern whites responded to the "great migration" of blacks in the early 19th century with their own brand of white collective terrorism. Illustrative of this trend was the murder of more than 500 African Americans by whites during "riots" that occurred from 1915 to 1919 (King, 1997). The data show that this unprecedented level of violence laid the groundwork for what scholars now refer to as

"American apartheid" (Massey, 1990). That is, "residential segregation is the institutional apparatus that supports other racially discriminatory processes and binds them together into a coherent and uniquely effective system of racial subordination" (Massey and Denton, 1993:8). We argue that the foundation for the continued racial subordination of African Americans—American apartheid—is the inimitable dislike that whites have toward African Americans. The data show that Americans hierarchically rank their preferences among minorities. They rank blacks as the least attractive minority they want as a neighbor (Charles, 2001, 2003; Sharkey, 2008).

This isolated concentration of African Americans into the most disadvantaged neighborhoods resulted in urban unrests—"race riots"—throughout the U.S. during the 1960s. As a result, African Americans witnessed the National Guard patrolling their neighborhoods, often with armed vehicles. A federal study of these urban unrests—the Kerner Commission—concluded that America was "moving toward two societies, one black, one white—separate and unequal" (Kerner, 1968). Notably, the urban unrests resulted in the passage of major civil reforms specifically designed to ameliorate the multifaceted forms of discrimination that African Americans encounter, such as the Fair Housing Act of 1968 and the Voting Rights Act of 1965. Despite these gains, the data indicate that severe racial segregation and its concomitant problems continue to disproportionately impact African Americans (Charles, 2001, 2003; Massey, 2005). A result of this continued racial subordination is the persistence of urban unrests as evidenced by the 1992 Los Angeles Civil Unrest, the 2001 Cincinnati urban disorder, and the 2010 Oakland, CA unrest (see also Hacker, 2003). Consistent with the prior unrests, these urban disruptions were triggered by perceived criminal justice injustices—in LA the acquittal of four Los Angeles police officers who were accused of the beating of the African American motorist, Rodney King, in Cincinnati the fatal shooting of an unarmed 19-year-old black male—Timothy Thomas—by a white police officer during an on-foot pursuit, and in Oakland the sentencing of a white transit police officer for involuntary manslaughter for the murder of an unarmed 22-year-old African American male—Oscar Grant.

This unprecedented level of persistent racial subordination has caused African Americans to have a cultural heritage and unique lived experiences that are not shared by any other racial or ethnic group within the U.S. That is, while other racial and ethnic minorities have encountered some racial or ethnic barriers along the way, no group has endured the same experiences as African Americans. For example, Irish Americans were despised when they arrived in America. More specifically, the Irish were viewed negatively, including the stereotypes that they were dirty, stupid, and drunks (Feagin and Feagin, 2008). They were also subjected to considerable religious persecution because of their adherence to Catholicism. But, as noted by Hawkins (1990:158): "After being the target of religious and ethnic prejudice for many decades and being regarded as prone to criminality, they are now said to be model Americans." In addition, research indicates that a significant proportion of the disadvantages some Latinos encounter (e.g., Puerto Ricans) is "clearly attributable to the persistence of a black racial identity among them" (Massey, 1990:354). Together, these studies highlight two salient issues. First, even though other groups (e.g., Irish Americans) were intensely despised, they were never enslaved, legally subordinated by Jim Crow laws, or persistently segregated in poor isolated neighborhoods. Second, the importance of skin color cannot be underestimated (Silberman, 1978). Having a light skin tone—white—and its corollary—a white racial identity—has advantages (Burton, Bonilla-Silva, Ray, Buckelew, and Freeman, 2010; Dixon and Maddox, 2005; Eberhardt, Davies, Purdie-Vaughns, and Johnson, 2006; Eberhardt, Goff, Purdie, and Davies, 2004; Keith and Herring, 1991; Williams, 2003).

A Black Criminology

We argue that any theory aimed at explaining criminal offending among African Americans must foundationally acknowledge that blacks share a unique worldview that has been shaped by their incomparable racial subordination; that is, their inimitable experiences with subtle and profound racial injustices. Our argument builds on the work of black criminologists who have long stated the need for a distinctive theory and body of research that is centered on African American offending.

Among the first black scholars to identify the need for such a body of work was W.E.B. Du Bois. In the late 1890s, Du Bois (1898:16) took stock of the social science research that had been done on blacks and wrote, "it is extremely doubtful if any satisfactory study of Negro crime and lynching can be made for a generation or more, in the present condition of the public mind, which renders it almost impossible to get at the facts and real conditions." In short, Du Bois argued that a true theory of African American offending will only be realized when the science of criminology elevates itself above the limiting constraints of racist beliefs and practices and examines the "real conditions" related to their offending.

Du Bois offered guidance as to what real conditions are specifically related to African American offending (Du Bois, 1899a, 1901; Du Bois and Dill, 1913; Hawkins, 1995; Gabbidon, 2007). One of Du Bois's more complete articulations on African American offending was published in his well-known publication, *The Philadelphia Negro* (1899b). This work is significant for two reasons. First, it represents, in our view, one of the earliest scholarly works that could be considered as "doing black criminology." Second, it also represents one of the earliest works that relates African American offending to their racial subordination. More specifically, Du Bois recognized that racial discrimination was a chief cause of African American offending. In fact, while he readily acknowledged that all African American offending in Philadelphia could not be attributed to race discrimination, Du Bois (1899b:351) writes that: "Certainly a great amount of crime can be without doubt traced to the discrimination against Negro boys and girls in the matter of employment." But Du Bois (1899b:351) also recognized the complexity of the relationship between racial discrimination and offending by stating that:

> The connection of crime and prejudice is, on the other hand, neither simple nor direct. The boy who is refused promotion in his job as a porter does not go out and snatch somebody's pocketbook. Conversely, the loafers ... and the thugs in the county prison are not usually graduates of high schools who have been refused work.

The connections are much more subtle and dangerous; it is the atmosphere of rebellion and discontent that unrewarded merit and reasonable but unsatisfied ambition make.

Du Bois's criminological work began an important dialogue on the salient and nuanced ways that racial discrimination is related to African American offending. His sophisticated insights recognize that there are multiple pathways through which racial subordination can impact African American offending, including the negative emotions of anger and defiance that flow from experiencing racial injustices.

Unfortunately and inexplicably, it was not until the 1990s that another scholar finally responded to Du Bois's clarion call for an unveiling of the "real conditions" related to African American offending. In 1992, Russell declared that "the discipline of criminology has failed to provide a well-developed, vibrant and cohesive subfield that seeks to explain crime committed by blacks," that is, scholars have failed to develop a "black criminology" (Russell, 1992:667). She argues that a holistic approach to explaining crime committed by African Americans has been ignored systematically by the discipline (Russell, 1992:679). She further asserts that this omission—that is, the absence of a black criminology—has placed the discipline of criminology in a "theoretical time warp" (Russell, 1992:675). Russell contends that a focus of black criminology should be on how African Americans have been treated in America and how they have internalized this treatment and, we add, how they externalize perceiving racial injustices. As part of this effort, she contends that researchers should develop, operationalize, and test perceived and objective measures of "racism" (Russell, 1992:673). She concludes that "the development of a black criminology would serve a function comparable to the development of feminist criminology: It would provide a framework for developing and testing new theories. The call for a black criminology is a call for criminologists to expand their theorizing and testing of the causes of crime committed by blacks" (Russell, 1992:681).

Subsequently, other scholars have recognized the poverty of criminology as it has failed to develop a black criminology that is grounded in their unique lived experiences (Onwudiwe and Lynch, 2000; Penn, 2003) or, in the British context, a more expansive approach that considers "minority perspectives" (Phillips and Bowling, 2003). Indeed, Noble (2006) calls much of the existing mainstream scholarly literature on race and crime "superficial." He argues that the "general theories of crime" (which have been developed only by white men) fail to or only superficially acknowledge that African American offending is inextricably related to and grounded in their resistance to racial subordination. Noble (2006:9) concludes that a theory grounded in the lived experiences of African Americans is needed that details "the precise connections between the personal, structural, and cultural factors that produce crime in the black community."

We assert that our theory offers a more holistic and fuller understanding of African American offending than previous attempts to explain the race–crime relationship (Russell, 1992). We recognize that other theories of crime have generated tremendous insights that are empirically verified as to why African Americans offend. Indeed, we integrate many of these findings into our own understanding of African American offending. Nevertheless, we fundamentally disagree with the assumption that underlies all "general" theories of crime; that is, that African Americans, whites, and other minorities offend for identical reasons. Our position is that obviously there are factors that are related to crime regardless of the offender's race or ethnicity, such as being raised in a severely dysfunctional household. However, we argue that there are other factors—such as the experience of being racially subordinated—that African Americans have uniquely experienced that explains their offending, even if the factors trumpeted by the general theories are taken into consideration.

General Theories on African American Offending

Criminologists have offered "general" theories of crime that they argue fully explain the disproportionate offending of African Americans. These theories claim to explain all criminality—irrespective of race, ethnicity, gender, crime type, etc. Therefore, in the eyes of general theorists, race-based theories are unnecessary (as well as feminist explanations).

The same reasons why whites offend—for example, resource-depleted neighborhoods—explain why African Americans engage in crime. Thus, general theorists simply argue that the only reason why African Americans disproportionately offend is that they are overexposed to the specific cause of crime highlighted by their theory, whether it is poor neighborhoods or delinquent peers. We reject the general theorist's assumption that race-based theories are redundant or superfluous. In fact, we argue that it is impossible to understand African American offending unless it is grounded in their unique lived experiences. However, we believe that general theories have important elements that can be used to help understand African American offending. Below, we review the more prominent general theory's explanation of African American offending.

Social Disorganization Theory

Social disorganization theory has its foundations in the work of the well-known Chicago school of sociology. This theory was formulated at the turn of the 20th century when the mass northern migration of southern blacks coupled with the heavy European immigration resulted in northern cities, such as Chicago, experiencing substantial growth in a relatively short span of time (Frazier, 1949; Park, Burgess, and McKenzie, 1925). A relatively sharp increase in an array of social problems including crime accompanied this rapid growth in the urban northern centers. The Chicago school attributed this increase in crime to the social disorganization that was occurring within the urban centers.

Elliot and Merrill (1934:20) define social disorganization as "a breakdown of the equilibrium of forces, a decay in the social structure, so that old habits and forms of social control no longer function effectively." Socially disorganized areas are typically characterized by fluctuating populations, high welfare rates, and several ethnic groups residing in one area (Shaw and McKay, 1942). The theory is also combined with the concentric zone approach formulated by Burgess (1925) and heavily influenced by his scholarship with Robert Park on human ecology. The concentric zone approach argues that cities can be broken down into areas that "expand radially from its central business district" (Park, 1925:5). Specifically, the approach separates cities such as Chicago into several zones that move from the center city out to the suburbs. The theory postulates that the center city and particularly the zone in transition where there are high levels of criminal activity will have the highest rates of social disorganization. Thus, of particular relevance to criminologists, is that the theory predicts that as one moves away from inner-city areas, characteristics of social disorganization will decrease—resulting in lower levels of offending.

It also must be noted that at the turn of the 20th century racist theories of crime were given scholarly consideration. These race-based theories attributed African American offending to their biological inferiority. Accordingly, we applaud the Chicago school criminologists for offering a race-neutral theory of crime, which directly undermined the validity of the argument that African Americans are inherently pathological. In short, this theory offers the compelling argument that offending is race neutral as it is not the product of something inherent to particular racial or ethnic groups but can be traced to the areas where they disproportionately reside.

More recently, Sampson, Raudenbush, and Earls (1997:918) expanded social disorganization with the introduction of the concept "collective efficacy," which they define as "social cohesion among neighbors combined with their willingness to intervene on behalf of the common good." Thus, crime principally occurs in areas where neighbors are not involved in the collective well-being of their neighborhood. Conversely, crime is less likely to occur, regardless of the race-ethnicity of its residents, in areas where residents engage in proactive–prosocial actions on behalf of their neighbors (Morenoff, Sampson, and Raudenbush, 2001; Sampson et al., 1997). In general, social disorganization theorists assert that the chief reason why African Americans disproportionately offend is because they disproportionately reside in disadvantaged areas with little collective efficacy. We do not dispute this contention. Indeed, we agree that people residing in areas with little collective efficacy will be more likely to offend, whether they are white or black. However, we argue that the everyday experiences of African

Americans with racism are related to both their collective and individual efficacy.

Hirschi's Social Control Theory

Travis Hirschi's control theory represents one of the most revered criminological theories. Formulated in the late 1960s, the theory did not seek to answer the more common question of why people commit crime but, instead, asked "Why *do* men obey the rules of society?" (Hirschi, 1969:10). Hirschi concluded that there are four key bonds that keep people from engaging in crime. First, Hirschi felt that persons who are *attached* to their spouses, family, and friends are less likely to engage in deviant behavior. Second, he argued that people who are *committed* to conventional activities such as their education and career are less likely to offend. Third, Hirschi argued that individuals who are *involved* in positive community activities are less likely to engage in crime. Fourth, he stipulated that people who believe (*belief*) in the legitimacy of the law and authority are less likely to offend. This bond rests on Hirschi's premise that there is a universal value system within society.

Hirschi in his classic *Causes of Delinquency* (1969) tested the core tenets of his control theory using a diverse sample (41 percent black) from California. Interestingly, Hirschi (1969:65) acknowledged the unique plight of African Americans, stating that: "Negroes occupy a highly disadvantageous position in the opportunity structure; the Negro's stake in conformity in conventional activities is decidedly small; Negro culture is lower-class in character; Negro family life produces faulty ego and superego development." In addition, he acknowledged that black communities were patrolled more by the police and that the police were "unusually" more likely to view African Americans as offenders. Nevertheless, Hirschi (1969:79) was adamant that "there is no reason to believe that the causes of crime among Negroes are different from those among whites."

In support of this position, Hirschi asserts that verbal achievement scores negate the relationship between delinquency and race. Control theorists reason that African Americans experience higher rates of street-related offenses because they have weaker bonds with conventional institutions than whites or other minority groups. These frail bonds primarily stem from African American youth being more weakly bonded to their families. Our theory integrates Hirschi's insights. We agree with Hirschi that African Americans are more likely to offend if they are weakly bonded to conventional institutions. However, we argue that racism undermines the ability of African Americans to build strong ties with "conventional" institutions.

Gottfredson and Hirschi's General Theory of Crime

In 1990, Gottfredson and Hirschi published *A General Theory of Crime*. This theory hinges on the concept of self-control. Gottfredson and Hirschi (1990:90) argue that "people who lack self-control will tend to be impulsive, insensitive, physical (as opposed to mental), risk-taking, short-sighted, and nonverbal, and they will tend therefore to engage in criminal and analogous acts." Gottfredson and Hirschi argue that low self-control is a product of "ineffective child-rearing." Ineffective child-rearing occurs when children are not properly monitored, their deviant behavior goes unrecognized, and they are not punished for the transgression. In addition, they argue that factors that inhibit the ability to develop self-control in children include parental criminality, family size, single-parent families, and mothers entering the workforce.

Gottfredson and Hirschi (1990) engage the question of race in their work. Notably, they affirm the generality of their theory by arguing that differences in offending between racial and ethnic groups can be explained by the disparities in self-control. However, they do not argue that African Americans inherently have less self-control, but, rather attribute their lack of self-control to lower "levels of direct supervision by family." Gottfredson and Hirschi (1990:172) urge researchers to "focus on differential child-rearing practices and abandon the fruitless effort to ascribe such differences to culture or strain." Recent tests with diverse samples have been mixed with some finding that the theory is not race-neutral (Higgins and Ricketts, 2005), while others find support for the race-neutral aspect of the general theory (Leiber, Mack, and Featherstone, 2009; Vazsonyi and Crosswhite, 2004). We do not dispute Gottfredson and Hirschi's (1990) contention that low self-control is related to offending (Pratt and Cullen, 2000). Indeed, we integrate this insight into our theory of African American offending. Yet, we add that there are other sources than family socialization experiences, that may cause African Americans to engage in impulsive behaviors.

Strain Theories

Merton's Strain Theory

Robert Merton's strain theory is among the most widely known criminological theories. His theory is based on the concept of anomie that was popularized by Emile Durkheim in the late 1800s. Anomie refers to a state of normlessness or the process whereby societal controls no longer have their desired impact and, consequently, citizens are likely to engage in nonconformist and/or deviant behavior (Merton, 1938). More specifically, Merton (1938:672) argued that in every society there are "culturally defined goals, purposes, and interest." Along with these societal goals (largely tied to financial success), there are also accepted institutional means to achieve the goals (e.g., work, education, etc.). However, when citizens adhere to the societal goal of achieving financial success and they are unable to achieve it using the prescribed means, a "strain" occurs and they turn to alternative (criminal) means.

Merton realized that people adapt to the strain from not being able to achieve success in multiple ways and, as a result, he conceptualized five "modes of adaptation." Of relevance to our discussion are two of Merton's modes of adaptation that are related to deviance-crime. First, he recognized that there were those citizens who adhered to the cultural goal of financial success, but being unable to achieve this success through conventional means, become "innovators" and create alternative (and often illegal) ways to achieve their financial aspirations. Second, he argued that there are "retreatists." These individuals are more likely to use illegal drugs because they both give up on achieving the American dream and the institutional means of achieving it.

On the surface, strain theory appears to be another race-neutral general theory. One would get little argument that both blacks and whites likely encounter anomic strains and become innovators or retreatists; however, Merton was not blind to the special circumstance of American blacks in the 1930s. In a neglected footnote in his classic article, Merton (1938:680) wrote: "Certain elements of the Negro population have assimilated the dominant caste's values of pecuniary success and advancement, but they recognize that social ascent is at present restricted to their own caste almost exclusively. The pressures upon the Negro which would otherwise derive from the structural inconsistencies we have noticed are hence not identical to those upon lower class whites."

Therefore, Merton represents one of the few early white theorists who openly recognized that black offending needs to be uniquely explained. In other words, he recognized that the challenges African Americans faced in society were not on par with those of whites. Undoubtedly, in the 1930s, the context of their existence included pervasive and caustic racial subordination at every turn—something Merton alludes to in his footnote but does not integrate as a prominent cause for African American offending in his classic article. Thus, classic strain theorists today would argue that the higher rates of offending among African Americans can be attributed to the existence of race-based structural inequalities; that is, a "level playing field" does not exist for blacks.

In general, because of its singular focus on economic strain, scholars turned away from Merton's strain theory (Bernard, 1984; Kornhauser, 1978). But, in the early 1990s, Robert Agnew presented his general strain theory, which provided a more expansive and nuanced view of the role of strains or stressors that can more readily explain African American offending.

Agnew's General Strain Theory

Agnew's (1992) general strain theory (GST) represents an important expansion of Merton's original formulation of strain theory. His expansion includes two new strains but incorporates Merton's original focus on strain being caused by a disjunction between aspirations and expectations. One new strain that Agnew identifies is the removal of positively valued stimuli from the individual. This can include a host of strains or stressors, including the death of a parent or close relative, the loss of a boyfriend/girlfriend, and moving to a new school. Agnew (1992:57–58) argues that: "The actual or anticipated loss of positively valued stimuli may lead to delinquency as the individual tries to prevent the loss of positively valued stimuli, retrieve the lost stimuli or obtain substitute stimuli, seek revenge against those responsible for the loss, or manage the negative effects caused by the loss by taking illicit drugs." The second strain Agnew introduces is the presentation of negative stimuli. Relying on the psychology literature, Agnew posits that the introduction of noxious stimuli (e.g., child abuse, negative relations with parents, criminal victimization, etc.) can lead to aggression and/ or delinquency. According to Agnew (1992:58), delinquency results because the individual tries to: "(1) escape from or avoid the negative stimuli; (2) terminate or alleviate the negative stimuli; (3) seek revenge against the source of the negative stimuli or related targets."

A decade after his pioneering article, Agnew (2001) expanded his theory to include experiences with prejudice and racial discrimination as potential stressors. More specifically, Agnew (2001:346–347) argues that: "Prejudice/racial discrimination may reduce social control, particularly attachment and commitment to those individuals and institutions associated with the prejudice and discrimination. Prejudice/discrimination may also create some pressure or incentive to engage in crime because the victim is exposed to others who violate strongly held social norms."

More recently, Kaufman, Rebellon, Thaxton, and Agnew (2008) clarified how GST can explain racial differences in offending. They argue that African Americans are more likely than other groups to experience: economic strains (poverty, high unemployment, etc.); familial strains (exposure to poor parenting practices); educational strains (poor grades, unfair discipline); community strains (high levels of economic disadvantage and violence); discrimination; and criminal victimizations. Because of their disadvantaged status, Kaufman et al. argue that African Americans are less likely to have the resources to cope with strain. In addition, they surmise that since African Americans are more likely than other racial/ethnic groups to live in single-parent households, they have less social support to buffer the effects of noxious stimuli and strains. It is noteworthy that since Agnew's initial clarification of the nuances of racial discrimination as a potential stressor, scholars have consistently found support for the theory (Eitle and Turner, 2003; Jang and Johnson, 2003, 2005; Jang and Lyons, 2006; Simons, Chen, Stewart, and Brody, 2003). Otherwise, in the absence of including perceived racial discrimination, GST has generated equivocal results for explaining racial disparities in crime (Piquero and Sealock, 2010).

We do not dispute the claims made by strain theorists in regards to African American offending. Indeed, we have found them to be particularly insightful and they inform our own theory. However, we argue, as Agnew (2001) recognizes, that group-based theories of crime are necessary to fully understand their offending. This is particularly the case as Agnew argues that there are no universal "objective strains," even though most people do not want to suffer from inadequate nutrition or shelter. Rather, he stipulates that every group has its own "objective strains." Agnew (2001) does not *a priori* predict the specific strains different groups will experience. Instead, he argues that these group-based strains can be revealed *post hoc* by, for example, surveying the members of the group or by assembling a panel of judges familiar with the group being examined. These responses are then averaged to create a list of objective strains particular to that group. Agnew (2001:353) calls for further group-based research as "it is likely that there are group differences in the extent to which certain strains are seen as unjust or high in magnitude."

Our theory creates a group-based theory of offending that is specific to African Americans. Our theory *a priori* articulates the strains that pervade the lived experiences of African Americans and how they relate to their offending. Equally importantly, our theory explains why these strains emerged and why they continue to compel some African Americans to offend. Thus, our theory begins with the argument that African Americans share a unique worldview that has been forged in the daily experiences of living within a conflicted, racially stratified society. We additionally assert that a theory of African American offending must recognize the systemic macro causes of racial subordination as they produce the stressors and strain that blacks disproportionately experience in their daily lived experiences. It also must be grounded in the history that African Americans uniquely experienced, share, and transmit across generations (Harrell, 2000). A theory without this history provides no context to situate why African Americans dispro-portionately experience the multifaceted forms of racial subordination and why they are related to their offending. In short, our theory reveals how the collective history and current lived experiences of African Americans are related to their likelihood of offending.

Aker's Social Learning Theory

Social learning theory has its origins in Edwin Sutherland's (1947) differential association theory. Sutherland's theory argues that criminal behavior is learned in the same way as any other behavior. That is, the motives and drives for engaging in crime are learned in intimate personal groups and people offend when they inculcate an excess of definitions favorable to the violation of law over definitions unfavorable to law viola-tions (Sutherland, 1947). In the mid-1960s, scholars began to challenge and revise Sutherland's work. Among the group of scholars who partici-pated in the revision of the theory was Ronald Akers.

In his first attempt to revise the theory, Akers and his colleague Robert Burgess constructed their differential association-reinforcement theory. They argued that Sutherland's theory did not consider the existing modern learning theory literature then being advanced by behavioral psychologists. This revision led to the development of what is now referred to as social learning theory. More specifically, the authors relied on the principle of operant conditioning that focuses on volun-tary behavior (Akers, Krohn, Lanza-Kaduce, and Radosevich 1979; Burgess and Akers, 1966). Operant behavior can be influenced by stimuli through classical conditioning. In brief, according to Akers (2009), social learning theory focuses on four major concepts: differen-tial association, differential reinforcement, imitation, and definitions. Akers (2009:50) provides the following overview of how these concepts work in tandem in social learning theory:

> The probability that persons will engage in criminal and deviant behavior is increased and the probability of their conforming

to the norm is decreased when they differentially associate with others who commit criminal behavior and espouse definitions favorable to it, are relatively more exposed in-person or symbolically to salient criminal/deviant models, define it as desirable or justified in a situation discriminative for the behavior, and have received in the past and anticipate in the current or future situation relatively greater reward than punishment for the behavior.

While there are limited race-specific tests of social learning theory in the literature (Higgins, 2010), the theory does assume that it will be applicable across races. Notably, in the original reformulation of the theory, Burgess and Akers (1966:142) addressed how their theory applies to minority groups:

> it has often been noted that most official criminal acts are committed by members of minority groups who live in slums. One distinguishing characteristic of a slum is the high level of deprivation of many important social reinforcers. Exacerbating this situation is the fact that these people, in contrast to other groups, lack the behavioral repertoires necessary to produce reinforcement in the prescribed ways. They have not been and are not now adequately reinforced for lawful or normative behavior.

In other words, according to the Burgess and Akers (1966), crime among inner-city blacks results from their overexposure to other African Americans who offend and the absence of being rewarded when they engage in conventional behaviors. Akers (2009) also includes race in his social structure social learning model. He views race as one of several sociodemographic/socioeconomic correlates that are "direct indicators of the differential location of groups or categories of individuals in the social structure" (Akers, 2009:333). Again, we do not dispute these general findings. Our theory incorporates the finding that African Americans are more likely to offend if they associate with delinquent peers but we argue that their inadequate reinforcement for engaging in conventional behaviors is related to their racial subordination.

Afrocentricity

We incorporate the insights from one other theoretical framework, Afrocentricity. Molefi Kete Asante is credited with founding the intellectual philosophy of Afrocentricity (Asante, 1980, 1988). Afrocentrists argue that the current focus in America and across the globe is Eurocentric and, as a result, privileges those ideas or people that are tied to Western society (Karenga, 2002). They also contend that Eurocentric researchers center their analyses on the history, contributions, and worldview of white Europeans while marginalizing the contributions made by other people— such as Africans—as they are deemed inferior to Western society.

Afrocentrists believe that in order to solve social problems in the black community, including elevated levels of criminal offending, blacks must adopt an Afrocentric cultural ideology. This ideology rejects the Eurocentric worldview that Afrocentric scholars argue is based on "control," "materialism," and "individualism." Oliver (1989b:26) contends that blacks can turn away from the harms attributable to Eurocentrism if they embrace African values:

> Afrocentric socialization refers to an interactive process by which black parents and adults structure their behavior and primary institutions to promote among black youth the internalization of values that emphasize love of self, awareness of their traditional African cultural heritage, and personal commitment to people of African descent.

Mazama (2001:387) adds that: "Afrocentricity contends that our main problem as African people is our usually unconscious adoption of the Western worldview and perspective and their attendant conceptual framework. The list of those ideas and theories that have invaded our lives as normal, natural, or even worse, ideal, is infinite." Consequently, Afrocentrists contend that an understanding of African Americans can only be attained if their behavior is situated within the lived experiences of being black in a conflicted racially stratified society that embraces Eurocentric values and rejects Afrocentric ideals.

Criminologist William Oliver was among the first to call for the incorporation of Afrocentricity into the study of black male criminality

(1984, 1989a, 1989b). Oliver (2003, 2006) argues that black male offending is the result of racial oppression; that is, "the result of structural pressures and dysfunctional cultural adaptations to those pressures. The term structural pressures is used to refer to patterns of American political, economic, social, and cultural organization designed to perpetuate White superiority and Black inferiority" (Oliver, 1989b:17). Oliver (1989b:17–18) asserts that black males are likely to inadequately respond to white racism if they do not embrace an Afrocentric cultural ideology. Oliver adds that black males who fail to embrace an Afrocentric cultural ideology are more likely to adopt a dysfunctional definition of their manhood. Thus, black males who inadequately respond to racial oppression are more likely to define their manhood in relation to being a "tough guy" or a "player of women."

Other Afrocentric scholars have added to the seminal work of Oliver. Schiele (1997, 2000) presents an Afrocentric perspective that relies heavily on Oliver's structural-cultural foundation. His perspective incorporates the roles of (1) political/economic oppression, (2) spiritual alienation, and (3) cultural misorientation. Schiele (2000:75) argues that: "This framework assumes that these factors, separately and together, can exert direct and indirect effects on many youths and can place them at risk of committing violent acts." The first aspect of Schiele's theory discusses the role of structural inequalities in the lives of blacks. Schiele (2000:75) notes that: "One of the most important ways in which political economic oppression manifests is through the occurrence of massive poverty, underemployment, and unemployment." Notably, Schiele (2000:76) specifies why poverty is related to African American offending: "The Afrocentric paradigm maintains that the discrepancy between the messages of meritocracy and youths' material conditions, and the sense of cynicism and despair that accompany this discrepancy, serve as the primary motivations for lower-income youth to commit violent crime." Furthermore, Schiele posits that many African American youths turn to the street economy because of their cynicism and despair (Sullivan, 1989; Venkatesh, 2006).

The second core aspect of Schiele's theory is spiritual alienation. He defines spiritual alienation as "the disconnection of nonmaterial and morally affirming values from concepts of human self-worth and from the character of social relationships" (Schiele, 1996:289). Thus, Schiele argues that American culture and its focus on individualism and the acquisition of material wealth leads to a "cutthroat morality." In turn, this produces spiritual alienation. Schiele believes that the mass media reinforces this alienation through its programming.

The final aspect of Schiele's theory addresses cultural misorientation or cultural oppression. Cultural misorientation is when one group "imposes the traditions, history, and interpretations of the dominant cultural group onto less powerful cultural groups in a manner that suppresses and marginalizes the traditions, history, and interpretations of these less powerful groups" (Schiele, 2000:88). He argues that cultural misorientation "manifests [itself] as a form of anti-self-expression or cultural self-hatred" (Schiele, 2000:88). Thus, blacks inflicted with cultural misorientation tend to reject their own history and traditions in favor of Eurocentric history and traditions including the racist belief that everything black is inferior (Akbar, 1991; Fanon, 1967a; Wilson, 1993). Afrocentric theorists argue that this hostility and rejection towards everything black contributes to the elevated levels of youth violence that is endemic among black youth (Schiele, 2000; Wilson, 1990, 1992, 1993, 1999).

Our work builds upon the fundamental assumption made by Afrocentists that an understanding of black offending can only be attained if their behavior is situated within the lived experiences of being African American in a conflicted, racially stratified society. We assert that any criminological theory that aims to explain black offending must place the black experience and their unique worldview at the core of its foundation. Our theory places the history and lived experiences of African American people at its center. We also fully embrace the Afrocentric assumption that African American offending is related to racial subordination. Thus, our work does not attempt to create a "general" theory of crime that applies to every American; instead, our theory explains how the unique experiences and worldview of blacks in America are related to their offending. In short, our theory draws on the strengths of both Afrocentricity and the Eurocentric canon.

Conclusion

In the chapters that follow, we detail how the experiences of living in a society with conflicted race relations are related to African American offending. We present our theory of African American offending out of a perplexed frustration. We are perplexed that most other criminologists have not developed a race-centered theory of African American offending given the incredible racial disparities in offending, especially in violent crimes. We are also perplexed that most other criminologists fail to fully recognize that racial subordination has something to do with African American offending. We are additionally perplexed that most other criminologists have not precisely outlined the multitude of profound and nuanced ways that racial subordination is related to African American offending. We are frustrated by their omission because it has been more than 100 years since the eminent scholar W.E.B. Du Bois argued that the maturation of criminology requires it to devote its theoretical promise to discovering the "real conditions" related to African American offending. We are further frustrated because it has been nearly 20 years since Russell-Brown (1992) prominently advocated for criminologists to create a subfield—a black criminology—that centers its analysis on race and racism.

2

AN AFRICAN AMERICAN WORLDVIEW

October 3, 1995, is a day burned in the memory of many Americans. Americans from all walks of life stopped everything that they were doing as the media announced the verdict of the O.J. Simpson trial for the alleged murder of his wife and Ronald Goldman. White Americans were literally stunned; their jaws dropped; they stood in total disbelief as the media blared that the jury had found him innocent of all charges after only four hours of deliberation. They were incredulous as they knew in their collective heart that O.J. was guilty; he had murdered his wife, Nicole Brown Simpson, and Ronald Goldman. But, the incredibility that was coursing through white America was exploded even further as the television cameras panned to groups of African Americans who had collectively gathered to watch the verdict. As the television scanned across these groups, white Americans witnessed African Americans in a rapturous joy as they spontaneously jumped up in unison to celebrate O.J. Simpson being set free. Poor and wealthy African Americans, men and women, young and old, college educated and those with little education, all collectively shared in a moment of celebration. White Americans were literally taken aback; it was unfathomable; how is it possible for their fellow African American citizens to celebrate the acquittal of a person who they "knew" killed his wife and another human being? Could it be, as one journalist opined, that whites "don't have anybody known to them as The Man?" (Littwin, 1995).[1]

This indelible moment in history forced Americans of all races and ethnicities to confront the reality that Americans do not speak with one voice; that is, that they do not share a collective worldview or cognitive landscape when it comes to how people perceive the criminal justice system. That is, African Americans and whites can witness the same event but interpret it quite differently. Indeed, the *New York Times/ CBS News*, October 1, 1995, poll shows that African Americans and whites viewed the O.J. trial from two worlds far apart. The survey revealed that 90 percent of African Americans in comparison with 30 percent of the whites thought that the O.J. verdict was right. And, 18 percent of African Americans in comparison with 87 percent of whites believed that O.J. was probably guilty. These differences in worldviews cannot be accounted for by other factors such as age, income, level of education, or political philosophy (whether they are liberals or conservatives).

Indeed, a NBC poll conducted in 2004 still indicated that African Americans and whites remain divided (NBC News, 2010). The survey revealed that 87 percent of whites in comparison with 29 percent of African Americans think that O.J. Simpson murdered his wife and Ronald Goldman; and, of interest, 17 percent of whites versus 63 percent of African Americans report that they would like to have dinner with O.J. Simpson. We present this short synopsis as a preliminary illustration that African Americans and whites may be two worlds far apart in their opinions of the criminal justice system.

The Basic Premise of Our Theory of African American Offending

A basic assumption of our theory of African American offending is that blacks have a unique worldview (or cosmology, axiology, aesthetics, cognitive landscape, collective memory) of the American social order that is not shared by whites and other minorities (see Coll, Lamberty, Jenkins, McAdoo, Crnic, Wasik, and García, 1996; Feagin, 2010; Gay, 2004; Harrell, 2000; Jean and Feagin, 1998; Mazama, 2001; Oliver,

2006). We argue that this worldview has been shaped by racial dynamics largely outside of their control. Thus, our theory assumes that African Americans, unlike any other racial group (e.g., whites) or other ethnic minorities (e.g., Hispanics), have a unique racial lens that informs their beliefs and behaviors especially as they relate to the salience of race and how racism impacts their lives in the U.S.

We argue that nearly every African American shares this worldview. A core belief of this worldview is that race and racism matters. This means that nearly every African American believes that they will encounter racial prejudice and racial discrimination during their lives because they are black. Thus, African Americans believe that they will not be treated as fairly as other races (e.g., whites) or other ethnicities (e.g., Hispanics). Put simply, they are aware that the playing field is not level; that is, they are aware that they will be discriminated against because of their race. In sum, we contend that the pivotal belief that solidifies and defines the worldview shared by African Americans is that the United States has been and continues to be a systematically racist society.

Scholars argue that blacks have developed this peerless worldview because there is a "long history of public dishonor and ritualized humiliation of African Americans by Euro-Americans" (Hagan et al., 2005:382). They also note that this worldview has been forged across generations as each successive generation has had to negotiate their encounters with the many variegated forms of racial subordination. Thus, over time, this worldview has become part of their "collective memory"; that is, how African Americans experience their present in light of their past. Jean and Feagin (1998:30) define this collective memory as:

> Memories of negative experiences with white Americans, accumulated and communicated by individuals, families, and communities, web together with memories of contending and resisting racial oppression. Beyond this collectively recorded experience are many family and other collective memories *not* associated with dealing with whites or white racism. All these collective memories and

knowledge become a major buttress of African American culture and communities.

Feagin (2010:213–214) adds that the assaults of blatant, covert, and subtle racism have strong effects not only on individual African Americans

> but also on their larger social circles, for the reality and pain of discriminatory acts are usually shared with relatives and friends as a way of coping with such inhumanity. Over time the long-term pain and memory of one individual becomes part of the pain and collective memories of larger networks, extended families, and communities. This negative impact requires the expenditure of much individual, family, and community energy to endure the oppression and to develop strategies for fighting back.

Thus, we concur with Harrell's (2000:46) assertion that the recognition and understanding of African American history "is necessary in order to appreciate the layers of racism-related dynamics" that reciprocally informs their peerless worldview and their daily lived experiences.[3]

We argue that the social construction of the African American worldview is a dynamic, evolving process. It includes a general recognition of the historical racial struggles that African Americans have gone through along with specific accounts of successful resistance. This means that the worldview has a historical-legacy component that acts as a racial lens that sensitizes African Americans to how race and racism shape the contours of their daily lived experiences. This worldview also evolves as its history is infused with the present collective racialized lived experiences of African Americans. But, all worldviews are just broad guides. They are not explicit detailed blueprints that precisely define how all African Americans should behave across immeasurable situations. Because of this imprecision, it is possible for the African American worldview to be both an inspiration for the majority of African Americans to successfully resist their racial subordination as well as a source of beliefs that cause a minority of blacks to offend.

Thus, the majority of blacks draw upon the strengths of the stories that describe how others have successfully resisted their racial subjugation. While the worldview for others causes them to be overwhelmed with the deleterious feelings associated with their awareness of how their race and racism will negatively impact their lives.

In sum, our theory contends that the worldview shared by African Americans provides the vast majority of blacks with the ability to fend off the deleterious consequences of racial subordination. However, it also provides a minority of blacks with the impetus to respond to racial subjugation with attitudes and behaviors that increase their likelihood of offending. Therefore, our task is twofold. First, we need to establish that African Americans have a unique shared worldview. Second, we have to highlight the racism-related dynamics that we assert are related to why a minority of African Americans engage in crime.

In this chapter, we begin this twofold process by first presenting unequivocal evidence that shows that African Americans share a unique worldview. This unique worldview is most clearly revealed when we examine issues related to the salience of race and racism. Second, we highlight two aspects of this worldview that our theory asserts are related to African American offending, that is, perceptions of criminal justice injustices and racial discrimination. We examine whether African Americans share the belief that the criminal justice system is racist and whether they perceive that they have been discriminated against because they are black. We hypothesize that African Americans who offend are more likely to perceive or experience criminal justice injustices and are more likely to experience the debilitating consequences of racial discrimination.

The Racial Divide

Evidence of a General Racial Divide

Evidence abounds that African Americans and whites do not share the same worldview across a variety of domains. Scholars often refer to these differences in viewpoints as the "racial divide" (Kinder and Sanders, 1996; Unnever, Cullen, and Jonson, 2008). Below we summarize a variety of surveys that have documented disparities in opinions between whites and African Americans. These include studies of public opinion related to Hurricane Katrina, whether race matters, the success of the civil rights movement, reparations, and race relations. We then follow with a discussion of the racial divide in public opinions about the criminal justice system.

Hurricane Katrina

Similar to the O.J. Simpson trial, the recent Hurricane Katrina catastrophe in New Orleans and its aftermath forced America to visually confront the fact that African Americans and whites do not always share the same lived experiences. Surveys showed that whites and African Americans reacted differently to the visual images of the Katrina aftermath that flashed across television and computer screens. Over three-quarters of African Americans (77 percent) expressed the view that the government's response to the crisis would have been faster if most of the storm's victims had been white, in comparison with only 17 percent of whites. African Americans and whites also differed in their interpretation of the acts of violence during the flooding; roughly a third of blacks (39 percent) thought that criminals were taking advantage of the flooding in comparison to 61 percent of whites (Pew Research Center, 2005).

Does Race Matter?

Surveys also show that African Americans and whites differ in their perceptions of the degree to which race shapes the contours of American life. A majority of blacks (53 percent) believe that major conflicts exist between the two races in comparison with a third of whites (35 percent) (Morin, 2009). According to a 2003 Pew Research survey, more blacks (93 percent) than whites (73 percent) agree with interracial dating. Additionally, whites and African Americans differ in their beliefs about equal educational opportunities; according to a 2007 Gallup survey, 80 percent of whites in comparison to 49 percent of blacks believe that African American and white children have equal educational opportunities. It is notable that this divide of 30 percentage points mirrors the gap between the high school graduation rate of African Americans and white males: 47 versus 78 percent (Schott Foundation for Public Education, 2010). Racial divides also extend into perceptions of whether housing and employment are equal for African Americans and whites; according to a 2007 Gallup survey, 44 percent of African Americans compared with 84 percent of whites believe that blacks and whites can get any housing they can afford; and, whites are twice as likely (76 percent) as African Americans (37 percent) to report that both races can get any kind of job for which they are qualified (Saad, 2007).

Success of the Civil Rights Movement

Furthermore, a 2008 Gallup survey indicates that African Americans and whites do not share the same worldview when considering the success of the civil rights movement. Twenty-nine percent of African Americans report that all or most of the civil rights movement's objectives regarding racial equality have been achieved in contrast to 46 percent of whites (Saad, 2007). And, there are wide gaps in the attitudes that African Americans and whites have as to how to resolve racial inequities. A quarter of African Americans (26 percent) believe that efforts to promote equal rights have gone too far, whereas nearly half of whites express this view (46 percent) (Pew Research Center, 2003). Not surprisingly, a substantial racial divide exists in support for affirmative action. A 2005 Gallup poll reveals that a majority of African Americans (72 percent) favor affirmative action in comparison with 49 percent of whites (Jones, 2006).

Reparations and Race Relations

Perhaps the clearest evidence that African Americans and whites have unique worldviews is revealed in opinions about reparations; that is, whether the federal government should pay blacks whose ancestors were slaves. The *2004 Racial Attitudes Survey* showed that 94 percent of African Americans support reparations versus only 6 percent of whites— a gap of 88 percentage points. The poll also revealed that African Americans vastly support the idea that the federal government should apologize to blacks for the slavery that once existed in this country

(77 percent). A minority of whites agree with offering blacks an apology (23 percent). A racial divide also exists in the belief of whether the relations between blacks and whites will always be a problem in the U.S. According to a 2006 Gallup survey, the majority of African Americans (55 percent) report that black–white relations will always be a problem, whereas the majority of whites (56 percent) are optimistic that a solution will emerge (Jones, 2006).

The Racial Divide in Perceptions of the Criminal Justice System

Our theory asserts that one of the aspects of the unique worldview shared by blacks that is related to offending is their attitudes toward the criminal justice system. The following assesses whether African Americans and whites share the same perceptions of the criminal justice system.

The Racial Divide in Support for the Death Penalty

Scholars have asserted that support for the death penalty—the ultimate weapon in a society's arsenal to combat crime—captures the "emotional angst" of American society (Unnever and Cullen, 2007; Vollum, Longmire, and Buffington-Vollum, 2004). Therefore, there is no reason to assume that support for capital punishment should generate any angst that is related to race or to feelings of racial animosity. It is a race-neutral policy; that is, unlike preferential treatment policies (e.g., racial quotas) that are specifically designed to benefit a racial group, the death penalty, as a law, is not intended to target any specific group (Unnever, Cullen, and Jones, 2008). Put more simply, capital punishment would be unconstitutional if its *intent* was to disproportionately execute African Americans.

There are two significant findings related to the relationship between race and support for capital punishment. First, studies have found that there is an enduring deep racial divide in support for the death penalty. In fact, research reveals that the majority of whites support capital punishment, whereas, a minority of African Americans support the death penalty (Unnever et al., 2008). Equally compelling, researchers have found that the racial divide in support for capital punishment, approximately a difference of 34 percentage points, has remained the same over the last 30 years (Unnever et al., 2008). Thus, despite the gains that African Americans have achieved and the moderation of the racial attitudes among whites over the last three decades, African Americans and whites still have significantly different opinions about whether it is appropriate for the U.S. to execute convicted murderers. In short, the racial divide in support for the death penalty is an enduring aspect of the American social order.

Second, scholars have found that one of the most salient predictors of support for capital punishment among whites is racial resentments. For example, Unnever and Cullen (2007) analyzed the 2000 National Election Study (NES) and examined whether a scale that measured racial resentment (e.g., "Over the last few years, blacks have gotten less than they deserve" and "It's really a matter of some people not trying hard enough; if blacks would only try harder they could be just as well off as whites") and report that roughly a third of the racial divide in support for the death penalty is explained by the level of racial animus among some whites. In other words, support of capital punishment is most fervently expressed among whites who most strongly embrace racial resentments (Unnever and Cullen, 2007, 2010). Scholars have argued that this concentrated level of support among racist whites stems from them associating crime with race and race with crime (Beckett and Sasson, 2003; Chiricos, Welch, and Gertz, 2004; Peffley and Hurwitz, 2002; Unnever and Cullen, 2010). Thus, racist whites are adamant supporters of the death penalty because they believe it will disproportionately impact people that they do not like, that is, convicted murderers, and individuals they particularly do not like, African Americans who have been convicted of homicide (Unnever and Cullen, 2010).

Relatedly, Johnson (2009) found that a significant percentage of the racial divide in punitive attitudes is caused by perceptions of criminal injustices among African Americans. Johnson (2009) analyzed the 2001 *Race, Crime and Public Opinion Study*, which was a representative national sample of 978 non-Hispanic white and 1,010 non-Hispanic black respondents living in U.S. households. She created a punitive index that summed across the responses to items such as, "Do you favor or oppose sentencing a criminal to life in prison if he or she has committed three violent felonies?" and "When it comes to granting parole to people in prison, should parole boards be more strict, less strict, or the same as they are now?" And, Johnson (2009) created a perceived racial bias index by averaging across three items ("How much confidence do you have in the police in terms of treating Blacks and Whites equally?", "How much confidence do you have in prosecutors in terms of treating Blacks and Whites equally?" and, "How much confidence do you have in judges in terms of treating Blacks and Whites equally?" She found that whites were more punitive than African Americans across the measures included in her punitive index and that the more African Americans and whites perceived that the criminal justice system was racially biased, the less likely they were to be punitive while controlling for other factors including age, education, gender, income, fear of crime, political conservatism, whether a friend or relative has been incarcerated, and individual attributions.

Together, this research clearly reveals that African Americans and whites employ quite distinct racial lenses when viewing the death penalty. It also shows that a significant segment of whites support punitive crime controls because of their animus toward blacks while opposition among African Americans is driven by their perceptions of criminal injustices. That is, blacks are unwilling to embrace the death penalty even though their communities disproportionately experience the brunt of crime because they believe these severe policies will unfairly target other African Americans while some whites specifically support harsh policies because they believe that more blacks will end up in prison (Johnson, 2009). Moreover, despite all the gains of the civil rights movement, blacks and whites remain two worlds far apart in their attitudes toward the death penalty. Thus, African Americans are confronted by a law—the death penalty—that they do not support, that disproportionately impacts their race, and that whites with racial resentments significantly endorse.

The Racial Divide in Perceptions of Injustice in the Criminal Justice System

The death penalty is one of the most symbolically important components of the criminal justice system. However, there are two other agencies within the criminal justice system that are much more likely to impact the daily routine lived experiences of both African Americans and whites, that is, the police and the courts.

As with the death penalty, the research is unambiguous: African Americans do not perceive the police in the same way as whites. That is, there is a vast body of research that shows that there are substantial racial divides in how African Americans and whites perceive the police. For example, Weitzer and Tuch (1999) report that 44.5 percent of African Americans believed that racist police practices were "very common" in comparison with 10.5 percent of whites. In a subsequent study, Weitzer and Tuch (2002) found that more African Americans (81.6 percent) than whites (60.2 percent) believed that racial profiling by the police is widespread. Further, Weitzer and Tuch (2002) showed that African Americans are eight times more likely than whites to believe that they had been stopped while driving because of their race. Weitzer (2002) also reported that African Americans are more likely than whites to be negatively influenced by cases of highly publicized police misconduct.

Relatedly, Johnson and Kuhns (2009) found that African Americans, but not whites, were less likely to support the police using excessive force if they perceived that the police were racially biased. These researchers conclude that: "These results suggest that blacks and whites interpret police–citizen interactions in different ways. Blacks' more negative response to a police officer striking a black offender than a white offender is rooted in the long-standing concern in the black community about racial bias in the criminal justice system" (Johnson and Kuhns, 2009:615).

Overall, the research on the racial divide in perceptions of the police indicates that there are significant gaps between African Americans and whites in their confidence in the police, whether police are racist, whether police engage in racial profiling, the police use of excessive force, and the extent to which racial profiling occurs (e.g., pulling over African Americans who are driving because they are black, which is often referred to as driving while black [DWB]); and that these gaps persist despite controlling for other known covariates of public opinions (Gabbidon and Higgins, 2009; Higgins, Gabbidon, and Vito, 2010; Noble, 2006: Weitzer and Tuch, 2004).

African Americans and whites also do not share the same worldview in their perceptions of whether the courts are race-neutral. For example, Buckler, Cullen, and Unnever (2007) report that African Americans are significantly more likely than whites to report that the courts are discriminatory, are not egalitarian (i.e., treat people with respect), and were less likely to express satisfaction with how the courts handled its cases. Similarly, Tyler (2001) found that African Americans are significantly more likely than whites and Hispanics to believe that the courts treat people unfairly (see also Higgins, Wolfe, Mahoney, and Walters, 2009).

Unnever (2008) further demonstrates the degree to which African Americans have a worldview of the criminal justice system that is not shared by whites. Analyzing *The Washington Post*, Henry J. Kaiser Family Foundation, and Harvard University 2006 African American Survey, his research investigated whether there is a racial divide in the perceptions of why African Americans are disproportionately imprisoned. Studies show that "mass incarceration" has disproportionately impacted black communities (Schlesinger, 2011; Tonry, 1996).

Indeed, Alexander (2010:6) argues in *The New Jim Crow: Mass Incarceration in the Age of Colorblindness* that the United States imprisons more of its racial or ethnic minorities than any other country in the world and, in fact, it incarcerates a larger percentage of its black population than South Africa did at the height of apartheid. She notes that this massive incarceration of African Americans has resulted in one in three young black men being currently under the control of the criminal justice system—in prison, in jail, on probation, or on parole. Alexander (2010:9) concludes that mass incarceration has "in fact, emerged as a stunningly comprehensive and well-disguised system of racialized social control that functions in a manner strikingly similar to Jim Crow." That is, the mass incarceration of African Americans has resulted in a new rigid racial caste system that equals the segregationist laws of the Jim Crow era—a term associated with a minstrel show character. In short, "mass incarceration operates as a tightly networked system of laws, policies, customs, and institutions that operate collectively to ensure the subordinate status of a group defined largely by race" (Alexander, 2010:13).

Unnever (2008) found that the number one reason why African Americans believe that blacks are disproportionately incarcerated is their belief that the police are biased against African Americans. Seventy-one percent of African Americans believed that police bias was a "big reason" for black imprisonment in comparison to 37 percent of whites. In addition, he found that 67 percent of blacks reported that a "big reason" why African Americans are imprisoned was their belief that the courts were more likely to convict black men than whites in contrast to only 28 percent of whites. Importantly, Unnever (2008) found that African Americans are *more* likely than whites to report that black male imprisonment is related to African American parents failing to teach their children right from wrong and from black men believing crime is not wrong.

The Racial Divide in Support for the "War on Drugs"

King and Mauer (2002) found that the war on drugs has resulted in the near-tripling of drug-related arrests from 580,900 in 1980 to 1,579,566 by 2000. They also report that the number of inmates incarcerated for drug offenses at all levels—state and federal prisons and local jails—increased by more than 1,000 percent from 40,000 in 1980 to 453,000 by 1999. Thus, by 2002, there were 251,200 drug offenders in state prisons incarcerated at a cost of about $5 billion annually. King and Mauer (2006) also found that since 1990, the focus of the war on drugs shifted to low-level marijuana offenses. From 1990 to 2002, 82 percent of the increase in drug arrests nationally (450,000) was for marijuana offenses, and virtually all of that increase was in possession offenses. In addition, these scholars report that over half (58 percent) of people in prison for drug-related charges had no history of violence or high-level drug activity. Relatedly, President Obama's newly released drug war budget allocates nearly twice the amount of money for the criminal justice system than for treatment and prevention and its record amount, $15.5 billion, is 31 times greater than President Richard Nixon's budget even after adjusting for inflation (Nixon initiated the war on drugs) (Mendoza, 2010).

Most relevant, King and Mauer (2002) found that four of every five drug prisoners are African American and that this percentage exceeds their respective rate of overall drug use. Scholars argue that law enforcement's emphasis on crack rather than powder cocaine especially in urban areas has further exacerbated the racial disparities in drug arrests (Provine, 2002). Fellner (2009) adds that law enforcement's emphasis on crack rather than powder cocaine, especially in urban areas, has further exacerbated the racial disparities in drug arrests. He also reports that urban blacks account for approximately 6 percent of the national population, yet they constituted 29.8 percent of all drug arrests in 2007. Fellner (2009) adds that in the largest American cities, drug arrests for African Americans rose at three times the rate for whites between 1980 and 2003, 225 percent compared with 70 percent, and that in 11 cities black drug arrests rose by more than 500 percent. He also notes that in the 75 largest counties in the United States, African Americans in 2002 accounted for 46 percent of drug offense arrests, even though they represented only 15.6 percent of the population. Moreover, these percentages are replicated at the state level. Schoenfeld (2010) states that between 1986 and 1990, the number of black offenders admitted to Florida's prisons for drug crimes increased by 850 percent, while admissions for white drug offenders increased by 210 percent. Consequently, Alexander (2010) argues that no other law and order policy has contributed more to the racial disparities in arrests and imprisonment than the war on drugs.

Scholars argue that the "crack versus powdered cocaine" controversy is a particularly racially divisive issue (Beckett and Sasson, 2003; Kennedy, 1994). Under current federal law, the possible punishment for possession and distribution of crack cocaine is 100 times more severe than for powdered cocaine. It is noteworthy that The Fair Sentencing Act that reduces the disparity from 100:1 to 18:1 was signed into law by President Barack Obama in August 2010. Nonetheless, at the height of the controversy surrounding the sentencing disparities, Bobo and Johnson (2004) investigated whether there is a racial divide in support for harsher punishments for crack cocaine in comparison to powdered cocaine. Their analysis of the 2001 *Race, Crime and Public Opinion Study*, which oversampled African Americans, revealed a substantial racial divide; that is, 23 percent of whites in contrast to 45 percent of blacks "strongly disapproved" of more severe punishments for crack versus powder cocaine. Bobo and Johnson (2004) also found that race produced the largest effect in their analyses of support for the harsher punishment of crack cocaine even after controlling for other attitudes, including the salience of crime. Moreover, they found that the whites who were most likely to support the harsher punishments for crack cocaine were those who held racial resentments. Their measure of racial resentments included questions such as, "It's really a matter of some people not trying hard enough; if blacks would only try harder, they could be just as well off as Whites" and "Irish, Italian, Jewish and many other minorities overcame prejudice and worked their way up. Blacks should do the same without any special favors" (Bobo and Johnson, 2004:158). Additionally, Bobo and Johnson (2004) report that perceptions of criminal justice injustices (i.e., "In general, do you believe the criminal justice system is biased in favor of blacks, gives blacks fair treatment, or is biased against blacks?") significantly decreased support among blacks for sentencing crack offenders more severely.

A Worldview that is Shared Among all African Americans

Below we review the research that focuses on whether African Americans are factionalized in their opinions about the criminal justice system.

Unnever, Gabbidon, and Higgins (2011) analyzed a 2008 Gallup poll and investigated whether factors that routinely predict whether whites believe the criminal justice system is racist, such as political ideology and education, also predict the opinions of African Americans. They examined two questions: "How much confidence do you have in the local police in your area to treat blacks and whites equally?" and, "Do you think the American justice system is—or is not—biased against blacks?"

Unnever et al. (2011) found that African Americans were almost three times more likely (15.9 percent) than whites (5.8 percent) to report that they have no confidence in their local police to treat blacks and whites equally. And, African Americans were more than two times more likely (74.5 percent) than whites (34.9 percent) to believe that the criminal justice system is biased against African Americans. In addition, they report that African Americans believe that the police and the criminal justice system are biased regardless of their age, gender, education, income level, political ideology, religious beliefs and practices, and their attitudes toward the election of Barack Obama. This finding that blacks are likeminded in their opinions of the criminal justice system replicates the research by Unnever (2008). He also found that only one factor, perceived racial discrimination, was related to the opinions of African Americans in relation to why blacks are disproportionately imprisoned.

Brunson's qualitative research focuses on how African American youths in a high crime area perceive the police (Brunson, 2007; Brunson and Miller, 2006). Brunson (2007) argues that scholars studying the "rift" between the police and the African American community rarely have investigated this divide from the perspective of African Americans. To address this omission, he qualitatively studied 40 African American young men's direct and vicarious experiences with racial discrimination by the St. Louis police and whether these experiences influenced their perceptions of the police. He asserts that the worldview that African American youth have toward the police in St. Louis is shaped by their cumulative exposure to police-related racial discrimination. Importantly, Brunson (2007) argues that racial discrimination by the police reverberates throughout the African American community. Consequently, the perceptions that African American youth have toward the police are shaped by both a direct experience of racial discrimination and their awareness of how other blacks are treated; that is, their perceptions of the criminal justice injustices are created from both direct and vicarious experiences.

Together, these studies clearly support the premises of our theory of African American offending. They illustrate that: (1) African Americans have a worldview that is not shared by whites; (2) this worldview includes the belief that the criminal justice system is biased against blacks; and (3) this belief about a racially biased criminal justice system is nearly universally embraced by all African Americans regardless of their individual differences. In short, these studies confirm our assertion that there is a shared consensus among African Americans that the criminal justice system is biased against blacks.[4]

Why African Americans Share this Perception of the Criminal Justice System

In April 1899, an African American, Sam Holt, was lynched by a mob of white men in Newman, Georgia. He was burned at the stake. What follows is a newspaper report of the lynching that was printed in the *Springfield Weekly Publication*:

> The Negro was deprived of his ears, fingers and genital parts of his body. He pleaded pitifully for his life while the mutilation was going on . . . before the body was cool, it was cut to pieces, the bones crushed into small bits . . . the Negro's heart was cut into several pieces, as was also his liver . . . small pieces of bones went for 25 cents . . . (Gado, 2010).

This lynching is an illustration of the argument made by Hagan et al. noted above (2005:382) that African Americans have a unique world-view because they have encountered brutal and humiliating acts at the hands of whites. We add that the worldview shared by African Americans features, or is galvanized around, perceptions of criminal justice injustices because the criminal justice system has committed some of the most known horrendous brutal humiliations of African Americans (Banner, 2006; Gabbidon and Greene, 2009; Holmes and Smith, 2008; Ogletree, 2002; Ogletree and Sarat, 2006; Oshinsky, 1997; Vandiver, 2006; Waldrep, 2006). Alexander (2010:227) adds that: "Since the days of slavery, black men have been depicted and understood as criminals, and their criminal 'nature' has been among the justifications for every caste system to date. The criminalization and demonization of black men is one habit America seems unlikely to break without addressing head-on the racial dynamics that have given rise to successive caste systems."

Scholars argue that historically, southern whites used diverse techniques to control African Americans. Before the Civil War, slaveholders were the chief agents of social control (Tolnay and Beck, 1992). With the passage of the Thirteenth Amendment to the U.S. Constitution ending slavery, the social control of African Americans was transferred officially to local criminal justice systems and unofficially to vigilante mobs acting in concert with local officials (Bass, 2001; Garland, 2005; Tolnay and Beck, 1992; Zimring, 2003). Ogletree (2002:4) concludes that the death penalty has been and continues to be the "black man's burden" and that: "At a fundamental level, lynching was an expression of racism and racial discrimination—it reflected an effort to assert the superiority of whites over blacks." Alexander (2010) adds that the social control of African Americans by chattel slavery was transformed into a control by segregationist laws within the framework of Jim Crow. She states that: "By the turn of the twentieth century, every state in the South had laws on the books that disenfranchised blacks and discriminated against them in virtually every sphere of life, lending sanction to a racial ostracism that extended to schools, churches, housing, jobs, restrooms, hotels, restaurants, hospitals, orphanages, prisons, funeral homes, morgues, and cemeteries. Politicians competed with each other by proposing and passing ever more stringent, oppressive, and downright ridiculous legislation (such as laws specifically prohibiting blacks and whites from playing chess together). The public symbols and constant reminders of black subjugation were supported by whites across the political spectrum" (Alexander, 2010:35).

Research documents show that in the south in the late 1800s and early 1900s there was an epidemic of lynchings. During this period, 73 percent of all lynching victims were African Americans (1,748 African American men, women, and children were lynched by white men), and more than 95 percent of those were tortured and killed in the south (Clarke, 1998; Tolnay, Deane, and Beck, 1996). All told, more than 4,700 people from 1882 to 1968, most of them black men, were lynched by white mobs. In fact, at the turn of the 20th century, more than 100 lynching incidents were reported each year, many of them publicly orchestrated to humiliate the victims and instill fear in others. Lynching occurred in all but four states in the contiguous United States, and fewer than 1 percent of the perpetrators were brought to justice

(Thomas-Lester, 2005). Tolnay et al. (1996) argue that the function of racially motivated lynchings was to perpetuate the hegemony of whites, especially the economic domination of whites. Clarke (1998:276) adds that public lynchings had a pernicious consequence on southern African American culture; they created a subculture of fear that "informed the actions of every black man, woman and child throughout the South."

Clarke further argues that this fear did not subside because of the eventual decline of lynchings by the 1920s. Rather, he asserts that the fear felt by African Americans endured because lynchings were replaced with an equally felt odorous form of violence that blacks disproportionately experienced—state executions. Indeed, southern white elites acknowledged that capital punishment could serve the same function as lynchings—the control and intimidation of African Americans. In fact, state-ordered executions were considered by both white and African American southerners as "legal lynchings" (Banner, 2006; Ogletree, 2006). Importantly, lynchings were just one part—but perhaps one of the most devastating aspects—of how the criminal justice system was implicated in the racial oppression of African Americans during the Jim Crow era (Vandiver, 2006). The criminal justice system was also instrumental in the enforcement of segregationist laws and it was a major supplier of cheap labor to white-owned businesses. "Convict laws" allowed local criminal justice officials to lease out its convicts to businesses including plantations (Oshinsky, 1997). Noble (2006) adds that African American males sentenced to the convict lease system faced conditions similar to those they experienced under slavery. Alexander (2010:32) concludes that: "The criminal justice system was strategically employed to force African Americans back into a system of extreme repression and control, a tactic that would continue to prove successful for generations to come."

It is important to note that the federal government passively supported the criminal justice system's oppression of African Americans; for example, even though the federal government was aware that thousands of individuals were being lynched, it failed to stop the mass terrorism of African Americans (Tolnay et al., 1996). Indeed, in 2005 the U.S. Senate finally approved a resolution apologizing to lynching victims, survivors, and their descendants and for its previous failure to enact federal anti-lynching legislation. Similar legislation to apologize for the federal government's complicity was thrice defeated by fiery Senate filibusters that included overt racist statements, such as the one made by segregationist Senator James Thomas Heflin (D-Ala.) in 1930: "Whenever a Negro crosses this dead line between the white and the Negro races and lays his black hand on a white woman, he deserves to die" (as quoted in Thomas-Lester, 2005). Recently, states have enacted similar legislation apologizing for racial atrocities such as the white-terrorist massacre in Rosewood, FL (Bassett, 1995; Dye, 1996). Today nearly 44 percent of those under a sentence of death are African American (Bonczar and Snell, 2004) and nearly half (46 percent) of the individuals exonerated since 1973 are blacks. Vandiver, Giacopassi, and Lofquist (2007) add that 90.6 percent of the recent executions occurred in states that supported the practice of slavery and conclude that the death penalty is one of the enduring legacies of American slavery. Together, these studies provide a context for understanding why the majority of African Americans oppose whereas the majority of whites support the death penalty for convicted murderers.

Butler (2009), in his *Let's Get Free: A Hip-Hop Theory of Justice*, adds that African Americans now interpret the mass incarceration of mostly young, poor, black men in the same way that past generations perceived slavery. Butler (2009:37) argues that slavery was a way of controlling blacks and now imprisonment serves the same function: "It causes many African Americans to harbor strong feelings of resentment against the government. Indeed, 'hate' would not be too strong a word to describe the feelings in some urban communities toward the criminal justice system and the police—the most visible agents of the state." Butler (2009:37), a former United States federal prosecutor, concludes "that mass incarceration is disastrous for race relations, and when it is gone, so too will be a major source of African American's disenfranchisement with their citizenship. They will be more a part of the fabric of America and they certainly will be freer."

We do not solely argue that the historical brutal oppression of African Americans by the criminal justice system and white mobs account for their unique worldview. Rather, we argue that this historical legacy provides a framework that sensitizes African Americans to any racist acts that are contemporarily perpetuated by the criminal justice system. We also assert that these current acts, whether they are committed by the police or the courts, reverberate throughout the African American community. Thus, the historical belief that the criminal justice system is racist is reaffirmed when African Americans personally or vicariously (see Brunson, 2007) experience criminal justice injustices, such as the beating of Rodney King, the killing of Amadou Diallo (shot 19 times, of 41 rounds fired, while reaching for his wallet) by four NYC police officers, the brutal sodomy of Abner Louima with a broken broom handle while other officers held him down (Hirschfield and Simon, 2010; Holmes and Smith, 2008). And, unfortunately, we suggest that there are enough of these racist acts, whether experienced locally or nationally, to continually reaffirm the belief among African Americans that the police are more likely to arrest blacks and the courts are more likely to convict and harshly sentence African Americans. It is also noteworthy that Johnson (2007) found that the willingness of African Americans to embrace "get tough" crime policies is negated by their perceptions of criminal injustices.

Thus, we argue that perceived racist acts by the police or courts become symbolically powerful events within the African American community. For example, we suggest that the arrest in 2009 of the African American Harvard scholar, Henry Louis Gates, was vicariously experienced by all African Americans (Thompson and Thompson, 2009). We posit that his arrest was especially felt by all African Americans because it intensified their feelings of vulnerability and potential humiliation. After all, Professor Gates was relatively wealthy, had an extremely prestigious occupation (a professor at Harvard), and had a PhD. Yet, from the African American perspective, none of these positive attributes could insulate him from the public shame of being arrested by a white police officer (Ogletree, 2010). That is, African Americans were saying to themselves: "if the police can arrest Gates, what can stop them from publicly humiliating me?" Indeed, a CNN poll indicates that blacks perceived the arrest of Professor Gates differently than whites. The survey revealed that two-thirds of whites rejected that a white homeowner would have been arrested for the same behavior in comparison to only 25 percent of African Americans (Steinhauser, 2009). Ogletree (2002:14) argues that: "The struggle for racial equality is inextricably tied to the struggle for fairness in the criminal justice system. And in both of these struggles, there is a long road ahead."

The Election of Barack Obama

There is little doubt that the election of the first African American president of the United States, Barack Obama, is a milestone in the history of American race relations. It is likely that 10 years prior to his election, the vast majority of whites and African Americans would not have predicted that a black man would be elected to be President of the U.S. Scholars also assert that his election marks a substantive turning point in race relations. That is, the "Obama effect" will reduce white racism while ameliorating the stereotype threat that inhibits African American achievement (Marx, Ko, and Friedman, 2009; Plant, Devine, Cox, Columb, Miller, Goplen, and Peruche, 2009).

However, central to our theory of offending, is whether the election of Barack Obama will fundamentally alter the worldview that African Americans have about the criminal justice system (Burton, Bonilla-Silva, Ray, Buckelew, and Freeman, 2010). This is a critical issue as our theory rests on the premise that African American offending is related to the belief that the criminal justice system is biased against blacks. The research by Unnever et al. (2011) directly addresses this issue. He and his colleagues examined whether the attitudes that African Americans have about the criminal justice system are related to their public opinions about the election of Barack Obama.

They found there was a racial divide in the attitudes that African Americans and whites have regarding whether the election of Barack Obama will positively impact race relations in the U.S. Whites were nearly twice as likely as African Americans to state that Obama's election will cause race relations to worsen. In addition, approximately 1 out of 4 whites discounted the impact that Obama's election will have on race relations by stating that his election would not be "that important." In comparison, 15 percent of African Americans expressed this opinion.

Although the percentage differences are not as large, they also found that whites were more likely to believe that Obama's election will not make it easier for African Americans to advance in their own careers and that his election will not open up opportunities for other blacks in national politics. In short, they found that African Americans were more optimistic than whites about whether Obama can positively impact race relations within the United States (see also Feagin and Wingfield, 2009).

Yet, Unnever et al. (2011) report that the favorable opinions that African Americans have about Obama were not related to their nearly uniform belief that the criminal justice system is biased. None of their Barack Obama measures significantly predicted African American opinions about whether the criminal justice system is racially biased. Their results reveal an ironic contradiction; African Americans are confident that Barack Obama will substantively improve race relations but their optimism had no impact on their perceptions of the fairness of the criminal justice system. This finding suggests that the long history of oppression that African Americans have experienced by the criminal justice system at the behest of whites has solidified and entrenched their worldview that the police and courts are biased against blacks. Their results further suggest that it will take more than the election of a black man as President of the United States to alter the worldview that African Americans share about the criminal justice system (Hagan et al., 2005; Ogletree, 2002; Oshinsky, 1997).

Perceived Racial Discrimination

Our theory asserts that there are two aspects of the worldview shared by African Americans that are related to their offending, perceptions of criminal justice injustices and perceived racial discrimination. The following provides evidence that the worldview shared by African Americans includes perceptions of racial injustices beyond their belief that the criminal justice system is biased against blacks.

We recognize that a good many of our readers, and perhaps our skeptics, will claim that racial discrimination is a "thing" of the past and is no longer a lived experience of African Americans. Others may claim that the level of racial discrimination has diminished to such an extent that it is no longer a salient factor for explaining black–white disparities (e.g., education, housing, economic, crime), especially with the election of Barack Obama. We do not dispute the fact that the level of overt racial discrimination has diminished. The data support this claim. For example, the level of acceptance of interracial marriage among whites has steadily increased, especially among younger cohorts (Pew Research Center, 2010). However, valid and reliable data simply do not support the claim that racial discrimination is no longer a meaningful factor that shapes the contours of America's race relations (Bonilla-Silva, 2008; Bonilla-Silva and Ray, 2009; Feagin, 2006; Feagin, Vera, and Batur, 2001; Feagin and Wingfield, 2009; Pager and Shepherd, 2008). Below, we highlight research that reveals the extent of racial discrimination in the 21st century and then we discuss the level of perceived discrimination among African Americans.

Would Employers Rather Hire Whites than African Americans?

Pager (2003) tested the degree to which a person's race in combination with a criminal record would affect their employment opportunities. Pager constructed four male testers, two African Americans and two whites. The two black testers formed one team and the two white testers the second team. The testers were 23-year-old university students who were matched on the basis of physical appearance and general style of presentation. All of the objective criteria, such as education and work experience, were made equal on their job applications. Within each team, one tester was randomly assigned a "criminal record" for the first week and then the pair was rotated so that the other member presented himself as the ex-offender for each successive week of employment searchers. Pager (2003) notes that varying which member of the pair presented themselves as having a criminal record negated any unobserved differences within the pairs. The pairs applied for jobs that required no previous experience and no education greater than high school.

The pairs were randomly assigned 15 job openings per week advertised in the newspaper. The white and black pairs were assigned separate sets of jobs with the same-race testers applying for the same job. One member of the testers applied first, with the second applying later in the same day. A total of 350 employers were contacted; 150 by the white pair and 200 by the black pair. Quite simply, Pager (2003) varied whether the tester had a criminal record but had a white and black apply for the same job who had the exact same application.

Not surprisingly, Pager reports that employers were significantly less likely to hire ex-offenders. However, her results regarding whether "race matters" were disconcerting. Pager (2003:960) found that: "Blacks are less than half as likely to receive consideration by employers, relative to their white counterparts, and black nonoffenders fall behind even whites with prior felony convictions." In other words, in 2003, employers would rather hire a white with a prior criminal record than a black who has never been arrested.

The research shows that racial discrimination is pervasive. Other "audit" studies (see Pager and Shepherd, 2008) using objectively matched African Americans and whites have documented strong evidence of racial discrimination in the context of housing searches (Yinger, 1986), car sales (Ayres and Siegelman, 1995), applications for insurance (Galster, Wissoker, and Zimmermann, 2001), home mortgages (Holloway, 1998; Turner and Skidmore, 2001), the provision of medical care (Schulman, Berlin, Harless, Kerner, Sistrunk, Gersh, Dube, Taleghani, Burke, and Williams,1999), in hiring at upscale restaurants (Bendick, Rodriguez, and Jayaraman, 2010), and in hailing taxis (Ridley, Bayton, and Outtz, 1989). Charles (2003:199) concludes that in terms of discrimination in housing the "use of audit methodology has forever altered the landscape of discussion regarding discrimination in the housing and lending markets, detailing widespread, current discrimination against blacks, Hispanics, and preliminarily Asians and Native Americans that occurs at virtually every point in the search process."

Perceptions of Racial Discrimination

The research unequivocally documents that racial discrimination has endured into the 21st century and is a lived reality for many African Americans. Thus, the research clearly shows that African American perceptions of racial discrimination are grounded in the objective conditions of their lives. Our theory of offending argues that the worldview of African Americans includes both the objective reality of being discriminated against and *perceptions* of racial discrimination.

Survey data support our contention that most African Americans, at some point in their lives, report that they have been personally discriminated against because of their race. A 2003 Gallup poll asked African Americans: "How often do you feel discriminated against in public life or employment because you are black—every day, every week, about once a month, a few times a year, less than once a year, (or) never?" Eighteen percent of African Americans report that every day they feel discriminated against, 8 percent every week, 13 percent about once a month, 25 percent a few times a year, and 15 percent report less than once a year. Most notably, only 19 percent of African Americans reported that they never have been discriminated against in public life or employment. Unnever et al. (2009) also reports that perceptions of discrimination among African Americans are widespread. He found that African Americans report experiencing different forms of discrimination, including being unfairly stopped by the police (51 percent), being denied a job that they were qualified for (28 percent), being physically threatened or attacked because of their race (26 percent), "people acting as if they are afraid of you" (21 percent), and "people acting as if they think you are not smart" (14 percent). Unnever et al. (2009) additionally reports that about two thirds (65 percent) felt that racial discrimination was a "big problem facing black men today." In addition, Dotterer, McHale, and Crouter (2009) report that a plurality of African American students report that they have personally experienced discrimination within their schools; that is, 48 percent of the black students reported that they have experienced discrimination from peers or teachers "a few times."

Studies further reveal that the vast majority of African Americans share the belief that blacks are routinely confronted by acts of racial discrimination. A 2008 Pew Research survey showed that two thirds of African Americans say blacks are "almost always" or "frequently" discriminated against when they apply for a job, 65 percent report discrimination when buying a house or renting an apartment, 43 percent report discrimination when applying to college, and 50 percent report discrimination when dining at restaurants or shopping in retail stores

(Morin, 2009; Rusche and Brewster, 2009; Harris, Henderson, and Williams, 2005). In fact, recent research has shown that blacks perceive that they are ten times more likely to be profiled as shoplifters in retail settings than whites (Gabbidon and Higgins, 2007, 2008; see also Harris, 2003; Harris, Henderson, and Williams, 2005; Gabbidon, Craig, Okafo, Marzette, and Peterson, 2008; Schreer, Smith, and Thomas, 2009). As in other studies, this finding holds true even when accounting for a host of variables including age, gender, and economic status. Also of interest, researchers have even found that there is a racial and ethnic divide in the degree to which Americans believe African Americans are confronted by racial discrimination. The data show that 67 percent of African Americans report that discrimination is commonly encountered when blacks apply for a job, in contrast to only 20 percent of whites and 36 percent of Hispanics (Pew Research Center, 2007).

In sum, the data confirm our assertion that a salient aspect of the worldview shared by African Americans is their experiences with racial discrimination. The research shows that few African Americans report that they have never personally experienced racial discrimination. Additionally, the research shows that few African Americans believe that other blacks have never experienced racial discrimination. In short, African Americans share a worldview that features the lived reality of being confronted by racial discrimination.

Conclusions

The fundamental assumption of our theory of offending is that African Americans have a unique worldview—a worldview that is not shared by others (i.e., whites, Hispanics, Asians). We argue that this worldview features two beliefs: perceptions of criminal justice injustices and perceptions of racial discrimination. The data presented throughout this chapter support our contention. The research shows that: (1) African Americans have a unique worldview; and (2) this unique worldview includes both perceptions of criminal justice injustices and perceptions of racial discrimination. In the following chapters, we discuss why these two perceptions increase the likelihood that some African Americans engage in crime.

3

PERCEPTIONS OF CRIMINAL JUSTICE INJUSTICES AND AFRICAN AMERICAN OFFENDING

We have established that the vast majority of African Americans have in common two beliefs: the belief that the criminal justice system is biased against blacks and that they have been or will be discriminated against because of their race. In this chapter, we outline why their perceptions of criminal justice injustices should be related to offending.

Perceptions of Criminal Justice Injustices

Our theory argues that there are two forms of racial oppression that are related to African American offending: criminal justice injustices and racial discrimination. Many scholars—both black and white—have prominently influenced our understanding of how these forms of racial oppression are related to African American offending. Below, we outline our theoretical reasons why African American offending should be related to perceptions of criminal justice injustices. Our analysis relies heavily on the well-known works of theorists Tyler (1990), Sherman (1993), and Hirschi (1969).

Why People Obey the Law

In the best of worlds, individuals obey the law and respect those responsible for its enforcement. People obey the law because it is perceived to

52

represent the collective interests of a society; that is, the law is perceived to be of, by, and for the people. Additionally, people perceive the police as instrumental in their lives because they serve and protect them and judges are exalted because they are perceived to blindly enforce the law, handing down the same sentence for like cases. In this consensual view, people obey the law because they perceive it to be legitimate. Sunshine and Tyler (2003:514) define the legitimacy of the law as: "a property of an authority or institution that leads people to feel that that authority or institution is entitled to be deferred to and obeyed." That is, people will voluntarily comply with the law because they believe that it is just and moral; that is, it is created from a moral consensus and it is applied fairly. As Tyler (1990:4) states: "Normative commitment through personal morality means obeying a law because one feels the law is just; normative commitment through legitimacy means obeying a law because one feels that the authority enforcing the law has the right to dictate behavior."

Thus, Tyler (1990) suggests that offending stems from how people perceive the law and the criminal justice system. For example, people may smoke marijuana even though it is illegal because they believe that the government does not have the right to legislate personal morality. Their moral position on the personal right to use drugs undermines the authority of the law to constrain their behavior. Tyler also hypothesizes that more serious and extensive offending occurs among individuals who perceive both the law and the criminal justice system as illegitimate. These individuals have little reason to obey the law because they perceive it as illegitimate and they believe that the criminal justice system has no legitimate authority to control their behavior. These beliefs define what he refers to as "procedural justice."

Procedural Justice

The concept of procedural justice assumes that individuals want to be treated respectfully by people in authority. More specifically, Tyler (2001) states that people want to be treated fairly and with dignity, they want their rights as citizens to be recognized, they want to feel the police care about their concerns, they need to feel that their views have been taken seriously, they need to believe that they or their case has not been prejudged, and to know that erroneous decisions will be reviewed and corrected. The concept of procedural justice also suggests that people primarily base their assessments of the legitimacy of the criminal justice system on perceptions of fair treatment rather than the fairness of outcomes. Thus, people can be arrested but still feel that the police who arrested them were "good cops" because the officers personally treated them with respect (Brunson and Weitzer, 2009).

Tyler (1990) tested his model of procedural justice with a panel study of over 1,500 Chicago residents. He created a self-report scale to measure the degree to which people violated six offenses (e.g., stole items from a store, drove a car while intoxicated). He then assessed whether the self-report crime scale was related to perceptions of the law (e.g., disobeying the law is seldom justified) and allegiance to legal authorities (e.g., how good of a job the police and courts are doing), while controlling for the effect of other measures (e.g., age and sex). The results strongly supported his normative model of procedural justice. "People who regard legal authorities as legitimate are found to comply with the law more frequently. This relationship holds across a variety of types of analysis and is robust across changes in methodology" (Tyler, 1990:64). Thus, the research shows that the relationship between perceiving criminal justice injustices and offending is robust.

In addition, Tyler (1990) reports that compliance with the law is most powerfully undermined when people feel that they have been mistreated by the criminal justice system. "If people feel unfairly treated when they deal with legal authorities, they then view the authorities as less legitimate and as a consequence obey the law less frequently in their everyday lives. Experiencing unfair procedures also leads people to base their compliance less strongly on assessment of legitimacy" (Tyler, 1990:108). Tyler (1990) also reports that peer support and personal morality were salient predictors of self-report offending.

In a related study, Sunshine and Tyler (2003) tested the procedural justice model using survey data collected in New York City. Controlling for other variables (e.g., ethnicity, education, age, income, gender, and other attitudinal variables), they found that individuals who strongly questioned the legitimacy of the police were both less likely to comply with the law and to cooperate with the police. In another study, using multiple datasets, Tyler (2001) found that personal contacts with the criminal justice system matter; that is, people who were arrested or went before the court and reported that they were not treated fairly were significantly less likely to positively evaluate the police and the courts.[1]

Legal Socialization

Tyler (1990) asserts that perceptions of criminal justice injustice and decisions to offend are constructed as individuals interact with others. More succinctly, he suggests that a person's "behavior is strongly affected by the normative climate created by others" (Tyler, 1990:24). Fagan and Tyler (2005) characterize this interaction process as legal socialization (see also Piquero, Fagan, Mulvey, and Steinberg, 2005). Fagan and Tyler (2005:220) define legal socialization as:

> a developmental capacity that is the product of accumulated social experiences in several contexts where children interact with legal and other social control authorities. In this framework, what adolescents see and experience through interactions with police and other legal actors subtly shapes their perceptions of the relation between individuals and society. These experiences influence the development of their notions of law, rules, and agreements among members of society, and the legitimacy of authority to deal fairly with citizens who violate society's rules.

They conclude that "children develop an orientation toward law and legal authorities early in life, and that this early orientation shapes both adolescent- and adult-law-related behavior" (Fagan and Tyler, 2005:219).

Thus, Fagan and Tyler (2005) suggest that children acquire their perceptions of criminal justice injustices as they contextually interact with their family, friends, and within the particular social milieu of their neighborhood. They describe this interactive process as "an integrative process that internalizes information derived from children's own experiences, their exposure to affective messages from others in response to their own experiences, and the cognitive frames that are prevalent within their neighborhood and peer group. That is, legal socialization is a process that is embedded in a set of interlocking social contexts and repeated social interactions over time in each of those settings" (Fagan and Tyler, 2005:222). In short, a person's decision to violate the law emerges from their personal perceptions of whether the law is just and whether the criminal justice system is fair and whether those perceptions are reinforced by the worldview in which they are immersed.[2]

Tyler (1990) further stipulates that it is possible for authorities (law-makers and the criminal justice system) to create a "reservoir of bad will" or a "sea of hostility" (see Noble, 2006:91). This reservoir reflects a belief "that the authorities are biased against a person or a person's group and should not be trusted or given discretionary authority" (Tyler, 1990:235). This suggests that it is possible for individuals to be immersed in a "reservoir of bad will" that gives rise to and reinforces their personal perceptions of criminal justice injustices. Other scholars note that there are significant race differences in perceptions of the legitimacy of the law, with African Americans having substantially lower legitimacy perceptions than whites (Piquero et al., 2005). Together, this research indicates that African Americans share a worldview—a sea of hostility—that includes perceptions of criminal justice injustices (Noble, 2006). In turn, the research indicates that African Americans, regardless of their age, that perceive criminal justice injustices are less likely to believe in the legitimacy of the law, and, therefore, are more likely to offend.

Fagan and Tyler (2005) found support for their thesis that legal socialization is an interactive process and that it impacts the probability of offending. They collected data from a community sample of adolescents, ages 10–16, from two racially and socio-economically contrasting neighborhoods in one of the five boroughs of New York City. Their analyses generated four findings that are particularly relevant to our theory of offending. First, they found that as children aged in these neighborhoods both their "legal cynicism" and perceptions of the legitimacy of the law decreased. Second, that "how children experience the law, or how they believe others experience the law, shapes their evaluations of legal actors and the underlying social norms that inform law" (Fagan and Tyler, 2005:231). Third, they found that parents impact the legal socialization of their children. And, fourth, their analyses showed that legal socialization (e.g., laws are made to be broken) is related to whether a person offends.

Perceptions of Criminal Justice Injustices and Defiance

The research by Tyler and his colleagues informs our theory of offending because it shows that individuals are more likely to offend if they perceive criminal justice injustices. However, we argue that a fuller understanding of why African Americans offend has to incorporate how perceptions of criminal justice injustice make people feel; that is, the emotions African Americans experience when they believe that the criminal justice system does not treat them fairly. Our theory of offending, therefore, argues that there are intervening attitudinal-emotive variables between the perception that the criminal justice system is biased and offending. We further argue that these emotive-attitudinal responses—master emotions—are the proximal cause of black offending. We now turn to the research by Sherman (1993) to identify the salient emotions and attitudes that intervene between African Americans perceiving criminal justice injustices and offending.

Shame, Anger, and Defiance

Sherman (1993) argues that perceived criminal justice injustices cause people to offend because being disrespected makes them ashamed of being ashamed; that is, it infuses them with a sense of self-righteous anger. This emotive response is defined by Sherman (1993) as defiance. He defines defiance as "the net increase in the prevalence, incidence, or seriousness of future offending against a sanctioning community caused by a proud, shameless reaction to the administration of a criminal sanction" (Sherman, 1993:459). This defiance stems from personal interactions (e.g., being personally disrespected by the police) or by vicarious experiences (i.e., knowledge that others have been disrespected). Sherman (1993) specifies four necessary conditions that cause people to act defiantly to perceived criminal justice injustices; that is, to offend. (1) The person must perceive the sanction as unfair. (2) The person must be weakly bonded to society.[3] (3) The person perceives the sanction as personally stigmatizing. And, (4) the individual refuses to acknowledge the indignation or shame that the sanction has caused him or her to suffer. In other words, Sherman (1993) suggests that perceptions of criminal justice injustice cause crime because: (1) it causes individuals to believe that sanctioning agencies (law-makers and the criminal justice system) are morally bankrupt and void of any legitimacy, and (2) individuals deny the indignation or shame of being treated unfairly and externalize these feelings by acting out with anger-rage-defiance.

Other scholars have found that perceptions of injustice are related to anger and that anger increases perceiving injustices (Brown, Abernethy, Gorsuch, and Dueck, 2010; Scher, 1997). The research also indicates that people associate feelings of disrespect with perceptions of being unfairly treated; that is, people believe they are being insulted or "dissed" when they perceive racial injustices (Mikula, Scherer, and Athenstaedt, 1998). In fact, scholars argue that the perception of disrespect is one of the most common sources of anger and aggression. Interestingly, the research shows that people become angry and aggressive because they believe that the unfair treatment—being disrespected—has diminished their prestige or status (Miller, 2001). In addition, scholars note that people who exhibit especially high levels of anger and aggression are more likely to perceive that other people are disrespectful (Dodge and Crick, 1990; Dodge, Price, Bachorowski, and Newman, 1990; Dodge and Somberg, 1987). Furthermore, the research shows that individuals are particularly likely to get angry and become aggressive if they feel that the perpetrators of the injustice are out-group members, have a higher status, purposefully treated them with disrespect, and if the insult was delivered in public (Mikula, 2003; Miller, 2001). Lastly, studies indicate that people retaliate in order to restore their self-image and to teach perpetrators of injustices that they do not tolerate being insulted (Miller, 2001). In sum, the extant research indicates that African Americans should be more likely to offend—externalize their anger-rage-defiance—in order to distance themselves from the shame that results from being unfairly singled out in public and unjustly treated by whites who show little remorse for their actions (Bouffard and Piquero, 2010).

Of interest, Sherman (1993) argues that defiant reactions to perceived or experienced criminal justice injustices are a cause for black on black crime (see also Schiele, 2000).[4] Sherman (1993) asserts that the righteous defiance felt by African Americans most often is displaced onto more vulnerable, more readily available others. Thus, the anger-defiance that African Americans have toward the criminal justice system is displaced and acted out within their own community, producing black on black crime (see also Fanon, 1967; Poussaint, 1983; Tatum, 1994; Wilson 1990). Sherman (1993) also argues that African Americans who perceive mistreatment may personally respond to a police encounter with "disrespect" toward the officer (thus, leading to higher rates of arrest for disorderly conduct or resisting arrest) (Belvedere, Worrall, and Tibbetts, 2005; Piquero and Bouffard, 2003).

In addition, scholars note that "race riots" are nearly universally triggered by an act of police brutality (Perez, Berg, and Myers, 2003). These riots spontaneously erupt as the perceived criminal justice injustices reverberate throughout the African American community (Holmes and Smith, 2008). Thus, the criminal justice injustice convulses through the community, causing individuals to feel a collective sense of outrage and defiance toward the criminal justice system. For example, Noble (2006:80) argues that in April of 2001, Cincinnati, Ohio, experienced "three nights of black rage" as a result of the shooting to death of an unarmed African American male, Timothy Thomas, and a subsequent outrage in September when the officer accused of shooting Mr. Thomas was found not guilty of negligent homicide. But, Sherman argues that often this outrage and defiance is contained within the black community. Consequently, the end result of this collective outrage is additional black on black crime.

However, Sherman (1993) notes that, at times, these criminal justice injustices can trigger race riots that result in violence that is not primarily contained within the African American community (i.e., resulting in higher rates of black on black crime) (Sunshine and Tyler, 2003). Indeed, Sherman (1993) argues that the Rodney King riot in Los Angeles illustrates how perceived criminal justice injustices can trigger widespread violence as African Americans targeted Korean and other Asian merchants operating in their neighborhoods even though their rage emanated from police brutality (see Kim, 1999).

Paternoster, Brame, Bachman, and Sherman (1997) tested the core hypotheses of Sherman's (1993) defiance theory. Their research analyzed data from the Milwaukee Domestic Violence Experiment. "In this experiment, all cases of misdemeanor domestic battery where probable cause to arrest existed were randomly assigned to one of three conditions: (1) warning with no arrest; (2) arrest with a brief detention period (average of 3 hours); and (3) arrest with a longer detention period (average of 11 hours)" (Paternoster et al., 1997:175). The experiment included 1,200 cases. They tested the hypothesis that the perception of fair treatment by the police, more so than perceptions of an unfair outcome, should restrain subsequent assaultive conduct. In other words, Paternoster et al. (1997) investigated whether people involved in domestic violence were less likely to offend if they perceived that the police treated them fairly (i.e., whether there is a relationship between offending and procedural justice).

Paternoster et al. (1997) found that the spouse assaulters' perceptions of procedural justice and fair treatment by the police were important factors related to the likelihood of future offending. They additionally discovered that perceived criminal justice injustices create the effect of anger and that this emotive response undermines the likelihood that individuals will feel compelled in the future to abide by the law or to acquiesce to the demands of the criminal justice system. Indeed, they conclude that the "recidivism-reducing effect of perceived procedural justice is comparable in magnitude to the various effects of arrest" (Paternoster et al., 1997:194).

In a related study, Bouffard and Piquero (2010) tested defiance theory within the context of life course explanations of persistent offending. They analyzed longitudinal data, the 1945 Philadelphia Birth Cohort, which allowed them to examine an individual's perceptions of his or her first encounter with police and how it relates to later offending. They specifically tested the defiance theory hypothesis that increased offending should occur among people who reacted defiantly because they perceived their treatment at the hands of sanctioning agents as unfair and stigmatizing, they refused to acknowledge their shame, and they had weak social bonds (while holding constant the effects of race, IQ, age of first contact with the police, and prior status offending).

Bouffard and Piquero's (2010) results support a strict interpretation of defiance theory. They found that individuals who define the sanction as unfair, were poorly bonded, and denied the shame of the sanction had the highest offending rates, which peaked later in the life course, and desisted at a much slower rate than the group that accepts the shame of the sanction. Bouffard and Piquero (2010) also argue that defiance theory can add to life course explanations of offending. They suggest that a defiant response to perceptions of criminal justice injustices may both cause individuals to engage in crime and to further distance themselves from conventional activities (e.g., completing school and full-time employment). Bouffard and Piquero (2010) argue that these reactions to perceptions of criminal justice injustices may add to the persistent offenders' experience of "cumulative continuity" (Sampson and Laub, 2004). That is, offending is more likely to occur when, for example, defiant individuals are channeled into environments that reinforce their angry-defiant attitudes, which, in turn progressively increases their likelihood of offending across their life course (Caspi, Bem, and Glen, 2006).

Research by Brownfield (2005) further supports Sherman's defiance theory. He analyzed urban youth in Canada to assess whether belonging to a gang was related to perceptions of the legitimacy of the police (e.g., the police treat most people fairly), feelings of shame (e.g., youths who would not care if they were picked up by the police), and pride (e.g., youths who were "excited" about the possibility of being picked up by the police). Brownfield (2005) found support for defiance theory; that is, gang members were more likely to believe that the police do not treat people fairly and they were excited about defying the police.

Hirschi's Control Theory and the Bond of Belief

The basic premise of control theory is that everyone is born with the predisposition to engage in criminal behavior. That is, the motivation to commit crime is equally distributed across all individuals. Accordingly, control theory eschews explanations of the origin of the motivation to commit crime and offers no explanation on why some individuals are more motivated than others to offend. Thus, the question for control theory becomes not why people engage in crime, but rather why some people, but not others, offend.

Hirschi (1969, 2003) argues that a person's belief in the moral validity of norms constrains their intrinsic desire to commit crime. Hirschi (2003:178) states:

> that there is variation in the extent to which people believe they should obey the rules of society, and, furthermore, that the less a person believes he should obey the rules, the more likely he is to violate them. In chronological order, then, a person's beliefs in the moral validity of norms are, for no teleological reason, weakened. The probability that he will commit delinquent acts is therefore increased. When and if he commits a delinquent act, we may justifiably use the weakness of his beliefs in explaining it, but no special motivation is required to explain either the weakness of his beliefs or, perhaps, his delinquent act.

Hirschi (2003:176) additionally assumes that there is a common value system "within the society or group whose norms are being violated." Thus, people do not have a separate belief system about what is right or wrong or in the legitimacy of law-makers and the criminal justice system. As Hirschi (1969:202) argues: "Attitudes toward the law are 'affectively neutral.' One does not love or hate the law." Of course, the question then becomes how control theory explains why there is "variation in belief in the moral validity of social rules" (Hirschi, 2003:178). Hirschi (1969, 2003) asserts that the reason why some individuals may question the moral validity of the laws or the legitimacy of law-makers and the criminal justice system is because they have weak social bonds with other conventional institutions. As Hirschi (1969:200) argues: "The chain of causation is thus from attachment to parents, through concern for the approval of persons in positions of authority, to belief that the rules of society are binding on one's conduct." Thus, control theory argues that the reason why African Americans question the legitimacy of the law is because their parents and other institutions, such as the educational system, failed to instill within them respect for the law and the criminal justice system.

It is particularly notable that one of the questions that Hirschi (1969:202) used to assess the variation in "belief" was: "I have a lot of respect for the Richmond police." And, his data show that in 1968 when the Richmond Youth Study data were collected, that people who strongly disagreed with the statement were four times (20 percent) more likely to self-report two or more delinquent acts than those who strongly expressed that they have a lot of respect for the Richmond police (5 percent). Thus, from a control theory perspective, these findings suggest that African American offending is related to their lack of respect for the police and that their lack of respect is caused by their parents and the educational system failing to inculcate them with a respect for the law and the criminal justice system. Hirschi (1969) also unequivocally assumes that the causes of why individuals do not have a strong belief system are the same for African Americans and whites.

We agree with the control theory's assumption that early socialization experiences are related to African American offending. In fact, a following chapter explicates how African American offending is related to racial socialization experiences. We also agree with his assumption that people who lack respect for the police should be more likely to offend. Indeed, Unnever, Cullen, Mathers, McClure, and Allison's (2009) reanalysis of the Richmond Youth Survey found that the more African Americans reported that they did not respect the Richmond police the more likely they were to self-report delinquent behavior, while controlling for the other social bonds and demographic characteristics.

But, we take issue with the control theory's assumption that the brutal oppression of African Americans by the criminal justice system is *not* a reason why they have "weak beliefs." We find this discounting especially perplexing given that Hirschi (1969) constructed his theory of "belief" when the U.S. was in the throes of the civil rights struggles with images emanating from the south of the police using weapons against blacks who were peacefully demanding civil right reforms and while cities on the coasts were aflame in race riots (Newark, NJ, 1967; Watts-Los Angeles, CA, 1965). Yet, in 1969, Hirschi presents a theory that assumes that the only reason why blacks disrespect the criminal justice system, the Richmond police, is because their parents and teachers failed to teach them to respect people in authority (Costello and Vowell, 1999).

Our theory argues that the distrust of the criminal justice system among African Americans is a salient, if not a defining, aspect of the worldview shared by blacks. As argued above, this perception of the criminal justice system has been "earned" and continually reinforced by widely publicized instances of the police using excessive force against African Americans (Holmes and Smith, 2008). We further assert that this worldview will only diminish when instances of racial bias within the criminal justice system are eliminated. Put more simply, perceptions of criminal justice injustices among African Americans are a natural outcome of widely known instances of racial bias by the criminal justice system. Thus, we conclude that there is a teleological reason why African Americans have weakened beliefs. This weak social bond is because of the past and present racially biased lived experiences that African Americans have with the criminal justice system.

In sum, we argue that weakened beliefs among African Americans can be caused by multiple sources. We agree with Hirschi (1969) that they can arise from the failure of parents and the educational system to instill within African Americans a sense of respect for authorities. In fact, we address this possibility in our chapter on racial socialization. However, we posit that African Americans should have weaker beliefs than whites and other minorities (e.g., Asians and Hispanics) because of the worldview they share and their experiences with racial injustices. More specifically, we argue that African Americans should have weaker beliefs than others because of their long history of being humiliated by whites in positions of authority such as the police (Hagan, Shedd, and Payne, 2005). Thus, as an extension of control theory, we hypothesize that higher rates of offending should occur among blacks who perceive criminal justice injustices and whose parents reinforced their perceptions of racial injustices.

Variations in African American Offending

The prior literature indicates that perceptions of criminal justice injustices are a salient predictor of offending (Bouffard and Piquero, 2010; Paternoster et al., 1997; Sampson and Bartusch, 1998; Sampson, Morenoff, and Raudenbush, 2005; Sunshine and Tyler, 2003; Tyler, 1990). The research also unequivocally reveals that African Americans are vastly more likely than whites to perceive criminal justice injustices and that this gap persists after controlling for the effects of other variables, including demographic characteristics, negative experiences with the police, and community disadvantages (Brunson and Weitzer, 2009; Gabbidon and Higgins, 2009; Schuck, Rosenbaum, and Hawkins, 2008). Scholars have also found that there are minimal differences among African Americans in their perceptions of criminal justice injustices (Unnever, 2008; Unnever, Gabbidon, and Higgins, 2011).[5] Therefore, the research indicates there should be little difference in offending among blacks as it relates to perceptions of injustice. That is, offending should occur among most African Americans because they nearly universally perceive criminal justice injustices. However, this is simply not the case; the vast majority of African Americans do not engage in crime even though they share the perception that the criminal justice system is biased against blacks. Below we initiate our explanation for why some African Americans but not others offend. We more fully explicate this explanation in the subsequent chapters.

Variations in the Degree to which African Americans Perceive Criminal Justice Injustices

We suggest that there are substantial individual differences among African Americans in the *degree* to which they perceive criminal justice injustices. However, we assert that researchers have failed to fully measure the *degree* to which African Americans perceive injustices. That is, we argue that researchers would find that there are significant differences among African Americans in their "legal cynicism" and that these differences will predict why some blacks but not others offend. In fact, we propose that researchers should assess the degree to which individual blacks perceive criminal justice injustices similarly to how they measure the severity of child abuse.

Thus, researchers should measure the age—the age of onset—that African Americans were first exposed to the belief that the criminal justice system is racist or had personal experiences of being mistreated by the criminal justice system (e.g. being personally mistreated by the police or having the courts "unfairly" take a parent away); who exposed the child to perceptions of criminal justice injustices (e.g. was it their parents, peers, or the community at large)?; to what degree was the person socialized into believing that the criminal justice system is biased against blacks (we discuss this aspect in our chapter on racial socialization)?; how often was the person exposed to instances of criminal justice injustices (e.g. did this come up in daily conversations, how often did they personally witness instances of police use of excessive force)?; and, over what length of time was the person exposed to the belief that the criminal justice system is racist (e.g. did it persist across their life span)? In short, we hypothesize that African American offending is related to the *degree* to which they perceive criminal justice injustices.

Variations in Place

The renowned scholar W.E.B. Du Bois (1903:103; see also Du Bois, 1899a) recognized how place negatively impacts African Americans and their likelihood of offending. Indeed, Du Bois (1903:16) argues that the "color-line"—racial segregation—is in itself a cause of crime:

> Draw lines of crime, of incompetency, of vice as tightly and uncompromisingly as you will, for these things must be proscribed but a color-line not only does not accomplish this purpose, but thwarts it.

Research confirms Du Bois's clear insights. That is, place matters in terms of African American offending. Peterson and Krivo (2010) found that African Americans are five times more likely to be arrested for violent crimes if they reside in the average black neighborhood in comparison to the typical white urban community. They also report that place matters, but less so, for property crimes. "Average property offense rates are about 30 percent and 50 percent higher for African American than for white and Latino communities, respectively" (Peterson and Krivo, 2010:111).

We argue that place matters because there are "pockets of legal cynicism" that enhance the probability that some African Americans will offend (Sampson and Bartusch, 1998; Sampson et al., 2005). Sampson and Bartusch (1998:786) identify legal cynicism as a "sense in which laws or rules are not considered binding in the existential, present lives of respondents" and it "taps variation in respondents' ratification of acting in ways that are 'outside' of law and social norms." Scholars characterize these pockets of legal cynicism as economically disadvantaged neighborhoods with high crime rates that are heavily policed (Carr, Napolitano, and Keating, 2007). Research reveals that African Americans are disproportionately more likely to reside in areas of concentrated poverty and isolated residential segregation (Kirk, 2008; Sampson et al., 2005). For example, Sampson and Bartusch (1998) reveal that in Chicago more than 50 percent of African Americans live in economically disadvantaged neighborhoods compared with 17 percent of Hispanics and only 2 percent of whites.

The research also indicates that African Americans residing in these poor areas—these pockets of legal cynicism—are more likely to have negative experiences with the police than blacks living in more affluent-less crime neighborhoods (Carr et al., 2007; Geller and Fagan, 2010; Weitzer, 2000). Indeed, Weitzer (2000:146) argues that middle-class black communities have more "social capital" than poor, high-crime African American neighborhoods and, therefore, are able to mobilize more resources to "hold officers accountable for their actions" (see also Sampson and Graif, 2009; Schuck et al., 2008; Weitzer, Tuch, and Skogan, 2008). In fact, Weitzer (1999) found that residents of a low-income African American neighborhood were between 4 and 7 times more likely than residents of a middle-class black community to report that the police had stopped people on the street unjustifiably, verbally abused residents, or used excessive force against them. These data parallel differences in African American offending, as Johnson (2007:3) notes that: "Within the black population, victimization rates also vary; the violent crime victimization rate between 1993 and 1998 was higher for younger blacks, for African Americans living in urban areas, and for blacks with incomes under $25,000 than for their respective counterparts."

We suggest that these pockets of legal cynicism are particularly criminogenic for some African Americans because they exacerbate the already shared belief among nearly all African Americans that the criminal justice system is racist and "is out to hassle them" (Brunson, 2007; Brunson and Weitzer, 2009; Gau and Brunson, 2010). That is, we argue that residing in these high-crime, police-saturated neighborhoods should substantially increase the probability that individual African Americans will be inculcated with the belief at an early age that is reinforced across the trajectory of their lives that the criminal justice system is biased against blacks. Johnson (2007) adds that in recent years perceptions of injustices within these pockets have been intensified as the "war on drugs" has principally targeted inner-city, predominantly black neighborhoods. As a consequence, African Americans residing in these pockets of legal cynicism may be hyper-vigilant in both perceiving and reacting to either personal or vicarious experiences with criminal justice injustices (Gau and Brunson, 2010).

Scholars have found that African Americans and whites residing in economically disadvantaged neighborhoods have substantially different perceptions of the police. More specifically, African Americans residing in economically disadvantaged neighborhoods are more likely to complain about perceived unjustified police stops and physically intrusive searches than similarly situated whites (Brunson and Weitzer, 2009).[6] That is, scholars have established that race matters in perceptions of criminal justice injustices even within urban areas of concentrated poverty. MacDonald, Stokes, Ridgeway and Riley (2007:2581) state "that Black and White residents with similar individual character-istics and perceptions of their neighbourhood environments, and who live in the same neighbourhood locations, still hold substantively different views of the police." Brunson and Weitzer (2009) add that in economically disadvantaged communities, whites have mixed opinions that include both favorable and unfavorable views of the police. In contrast, their research indicates that African Americans living in the same areas had "virtually *no* conception of the police as guardians" and considered them as "bullies in uniform" (emphasis in original) (Brunson and Weitzer, 2009).

It is also ironic that research reveals a reciprocal process whereby places with more concentrated disadvantage experience an increase in crime over time, which in turn causes these high-crime neighborhoods to experience a greater increase in concentrated disadvantage (e.g., a decrease in retail activity, more vacant buildings, an increase in liquor stores) (Hipp, 2010). Of note, scholars report that being chronically exposed to violent crime—homicide—reduces the scores on cognitive assessments (applied problems tests) for African American youths but not Hispanics (Sharkey, forthcoming). In addition, Hipp (2010) found that this process results in greater concentrations of African Americans. That is, (1) whites that perceive more crime in a neighborhood are more likely to move out, (2) whites are significantly less likely to move into a neighborhood with more commonly perceived crime, and (3) African Americans are more likely to move into the area (Hipp, 2010b; Xie and McDowall, 2010). We assert that these cumulative processes should intensify the likelihood that African Americans will experience racial injustices. Thus, these data suggest that the racist policies that created higher rates of crime in "ghettos" are exacerbating the likelihood that more African Americans will encounter criminal justice injustices, which in turn, should increase their rate of offending.

Of note, Weitzer (2010) argues that isolated racial segregation may have a complex impact on African Americans' perceptions of criminal justice injustices. He argues that isolated racial segregation geographically "contains" offending, which, in turn, may cause whites to feel less threat-ened by crime. In turn, this may result in the depolicing of these isolated racially segregated areas. African Americans, who usually demand greater police resources, may therefore negatively respond to the diminished presence of police, whereas those who believe the police are out to hassle them may be relieved by fewer police being in their neighborhoods. In short, Weitzer (2010) argues that these dual orientations, segregation, and its potential corollary, depolicing, may have a mixed effect on the opinions of the African Americans residing in isolated, racially segregated neighborhoods.

Variations in Defiance

Our theory further hypothesizes that African American offending should be related to the *degree* to which blacks take a defiant stand against authority. Thus, we hypothesize that African American offending is most likely to occur among those who most intensely perceive criminal justice injustices and most intensely embrace a defiant stand against authority. Our theory further argues that the likelihood of African Americans intensely perceiving criminal injustices and righteously embracing a defiant reaction is related to their place of residence. More specifically, we posit that African Americans that reside in a pocket of cynicism are more likely to intensely perceive criminal justice injustices and to more intensely react to their perceptions with defiance. We assert that this process of escalation or intensification occurs because individuals who embrace these attitudes are immersed in a network within these pockets of legal cynicism that reinforce both the perception of criminal injustices and a defiant reaction.

Variations by Gender

Our theory can also add to the explanations of gender differences in African American offending. The data clearly indicate that African American women are far less likely to offend than black men. Our focus here is whether there are gender differences in perceptions of criminal justice injustices that can supplement the explanations related to gender disparities in African American offending.

The prior research shows that African American women—like their male counterparts—have little trust in the police (Brunson and Miller,

2006; Fine and Weiss, 1998). However, Weitzer and Tuch (2002:443) found that young black males (ages 18–34) were nearly twice as likely as young African American females to report feeling that they had been unfairly stopped by the police because of their race (37.7 percent vs. 72.7 percent). More recently, Weitzer and Tuch (2006:86) again found that young black men were nearly twice as likely to report having experienced police bias in their city than young African American women (41 percent vs. 23 percent). Notably, black women reported experiencing police bias at rates higher than that of young white men (3%) and nearly on par with the rates of young Hispanic *males* (26%). Relatedly, Gabbidon, Higgins, and Potter (2011) explored the recent experiences of African Americans with the police and found that when asked whether they had encountered unfair treatment by the police in the last 30 days, slightly more black males (30%) than females (21%) answered yes.

Together, the research indicates that perceptions of criminal justice injustices pervade the African American community, impacting both males and females. Yet, the data suggest that black males are more likely to perceive criminal justice injustices, especially as they relate to the police. Thus, we contend that part of the gender disparity in African American offending can stem from the gender differences in percep-tions of criminal justice injustices. We hypothesize that because African American men may perceive greater criminal justice injustices they should have weaker beliefs in the legitimacy of the criminal justice system and should experience higher rates of anger-defiance than black women. Consequently, African American men should have higher rates of offending because of their weaker beliefs and their greater propensity to experience the negative emotions that are related to perceiving criminal justice injustices.

In sum, the literature is unequivocal; it shows that perceptions of criminal justice injustices are an integral and salient component of the worldview of African Americans. Our theory of offending assumes that the degree to which African Americans perceive criminal justice injust-ices varies across individuals and places. We hypothesize that higher rates of offending should occur among African Americans who deeply

perceive criminal justice injustices and intensely react to these perceptions with defiance. We further posit that these beliefs are more likely
to be expressed and intensified among African Americans who reside in
"pockets of legal cynicism." Thus, we assert that the highest levels of
African American offending should occur among those who strongly
perceive that the criminal justice system is racist, strongly react to these
perceptions with defiance, and reside in areas of legal cynicism.

4

RACIAL DISCRIMINATION, NEGATIVE STEREOTYPES, STEREOTYPE THREATS, AND AFRICAN AMERICAN OFFENDING

The history of black America is a history of African Americans encountering the painful experiences of racial discrimination and pejorative stereotypes. The ability of a group to discriminate against another group is power (Feagin, 2006). This means that there are two groups: that is, the superordinate group, which has more power and uses it to discriminate against the less powerful group, that is, the subordinate group. Discrimination occurs when members of the superordinate group use their power to deny subordinate group members the ability to maximize their human potential. Thus, discrimination in all of its facets is a form of injustice—being "dissed"—and as Butler (2009:135) argues, to "'dis' someone is worse than to insult them—it is to deny his or her humanity" (see also Miller, 2001). Accordingly, when members of the superordinate group discriminate against members of the subordinate group, regardless of whether it is unconsciousness, conscious, or institutional-systemic, it is at the subordinate group member's immediate and long-term expense. In the United States, the superordinate group consists of whites and the research shows that they have and continue to use their power to discriminate against African Americans (Bobo and Charles, 2009; Bonilla-Silva 2006, 2008; Bonilla-Silva and Ray 2009).

In this chapter, we outline how African American offending is related to three forms of racism, racial discrimination, pejorative stereotypes, and stereotype threats. Our theory of offending asserts that these forms of racism cause blacks to develop weak social bonds with conventional institutions and they cause African Americans to experience negative emotions, such as, hopelessness-depression and anger-defiance. Indeed, Feagin and Sikes (1995:293) argue that: "Most white Americans do not have any inkling of the rage over racism that is repressed by African-Americans. . . . The psychological costs to African-Americans of widespread prejudice and discrimination include this rage, as well as humiliation, frustration, resignation, and depression" (see also Clark, 1965; Grier and Cobbs, 1996; Noble, 2006). We further assert that racism undermines the ability of African Americans to create strong bonds with American institutions which in turn is related to their offending (Giordano, Schroeder, and Cernkovich, 2007; Schiele, 1997, 2000).

We posit that general theories of crime have tended to largely omit from their analysis the possibility that different forms of racism are a salient cause of crime among African Americans. This omission cannot be attributed to the lack of insight by black scholars on the unique causes of crime among African Americans (Caldwell and Greene, 1980; Gabbidon, 2007, 2010; Gabbidon, Greene, and Young, 2002; Greene, 1979; Greene and Gabbidon, 2000; Ross, 1998; Sulton, 1994; Young and Greene, 1995). For example, Du Bois clearly identified that racial discrimination—a unique lived experience among blacks—is related to black offending. Yet, we argue that Du Bois's insights were largely ignored in the historical development of the general theories of crime (Gabbidon, 2010). That is, "race-neutral" theories of crime, by definition, have to deny the possibility that racial discrimination is a cause of African American offending because it would limit their explanation to only blacks. This is not to say that the development of crime theories was purposefully racist. Indeed, we argue that the aspiration to develop race-neutral theories of crime had an admirable goal given the context in which they were created. These theories were developed at a time of rampant overt racism that, at times, pervaded the academic literature. Indeed, articles were published that related crime to the genetic or cultural inferiority of African Americans (Gabbidon, 2010). Thus, white general theoreticians, such as Hirschi (1969), had the well-meaning intent of arguing that blacks and whites are not biologically or in any other way different or inferior to whites; that is, the intent of many of these general theories of crime was to argue that higher rates of offending among blacks is simply a result of them being disproportionately exposed to the social forces that also cause whites to engage in crime (Wright and Younts, 2009). In other words, the same forces compel both blacks and whites to engage in crime; it is just that African Americans encounter these social forces more often than whites.

We argue that this reasoning has "thrown the baby out with the bath water." This is rather evident in the fact that racial discrimination as a cause of crime among African Americans has been essentially ignored by most criminologists. This is not to say that racial discrimination is not a prominent, if not a chief, concern among many criminologists. Indeed, post-World War II, a dominant admirable theme among criminologists has been to expose how racism manifests itself within the criminal justice system. There are literally thousands of criminological studies that reveal the overt and subtle ways in which racism pervades the decisions of the police or how racial discrimination is systemic within the courts (e.g., whites get probation while blacks get sentenced to prison). Scholars recognize that stereotypes are distinct from both racial discrimination and racial prejudice. They define "stereotypes as cognitive structures composed of consensual knowledge, beliefs, and expectations about social groups that may result in both positive and negative associations for a single specific group" and argue that they are "distinct from racial attitudes, which reflect affective evaluations or preferences, where one group is consistently considered more positively and another more negatively" (Pauker, Ambady, and Apfelbaum, 2010: 1799).

In the last chapter, we argued that criminal justice injustices are, in fact, a cause of African American offending. Yet, we scratch our heads and wonder how has it been possible for the vast majority of criminologists to ignore that one of the most obvious and detrimental forces in the lives of African Americans—racism—is a cause of their offending. Our theory of offending corrects this imbalance. We center our analysis of African American offending on their experiences with different forms of racism. We assert that this emphasis is warranted, as the data show that 98 percent of African American adults reported experiencing some form of racial discrimination in the past year (Klonoff, Landrine, and Ullman, 1999). In this chapter, we explain how perceived racial discrimination, negative stereotypes of African Americans, and stereotype threats are related to the probability of African American offending.[1]

Racial Discrimination and the General Well-Being of African Americans

The literature is replete with analysis of how African Americans suffer because of their exposure to different aspects of racial discrimination (Blistein, 2009; Gabbidon and Peterson, 2006; Geronimus, Hicken, Keene, and Bound, 2006; Geronimus and Thompson, 2004; Harrell, 2000; Klonoff et al., 1999; Major and O'Brien, 2005). Scholars have studied the effect that racial discrimination has on African Americans on diminished mental health, stress, high blood pressure, cognitive processing, substance abuse, depression, coronary heart disease, and hypertension (for reviews of this literature, see Brondolo, ver Halen, Pencille, Beatty, and Contrada, 2009; Clark, Anderson, Clark, and Williams, 1999; Williams, Neighbors, and Jackson, 2003; Williams, Neighbors, and Jackson, 2008). Yet, nearly all of this research shows the deleterious health-related, not criminogenic (crime-causing), consequences of racial discrimination. Below we briefly review a few studies (the literature is exponential) that show that perceived discrimination has negative effects on the well-being of African Americans regardless of their age, class, or gender.

Keith, Lincoln, Taylor and Jackson (2010) analyzed data from the National Survey of American Life and investigated the relationship between perceived discrimination and depressive symptoms among African American women aged 18–98 years. Keith et al. (2010:48) found that: "discrimination is a major threat to African American women's mental health. They are vulnerable to discrimination, in part, because discrimination undermines their beliefs in mastery making them less psychologically resilient." Perceived racial discrimination was measured with items such as, "called names or insulted," "threatened or harassed," and "followed around in stores," and mastery was assessed with items such as, "no way I can solve problems" and "I have little control over what happens" (see also Odom and Vernon-Feagans, 2010).

African American youth are also vulnerable to the negative consequences of racial discrimination (Seaton, Yip, and Sellers, 2009; Seaton, 2010). Seaton and Yip (2009) analyzed data collected on 252 urban African American adolescents (ages 13 to 18). They found a negative relationship between perceived discrimination and the youth's self-esteem and a positive relationship between perceived discrimination and depressive symptoms. The more these youths perceived racial discrimination, the more likely they were to be depressed and to lack self-esteem. Measures that Seaton and Yip (2009) used to assess perceived discrimination included, "White people have treated you as if you were stupid and needed things explained to you slowly or several times" and "You think you did not receive a school award you deserved because you are Black." Self-esteem was measured with the Rosenberg scale, which included items such as "On the whole, I am satisfied with myself." They measured depressive symptoms using the Center for Epidemiological Studies Depression Scale (CES-D), which included items such as, "I did not feel like eating, my appetite was poor." Relatedly, Brody, Chen, Murry, Ge, Simons, Gibbons, Gerrard, and Cutrona (2006:1183) analyzed three waves of longitudinal data from the Family and Community Health Study and found that perceived discrimination was related "to conduct problems and depressive symptoms among African American youths across late childhood and early adolescence." They used a scale that assessed perceived discrimination over the past year ("a store owner or sales person working at a business treated you in a disrespectful way because you are African American," "someone yelled a racial insult at you because you are African American," and "you encountered Whites who didn't expect you to do well because you are African American").

Furthermore, perceived racial discrimination has been found to diminish the well-being among African American men. African

American men have the highest age-adjusted death rate of any group, experience higher rates of preventable illness, and suffer an increased incidence of preventable deaths while having lower alcohol-use rates than white men (Sellers, Bonham, Neighbors, and Amell, 2009). Sellers et al. (2009) analyzed a sample of 399 middle-class, well-educated African American men to assess whether they suffered the deleterious effects of racial discrimination. They used the Jackson and Williams discrimination stress scale (e.g., the men were asked whether because of their race they have been unfairly fired or denied a promotion, unfairly not hired for a job, unfairly stopped by the police, unfairly discouraged by a teacher from continuing education, or unfairly prevented from moving into a neighborhood) and examined whether it was related to their measures of the person's mental health (they used the SF-12 scale to assess mental health). Sellers et al. (2009) found that mental health problems are related to increases in perceived racial discrimination, even among middle-class, well-educated black men. Together, these studies indisputably show that "discrimination ranks in significance with major stressful life events such as divorce, job loss, and death of a loved one" (Sellers et al., 2009:33).

Racial Discrimination and African American Offending

Just within the last decade, criminologists have begun to more fully investigate whether perceived racial discrimination is a factor that significantly predicts African American offending. Analyzing data from the Family and Community Health Study, researchers marshal compelling evidence that shows that perceived racial discrimination predicts higher rates of offending among African American youths (Brody et al., 2006; Gibbons, Gerrard, Cleveland, Wills, and Brody, 2004; Simons, Chen, Stewart, and Brody, 2003; Simons, Simons, Burt, Drummund, Stewart, Brody, Gibbons, and Cutrona, 2006; Stewart, Schreck, and Simons, 2006; Stewart and Simons, 2006). The Family and Community Health Study is a longitudinal study of African American families residing in Georgia and Iowa. Waves of data were collected beginning in 1997. Every family included in the first wave had a child in the fifth grade.

Perceived racial discrimination was measured with an instrument that included questions such as: "How often has someone yelled a racial slur or racial insult at you just because you are African American?" and "How often have the police hassled you just because you are African American?" (Simons et al., 2003:837). Delinquency was measured using the children's self-reports on the conduct-disorder section of the Diagnostic Interview Schedule for Children. In addition, different theories of crime—including control theory, differential association-social learning theory, strain theory (Cloward and Ohlin, 1960), and general strain theory—were operationalized. For example, measures of the different dimensions of parenting (warmth and monitoring), school efficacy (commitment and involvement in school), association with prosocial peers, association with delinquent peers, a scale measuring aggressive attitudes, a scale measuring the degree to which the adolescents "blamed the system," and scales measuring anger and depression were included. Even with these measures included, perceived racial discrimination was a significant predictor of black offending.

Scholars have reproduced the relationship between perceived racial discrimination and offending among African Americans using datasets other than the Family and Community Health Study. Most notably, Unnever et al. (2009) reanalyzed the Richmond Youth Survey, the dataset that Hirschi (1969) used to construct his social bond theory, and found that perceived racial discrimination was a salient predictor of African American adolescent offending while controlling for the strength of the other social bonds, including attachment, beliefs, commitment, and involvement.

In addition, researchers have found that perceived racial discrimination is a strong predictor of violent behavior for both male and female African Americans even after controlling for adolescent risk factors (e.g., ninth grade GPA, SES, racial identity, and prior violent behaviors). Caldwell, Kohn-Wood, Schmeelk-Cone, Chavous, and Zimmerman (2004:99) conclude that for both African American males and females the "experience with racial discrimination was the strongest risk factor for young adult violent behavior, which highlights the significance of race-relations as a critical social context for understanding violent behavior as a response to oppression."

Racial Discrimination and Weak School Bonds

The data reveal vast differences in the ability of African Americans, especially black males, to achieve educational success. The gap between the high school graduation rates of African Americans and white males is glaring, 47 versus 78 percent. Perhaps more disconcerting, the data show that in some school districts (e.g., Pinellas County, FL and Charleston County, SC) less than 25 percent of African American males graduate from high school (in comparison to over 50 percent of white males) (Schott Foundation for Public Education, 2010).

Our theory asserts that racial discrimination can increase the probability of black offending by undermining the ability of African Americans to develop strong bonds with conventional institutions. We focus on the educational system to illustrate how racial discrimination weakens the ties that African Americans have with institutions because school failure is related to youth offending (Noble, 2006; Zahn, Agnew, Fishbein, Miller, Winn, Dakoff, Kruttschnitt, Giordano, Gottfredson, Payne, Feld, and Chesney-Lind, 2010). For example, Payne (2008:450) reports "that students who are more attached to their school and teachers and more committed to their education and who give more legitimacy to the school rules and norms will be involved in less delinquency." And, Carswell (2007) specifically found that African American students are less likely to engage in delinquency when they have strong bonds with their school. It is also noteworthy that scholars have found that African Americans are as strongly bonded to schools as whites and that the effect of weak school bonds on offending is equivalent for blacks and whites (Cernkovich and Giordano, 1992). Scholars have further found that school failure is related to other life course turning points such as unemployment, which in turn is related to adult offending (see also Baron, 2008; Crutchfield and Pitchford, 1997; Farrington, Gallagher, Morley, Ledger, and West, 1986; Giordano et al., 2007; Uggen, 2000). Hip-hop artist Gang Starr succinctly captures the reason why we focus on education: "The educational system presumes you fail/The next place is the corner then after that jail."

Thus, our thesis is straightforward. We assert that African Americans encounter a unique lived experience within their schools—that is, an experience not shared by whites—that causes them to develop weak bonds with the educational system. We argue that African Americans encounter the many variegated forms of racial discrimination within their schools.

As previously discussed, social bond theory argues that the fundamental cause for why African Americans and whites fail to develop strong ties with conventional institutions (e.g., attachment and commitment), such as with the educational system, is the failure of parents to bond with their children. Therefore, the failure of parents to develop strong ties with their children cascades into the person having difficulties bonding to other institutions such as with their schools and the legal system. As Hirschi (1969:94) states: "The more strongly a child is attached to his parents, the more strongly he is bound to their expectations, and therefore the more strongly he is bound to conformity with the legal norms of the larger society." Our theory of offending assumes that parenting can provide African American children with a solid foundation upon which other strong bonds are developed. Indeed, we discuss this process in our next chapter on racial socialization. However, our theory also posits that there are other reasons than poor parenting for why African Americans may develop weak bonds with conventional institutions. We assert that different forms of racial discrimination cause African Americans to develop weak ties with conventional institutions.

There are a multitude of ways that African Americans can encounter racial discrimination within their schools including, but not limited to, their white peers rejecting them because of their race (e.g., not allowed access to the "in-group"), being called racist epithets (e.g., the "N" word), being told racist jokes, being bullied because of their race, being physically attacked, teachers only calling on white students, teachers belittling black students, teachers assuming that they are "lazy" or prone to violence (i.e., invoking a stereotype threat), incidents of hate crimes targeting African Americans (e.g., a display of a white doll dressed in a

Ku Klux Klan robe and a black doll with a noose around its neck), racially biased texts and curricula, racial tracking, discriminatory penalties (e.g., whites get detention while blacks get suspended from school for the same incident), disproportionately placing African American students in special education classes, lowered teacher expectations, less encouragement to take advanced courses, and the school authorities' denial and refusal to acknowledge that there is racism within their schools—that is, that racial stratification exists (Alliman-Brissett and Turner, 2010; Donaldson, 1996; Goldsmith, 2004; Mattison and Aber, 2007; Noble, 2006; Rosenbloom and Way, 2004; Wong, Eccles, and Sameroff, 2003). For example, the research indicates that 46 percent of African American students reported that they were given a lower grade than they deserve because of their race (Rivas-Drake, Hughes, and Way, 2009). And, Gregory and Weinstein (2008) found that African American students behaved more defiantly and less cooperatively when interacting with teachers that they perceived as being untrustworthy.

Scholars have found that pejorative stereotypes of African Americans pervade the classroom. Research indicates that teachers perceive African American middle school students as more defiant, disrespectful, and rule-breaking than other groups (Gregory and Weinstein, 2008). Therefore, not surprisingly, research shows that 51 percent of black students believe they are more likely to be suspended and 51 percent believe that the school is more likely to call the police because of their race (Ruck and Wortley, 2002). These percentages become more glaring when compared with whites. Ruck and Wortley (2002:192) note that "Black students were approximately 32 times more likely than White students to perceive discrimination with respect to the use of police at school and 27 times more likely to perceive that they would be treated worse by the police at school." Of note, in 2004 suspension data from the U.S. Department of Education Office for Civil Rights showed that African Americans were approximately three times more likely to be suspended than other groups and that these differences remained significant after controlling for the student's socioeconomic status (Gregory and Weinstein, 2008).

Importantly, the toxic effects of peer-based discrimination on weakening the ties that African American youths have with their schools should not be underestimated (Chavous, Rivas-Drake, Smalls, Griffin, and Cogburn, 2008). Scholars have found that within the context of schools, peer-based discrimination is particularly salient for how African Americans perceive their own race (i.e., their public regard). The more African American students perceived being racially discriminated against by their peers the more negatively they perceived their race (Rivas-Drake et al., 2009). Ruck and Wortley (2002) add that African American youths are more likely to perceive differential treatment, have less positive attitudes toward students of other groups, and have fewer positive out-group interactions in schools that are racially and ethnically self-segregated. In short, African American students confront a different reality than whites when they open the door to their school. For some African American students, whether they attend integrated or what has been referred to as "apartheid schools" that are populated by all blacks or minorities (Frankenburg, Lee, and Orfield, 2003), it may be a toxic racist environment contaminated with both pervasive negative stereotypes that "put them down" and instances of discrimination because they are African American.

Evidence is accumulating that supports our thesis that perceived racial discrimination undermines the ability of black youths to develop strong bonds with their schools. Wong et al. (2003) analyzed data from a longitudinal study (from seventh grade to the completion of the eighth grade) of an economically diverse sample of African American adolescents living in Maryland. Discrimination within the school by peers was measured with items such as the frequency that African Americans felt they got into fights, were not associated with, and not picked for particular teams or activities because of their race. Measures of teacher-based discrimination included how often students felt that their teachers called on them less, graded them more harshly, disciplined them more harshly, discouraged them from taking a class, and thought they were less smart because of their race. Consistent with our thesis, Wong et al. (2003) found that experiences of racial discrimination at school from one's teachers and peers predicted declines in grades, academic ability, self-concepts, and academic task values (see also Chavous et al., 2008). Also of interest, Wong et al. (2003) found that racial discrimination predicted increases in the proportion of peers who were not interested in school. Notably, these scholars found that perceived racial discrimination was related to delinquent behavior even after controlling for a host of other covariates.

In a related study, Dotterer, McHale, and Crouter (2009) examined whether weak school bonds developed among African American youths who perceived discrimination by their school peers (e.g., "how often have kids at school excluded you from their activities because you are African American?") and teachers (e.g., "how often have you had to work harder in school than white kids to get the same praise or the same grades from your teachers because you are African American?"). Using the first phase of a longitudinal dataset collected from two large eastern cities, they analyzed three dimensions of school bonds: (1) school self-esteem (e.g., "I usually have been proud of my report card"); (2) school bonding (e.g., "I feel close to people at my school"); and (3) school grades (GPA). Dotterer et al. (2009) found that personal discrimination experiences were a significant and negative predictor of school self-esteem and school bonding. That is, the more African American students reported personal experiences with racial discrimination, the less likely they were to identify with doing well in school and were less attached to their schools. Of note, they did not find a relationship between perceived racial discrimination and lower grades.

Mattison and Aber (2007) surveyed 1,838 high school students including 382 African Americans in two public schools in the Midwest to investigate whether their perceptions of the school's racial climate impacted their achievement and discipline-related problems. Three dimensions of the school's racial climate were assessed: (1) racial fairness (e.g., "At my school, students are disciplined fairly regardless of race" and "Black students are treated fairly at my school"); (2) experiences of racism (e.g., "How often has a teacher treated you badly because of your race?" and "How often has another student treated you badly because of your race?"); and (3) a "Need for Change subscale" (e.g., "The school district should reduce the difference in gifted and talented enrollment between Black and White students" and "The school district should reduce the difference in special education enrollment between Black and White students"). They examined whether these measures of the school's racial climate were related to the student's self-reported GPA and whether they had been suspended or their number of school-based detentions. Mattison and Aber (2007) found that 51 percent of the white students agreed they were treated and disciplined fairly regardless of race compared with 31 percent of the African Americans, black students were two and a half times (8 percent) more likely to report that they experienced racism than whites (3 percent), and about 10 percent of white students agreed schools needed to change compared with 40 percent of African American students. They also report that African American students were eight times more likely to be suspended and received twice as many detentions as whites. Their multivariate analyses revealed that perceptions of a negative racial climate were related to lower grades and more disciplinary actions for both African Americans and whites. Mattison and Aber (2007) conclude that a climate of racism may create disincentives for students to engage in schoolwork, which in turn promotes delinquent behaviors. Thus, "perceptions that the school is racist may set in motion a series of reactions including fighting, insubordination, etc., for which students are disciplined. In this case, misbehavior may be precipitated by perceived racist school structures or racist interactions with students and staff" (Mattison and Aber, 2007:9).

Scholars also have put forth a "resistance theory" that parallels our previous hypothesis that perceived criminal justice injustices are a source of anger and defiance among African Americans. The resistance theory argues that African American students employ "right to respect" coping strategies or exude a tough defiant facade in response to explicit or implicit racism in schools (Spencer, Noll, Stolzfus, and Harpalani, 2001). Gregory and Weinstein (2008), in their study in an urban high school in a mid-size city, found that African American students comprised 30 percent of the school enrollment, but they were 58 percent of the students who teachers referred for disciplinary actions because of "defiance." In contrast, they found that white students were 37 percent of the school enrollment, but only comprised 5 percent of students referred for defiance (see also Gregory, Skiba, and Noguera, 2010; Ruck and Wortley, 2002).

Gregory and Weinstein (2008) argue that African Americans are particularly likely to be defiant when they perceive that teachers are underestimating their academic ability or that they are uncaring because of their race. Indeed, they found that African American students critically discern among teachers that they perceive to be either racists or nonracists. Thus, in support of the resistance theory, these scholars found that "African American students reported uncaring treatment and low academic expectations from teachers with whom they behaved more defiantly and less cooperatively, as rated by themselves and by these teachers. In contrast, the students reported that their nominated teachers treated them with care and high expectations. Moreover, students expressed a willingness to comply with the authority of teachers who had earned trust and legitimacy" (Gregory and Weinstein, 2008:469). In short, these data support our thesis that African Americans are likely to become angry-defiant when they perceive racial injustices, whether they occur in the classroom or on the streets.

We last discuss a study conducted by Unnever, Cullen, Mathers, McClure, and Allison (2009). These scholars reanalyzed the same dataset used by Hirschi (1969), the Richmond Youth Study, to examine whether Hirschi omitted from his analysis the possibility that perceived racial discrimination is a cause of African American youth offending, while controlling for his other bond measures of involvement, commitment, attachment, and beliefs. More specifically, these researchers examined whether personal perceptions of racial discrimination within the context of the school were related to African American offending. They created a measure of perceived school discrimination by summing across three items: (1) whether the black students thought their teachers did not like them, (2) how well they got along with the white students, and (3) whether the black and white students interacted with one another. Unfortunately, Unnever et al. (2009) did not test whether these perceptions of a racially toxic school environment were related to

African American students developing weak school bonds. However, they did examine whether these perceptions of a toxic racist school environment predicted black offending. Unnever et al. (2009:396) found that "African American youths who perceived that their school was antagonistic to members of their race were significantly more likely to offend."[2] They concluded that African American youths are more likely to offend if they perceive their school climate to be discriminatory and hostile.

Of interest, Unnever et al. (2009) also examined whether the black youths' perception of racial discrimination in domains outside of school were related to their probability of offending. They investigated whether African American youths in the late 1960s were more likely to offend if they perceived whether blacks were discriminated against in income ("Do you think a person of your race would get paid as much as a person of other racial groups for doing the same kind of work?"), in housing ("If a family of your racial group rented the same kind of house as a family of other racial groups, do you think they would have to pay the same amount of rent?"), and in employment ("In the city where you live, do you think that Negroes are discriminated against when people are being hired for jobs?"). Unnever et al. (2009) found that personal experiences with racial discrimination ("Have you personally ever been treated badly because of your race?") and perceptions of a toxic racist school environment were related to African Americans engaging in delinquent behavior, but, none of their vicarious perceptions of racial discrimination outside of their school predicted black offending.

In sum, the totality of the research indicates that perceived racial discrimination not only places the physical and mental well-being of African Americans at risk, it also causes black males and females to have a greater probability of offending. These results have been replicated at different times, have controlled for a wide array of correlates, have been found across different geographical locales, and when employing and representing different methodologies (e.g., cross-sectional and longitudinal surveys). In short, the data indicate that racial discrimination is related to African American offending.

Stereotypes of African Americans

We assert that the effects of racial discrimination on African American offending extend beyond the immediate experience of blacks perceiving that they have been discriminated against because of their race (e.g., being denied employment because the person is African American, being given a lower grade in school because they are black). Our theory posits that racist stereotypes are another form of racism that is related to African American offending. Below we first provide evidence that pejorative stereotypes of African Americans are pervasive and then outline why these negative depictions are related to black offending.

Prevailing Racial Stereotypes

Scholars argue that an attribute of racialized societies are negative racial and ethnic stereotypes (Beckett and Sasson, 2003; Bobo and Charles, 2009; Bonilla-Silva, 2006, 2008; Bonilla-Silva and Ray 2009; O'Brien, Crandall, Horstman-Reser, Warner, Alsbrooks, and Blodorn, 2010). Lynch (2006:185) states that "stereotypes distort perceptions of out-groups, create social distance between in-group and out-group members, and may help justify negative feelings toward out-groups." These negative stereotypes flow from a racial ideology that reproduces the ever-changing dynamics of groups differentially positioned because of their race or ethnic background (Bobo, 2000). Bonilla-Silva (1997:474) argues that pejorative stereotypes define what "common sense" becomes and provide the rules for "perceiving and dealing with the 'other' in a racialized society." Scholars refer to stereotypes as "pictures in the head" (Lippman, 1922; Peffley and Hurwitz, 1998; Hurwitz and Peffley, 1997; Peffley, Hurwitz, and Sniderman, 1997). These images create expectations of others, and they tend to filter out information that is inconsistent with their preconceived opinions of these groups (Sigelman and Tuch, 1997).

Negative stereotypes arise from a number of distinctive social and racial and ethnic experiences and can cut across both racial and ethnic groups (Bobo and Charles, 2009; Hochschild and Weaver, 2007). For example, researchers have routinely documented that African Americans are significantly more likely to be depicted as criminals on news programs (see, e.g., Dixon, 2000, 2007, 2008; Dixon and Linz, 2000, 2006; Entman, 1994; Entman and Rojecki, 2001). Note that it is possible for stereotypes to have a "kernel of truth" associated with them (Niemann, 2001). Official data indicate that 1 in 15 African American and 1 in 36 Hispanic men are incarcerated in comparison with 1 in 106 white men (Pew Center on the States, 2009). Therefore, for example, it could be argued that whites who identify African Americans as being more criminal than members of their own race are not stereotyping but rather are just "letting the data do the talking."

The eminent scholar W.E.B. Du Bois recognized this insidious aspect of stereotypes in his classic *The Philadelphia Negro*: "Being few in number compared with the whites the crime or carelessness of a few of his race is easily imputed to all, and the reputation of the good, industrious and reliable suffer thereby" (Du Bois [1899] 1996:323). Jones (1997:169) adds to Du Bois's dismissal of the "kernel of truth" justification for negative stereotypes, "that even when a stereotype is largely true, it reflects no more than a probability that a member of the group will possess the trait on which the group is being stereotyped." In addition, Quillian and Pager (2001) argue that negative stereotypes of African Americans cause individuals to systematically overestimate the true rate of behavior. For example, they argue that a combination of negative media depictions of African Americans, historical stereotypes, and ethnocentric biases combine to form distorted perceptions in which the association of blackness and criminality is systematically overestimated. In short, there is no legitimate justification for embracing stereotypes, whether they are positive or negative, because they cannot be applied to *every* member of the out-group and they create distorted images that cannot be verified.

Empirical studies unequivocally indicate that pejorative stereotypes of African Americans are a prevailing and enduring component of the American cultural landscape (Devine, 1989; Trawalter, Todd, Baird, and Richeson, 2008; Wood and Chesser, 1994). Bobo and Charles (2009) note that negative racial stereotypes remain the norm in white America with between half and three quarters of whites in the United States still expressing some degree of negative stereotyping of blacks and Latinos, with a smaller share of whites expressing negative stereotypes of Asians (between one tenth and two fifths).

Devine and Elliot (1995:1142), in a follow-up to the classic Princeton trilogy studies, provided 147 students a checklist composed of 93 adjectives and asked them to mark those that "make up the cultural stereotype of Blacks." Note that, based on recent free-response data, they decided to add the concepts of "criminal" and "hostile" to the original checklist of 84 adjectives. Devine and Elliot found that from 1933 to the mid-1990s, a consistent and negative stereotype of African Americans has endured. Devine and Elliot (1995) found that the top nine list of adjectives that whites checked to describe African Americans were, in order: athletic, rhythmic, low in intelligence, lazy and poor (these were tied), loud, criminal, hostile, and ignorant. In contrast, no whites checked, for example, that African Americans are ambitious, tradition loving, sensitive, or gregarious.

Scholars argue that the "war on drugs" has profoundly impacted the racial stereotyping of African Americans, particularly African American men. That is, they argue that the "war on drugs" has caused most Americans to conflate crime with race and race with crime. Russell-Brown (2009) captures the pervasiveness of this gendered pejorative stereotype of African American men in her provocative label, the *criminalblackman*. Feagin (2001:113) states that the common white stereotype of the dangerous black man is "the staple of white thinking, including the thinking of white leaders and intellectuals speaking or writing about the black 'underclass'" (see also James, 2010). Bjornstrom, Kaufman, Peterson, and Slater (2010) analyzed data from a stratified random sample of television newscasts in 2002–03 and found that the media actively perpetuates these toxic stereotypes. They report that television news over-report crimes committed by African Americans when compared with whites and that blacks are less likely to be portrayed as victims than whites. Furthermore, scholars contend that this more crystallized master stereotype—of the *criminalblackman*—is the basis for the creation of a "New Jim Crow" (Alexander, 2010; Bass, 2001; Noble, 2006; Russell-Brown, 2009). This New Jim Crow is characterized by the mass incarceration and disenfranchisement of millions of African Americans (mostly black men), which is being facilitated by the war on drugs and legitimated by the racial stereotype of the *criminalblackman* (Alexander, 2010). Thus, African Americans are now confronted by the fact that most Americans think of them as being criminals, especially black men.

Research supports the argument that African Americans, particularly African American men, are portrayed as dangerous, violent, super-predators (Barkan and Cohn, 1994; Bobo and Charles, 2009; Chiricos, Welch, and Gertz, 2004; Devine, 1989; Gabbidon, 2010; Gabbidon and Greene, 2009; Jones, 1997; Maykovich, 1972; Trawalter et al., 2008; Walker, Spohn, DeLone, 2007; Welch, 2007). Fishman (2006:199) argues that this stereotype was resurrected from the legacy of slavery as African American men were depicted as "menacing black brutes" that are animalistic, aggressive, and brutal. She also notes that African American women during and immediately after the end of slavery were portrayed as "wanton, hot-blooded, highly sexed, and exotic, as well as very fertile." Feagin (2001:113) adds that this perception of black men runs deep in American culture as "during the first centuries of American development, whites constructed a view of enslaved black men as dangerous 'beasts' a stereotyped view that has rationalized much discrimination over the centuries, including bloody lynchings." Beckett, Nyrop, and Pfingst (2006:130) add that the *criminalblackman* has embedded within it the portrayal of young African American males as "dangerous black crack offenders" (see also Beckett, Nyrop, Pfingst, and Bowen, 2005).

Eberhardt, Goff, Purdie, and Davies (2004:876) add that "not only is the association between blacks and crime strong (i.e., consistent and frequent), it also appears to be automatic (i.e., not subject to intentional control)." They further assert that this automatic stereotype has dire consequences in that the mere presence of an African American man can trigger thoughts among whites that he is violent and criminal.

Based on their research with white students, Eberhardt et al. (2004) found that the stereotype that associates African Americans with crime is bidirectional. That is, among whites, thinking about crime triggers images of African Americans and that thinking about African

Americans triggers thoughts about crime. Eberhardt et al. (2004) conclude that the coupling between African Americans and crime is so deeply embedded among whites that blacks are the prototypical embodiment of crime.

This conflating of crime with race and race with crime is further evidenced in a study that asked approximately 400 persons in the Washington, D.C., area: "Would you close your eyes for a second, envision a drug user, and describe that person to me?" The data show that more than 95 percent of the respondents identified the person as an African American. Notably, the pervasiveness of this pejorative stereotype is illustrated by the fact that blacks also indicated that the image in their head of a drug user was an African American (Burston, Jones, and Roberson-Saunders, 1995).

In addition, in an analysis of the General Social Survey (GSS), Unnever and Cullen (2011) found that in 1990, whites considered African Americans 15 times more likely to be violent than members of their own race. They also found that the degree to which whites negatively depict African Americans as prone to violence changes over time. Taken together, these studies clearly demonstrate that a prevailing cultural belief within the United States is that African Americans tend to be "lazy," "poor," and prone to violent crime.

The Impact that Negative Stereotypes Have on African Americans

Scholars argue that these toxic stereotypes permeate the worldview of those who are stigmatized—that is, African Americans. Major and O'Brien (2005:399) state that: "Based on their prior experiences as well as their exposure to the dominant culture, members of stigmatized groups develop shared understandings of the dominant view of their stigmatized status in society [Crocker 1999, Crocker et al. 1998, Steele 1997]. These collective representations include awareness that they are devalued in the eyes of others, knowledge of the dominant cultural stereotypes of their stigmatized identity, and recognition that they could be victims of discrimination [Crocker et al. 1998]. Virtually all members of a culture, including members of stigmatized groups, are aware of cultural stereotypes, even if they do not personally endorse them." Thus, African Americans, even before the age of 10, are aware that other groups perceive them as "less than" and may modify their behavior based on the toxic judgments of others.

The noted artist Gang Starr raps about the insidiousness of the *criminalblackman* pejorative stereotype in his song "Conspiracy" (from the album *Daily Operation*):

> You can't tell me life was meant to be like this
> a black man in a world dominated by whiteness
> Ever since the declaration of independence
> we've been easily brainwashed by just one sentence
> It goes: all men are created equal
> that's why corrupt governments kill innocent people
> With chemical warfare they created crack and AIDS
> got the public thinking these were things that black folks made
> And every time there's violence shown in the media
> usually it's a black thing so where are they leading ya
> To a world full of ignorance, hatred, and prejudice
> TV and the news for years they have fed you this
> foolish notion that blacks are all criminals
> violent, low lifes, and then even animals
> I'm telling the truth so some suckers are fearing me
> but I must do my part to combat the conspiracy

Stereotypes and Offending

Our theory asserts that negative stereotypes of African Americans can increase African American offending. Research shows that children develop a stereotype-consciousness—the awareness of others' stereotypes—in middle childhood (between the ages of 5 and 10) (McKown and Strambler, 2009). McKown and Weinstein (2008) found that between the ages of 6 and 10, African American children were more likely to express knowledge of broadly held stereotypes than white and Asian students and they concluded that the different lived experiences of minorities influence the age of onset of stereotype-consciousness. Indeed, McKown and Strambler (2009) report that by age 11, African American children have mastered all aspects of stereotype-consciousness.

Brown and Bigler (2005) stipulate that stereotype-consciousness causes African Americans to perceive that they and other blacks will be the target of discrimination and that these beliefs have deleterious consequences that are not domain-specific. Consequently, our theory of offending assumes that the worldview shared by African Americans includes an explicit awareness of the pejorative stereotypes that depict them as "less than" whites.

Below, we first outline how pejorative stereotypes can impede the ability of African Americans to develop strong bonds with white-dominated institutions, such as with their schools. This argument is centered within the research on "stereotype threats" (Steele and Aronson, 1995; Steele 1997). Second, we present the hypothesis that some African Americans internalize the stereotype that blacks are criminal. Third, we hypothesize that negative stereotypes deplete the emotional resources of African Americans, increasing their likelihood of experiencing negative emotions—such as, hopelessness-depression and anger-defiance—which in turn, are related to higher rates of offending.

Stereotype Threat and Weak Social Bonds

Stereotype Threats

We have established that African Americans are immersed in a dominant culture that has pervasive negative stereotypes that depict blacks as "less than" whites (e.g., lazy, poor, and prone to offending). This suggests that the daily interactions between African Americans and whites are contaminated by these negative depictions of blacks. Of course, some whites do not implicitly embrace or explicitly express these negative stereotypes. Indeed, some whites outright reject these harmful depictions. Nevertheless, both blacks and whites are aware of these depictions and have to uncomfortably negotiate around them in the minutia of their interactions (Frantz, Cuddy, Burnett, Ray, and Hart, 2004; Schmader, Johns, and Forbes, 2008). It is our thesis that the awareness of these negative typifications among African Americans is related to their offending (McKown and Strambler, 2009).

We couch our principal argument that pervasive negative depictions of African Americans are related to black offending within the "stereotype threat" literature (Gates and Steele, 2009). This literature has generated consistent and clear findings; negative racial stereotypes that are "in the air" have profound measurable deleterious consequences on domain-specific African American behaviors (Alter, Aronson, Darley, Rodriguez, and Ruble, 2010; Arbuthnot, 2009; Steele, 1997; Steele and Aronson, 1995). That is, pejorative stereotypes of African Americans, such as that they are low in intelligence, can result in domain-specific "stereotype threats" that diminish the quality of the interactions that African Americans have within institutions.

In their modern classic study, Steele and Aronson (1995:797) define stereotype threat as "being at risk of confirming, as self-characteristic, a negative stereotype about one's group." In other words, stereotype threats heighten African Americans' concerns that they will be judged stereo-typically or that they may conform to the validity of the relevant stereo-type through their behavior. That is, African Americans have to contend with the felt experience that anything they say or do can confirm toxic stereotypes about being black (Brown and Pinel, 2003; Inzlicht, McKay, and Aronson, 2006).[3]

Steele and Aronson's (1995) initial study was groundbreaking. They found that how well blacks perform on standardized tests depends on their perceptions of negative stereotypes. Steele and Aronson (1995:808) report that "making African American participants vulnerable to judg-ment by negative stereotypes about their group's intellectual ability depressed their standardized test performance relative to White partici-pants." Schmader et al. (2008:337) argue that stereotype threats diminish the performance of African Americans because they:

> pose significant threat to self-integrity, the sense of oneself as a coherent and valued entity that is adaptable to the environment [Steele, 1988]. This self-integrity threat stems from a state of cognitive imbalance in which one's concept of self and expectation

for success conflict with primed social stereotypes suggesting poor performance. This state of imbalance acts as an acute stressor that sets in motion physiological manifestations of stress, cognitive monitoring and interpretative processes, affective responses, and efforts to cope with these aversive experiences.

They conclude that "for those who contend with negative stereotypes about their abilities, the chronic experience of stress, heightened vigilance, self-doubt, and emotional suppression not only can impair performance directly but also can lead them to avoid situations where these aversive phenomena reside" (Schmader et al., 2008:352). It is interesting, however, that stereotype threats function to undermine the ability of African Americans to be successful but do not necessarily cause a loss of self-esteem (Gates and Steele, 2009). In short, when a negative stereotype is applicable to a domain-specific behavior (i.e., tests in schools), the performance of African Americans diminishes.

Notably, recent research indicates that stereotype threats may have a "spillover" effect. Inzlicht and Kang (2010) found that stereotype and social identity threats have effects that extend beyond the stereotyped domain. They report, based on a series of experiments, that even after African Americans (and other minorities including women) leave a domain-specific situation (e.g., their school) where they faced negative stereotypes, the effects of coping with that situation persist. More specifically, Inzlicht and Kang's (2010) research indicates that African Americans are more likely to be aggressive, exhibit a lack of self-control, have trouble making good rational decisions, and overindulge on unhealthy foods after they have perceived prejudice in a given situation. In short, the research shows that stereotype threats exhaust the emotional capital of African Americans, leaving them more vulnerable to impulsively responding to their racial subordination.

Stereotype Threat, Weak Bonds, and African American Offending

The stereotype threat literature clearly indicates that African Americans physiologically and emotionally suffer as a consequence of pejorative depictions of blacks; that is, stereotype threats become a chronic experience that alters their behaviors. Our theory hypothesizes that stereotype threats increase the likelihood that African Americans offend by undermining their ability to build strong bonds with conventional institutions. Below we illustrate how stereotype threats cause black offending by weakening the bonds that African Americans have with their schools.[4]

Steele (1997:613) argues that African Americans develop strong bonds with their school when they identify with their academic achievement: that is, they become part of their self-definition, a self-identity to which they hold themselves accountable. This accountability—that good self-feelings depend upon positive achievements in school—translates into sustained achievement motivation. That is, African Americans are likely to be motivated when they perceive that they have the interests, skills, resources, and opportunities to succeed in school. Their motivation to do well in school is also related to believing that they are accepted, valued, and that they belong in school. However, Steele (1997) argues that negative depictions of African Americans threaten their ability to perform well in school. Furthermore, he argues that poor performances because of stereotype threats spiral into sustained patterns of failures, especially among those who initially desired to develop strong bonds with their schools. That is, strings of failures over time undermine the enthusiasm that African American students initially had toward their schools. Steele (1997:614) defines this process as "disidentification" whereby African American students reconceptualize their self and their values in order to remove performing well in school as a basis for self-evaluation. Thus, disidentification offers the retreat of not caring about doing well in school as a basis of self-evaluation. However, Steele argues that as it protects in this way, it can undermine sustained motivation and that this new self-identity can be costly when the domain is as important as doing well in school. Indeed, scholars argue that racial differences in educational achievement can be accounted for by the relationship between stereotype threats and the underperformance of African Americans rather than any alleged differences in lack of ability or incompetence (Haslam, Salvatore, Kessler, and Reicher, 2008).

Our theory of offending argues that negative depictions of African Americans are related to offending because they undermine the motivation for blacks to develop strong bonds with their school. These weakened social bonds have profound consequences. Steele (1997) argues that disidentified African American youths—those with weak social bonds—engage in behaviors that allow them to create a self-identity within "domains in which their prospects are better" than school-related activities (Steele, 1997:623). We assert that one of the domains that disidentified black youths are likely to choose is delinquency, a behavior that most often does not demand a high level of competence (Gottfredson and Hirschi, 1990). Thus, delinquent behavior offers an opportunity for disidentified black youth to gain a sense of self-importance; that is, an identity that is not diminished by their tenuous relationship with their school. This assertion is consistent with Steele's (1997) thesis that as blacks retreat from their attachment, commitment, and involvement in their schools they may engage in compensatory behaviors (e.g., acting in grandiose ways) in order to bolster their sense of their self-worth.

Pejorative Stereotypes and Offending

Thus far, we have outlined how toxic stereotypes result in stereotype threats that permeate the interactions that African Americans have within specific institutions, such as their schools. However, we argue that negative stereotypes of African Americans also have more general deleterious consequences—that is, that are not domain-specific—that are related to offending.

First, we argue that some African Americans internalize the negative depictions that are embedded in racist stereotypes—more specifically, the stereotype that they are criminal—and take on that label as their self-identity (Harrell, 2000). Research on negative stereotypes "have depicted a fairly standard sequence of events: Through long exposure to negative stereotypes about their group, members of prejudiced-against groups often internalize the stereotypes, and the resulting sense of inadequacy becomes part of their personality" (Steele, 1997:617). Thus, it is likely that some African Americans may simply say to themselves: "Why bother?

I might as well be a criminal if that is the only thing people think that I am." This argument is consistent with labeling theory's "secondary deviance" hypothesis (Bouffard and Piquero, 2010; Lemert, 1972; Schur, 1971; Winnick and Bodkin, 2008, 2009). Black feminist bell hooks (2004:49) describes the nature of secondary deviance among black males as:

> Nonviolent black males daily face a world that sees them as violent. Black men who are not sexual harassers or rapists confront a public that relate to them as though this is who they are underneath the skin. In actuality many black males explain their decision to become the "beast" as a surrender to realities they cannot change. And if you are going to be seen as a beast you may as well act like one. Young black males, particularly underclass males, often derive a sense of satisfaction from being able to create fear in others, particularly in white folks.

hooks' quote clearly illuminates the secondary deviance hypothesis that some African Americans may internalize the widespread belief that they are a criminal and adjust their behavior to make it consistent with how others define them, particularly when those who are applying the label have a higher status. Of course, we recognize that African Americans will more likely internalize and act out the criminal label if they encounter criminal justice injustices, racial discrimination, and domain-specific stereotype threats (Markowitz, 1998).

Second, we hypothesize that pejorative stereotypes—particularly when there is chronic exposure—are debilitating. That is, they deplete ego resources as African Americans are continually confronted with the negative emotions that arise from being "dissed" or insulted by stereotypes that "put them down." We assert that the negative emotions that arise can oscillate between depression-humiliation and anger-defiance. Brunson and Weitzer (2009:879) succinctly capture how stereotypes that associate blacks with crime can create a sense of hopelessness (i.e., depressive symptoms) among African American youth: "Black respondents expressed hopelessness regarding the situation because they felt that officers would never see them as anything other than symbolic assailants, even when they were engaged in entirely lawful activity." Burt, Simons, and Gibbons (2010) states that depression is related to offending as it increases impatience, irritability, reduces inhibitions and self-regulation, reduces empathy, and decreases a person's stake in conformity (see also, Simons et al., 2002).

The research also suggests that the anger caused by being "dissed" or insulted should be related to offending (Miller, 2001). Brezina (2010) argues that anger is related to offending because it strengthens aggressive attitudes, weakens the belief that crime is wrong by fostering the belief that offending is justifiable, and increases the likelihood that individuals will associate with criminal peers. Research reveals that both anger and depression are related to conduct problems and crime after controlling for other correlates of offending, including the person's current level of social bonding, prior criminal activity, nurturant-involved parenting, affiliation with prosocial peers, and school efficacy (Agnew, Brezina, Wright, and Cullen, 2002; Aseltine, Gore, and Gordon, 2000; Brezina, 1996; Brody et al., 2006; Giordano et al., 2007; Hagan and Foster, 2003; Mazerolle, Burton, Cullen, Evans, and Payne, 2000; Mazerolle, Piquero, and Capowich, 2003). Relatedly, Simons et al.'s (2003) longitudinal research shows that perceived racial discrimination creates heightened states of anger and depression among African Americans. They further found that anger and psychological depression mediated a significant portion of the relationship between discrimination and delinquency and that this pattern held for both boys and girls. Thus, African Americans who respond to racial stereotypes with humiliation-depression and anger-defiance should have higher rates of offending because it energizes them to action, lowers their inhibitions, increases their felt injury, increases their likelihood of associating with other disidentified individuals, and creates desires for retaliation and revenge (Agnew, 1992; Brezina, 2010). In short, our theory hypothesizes that offending becomes an ill-fated attempt by some African Americans to reestablish a sense of control and status in their life, which is lost when they are confronted by toxic racist stereotypes (Miller, 2001).

Summary

Unlike whites, African Americans are immersed in a social milieu that includes stereotypes that "put them down" and encounters with racial discrimination. African Americans can experience these forms of racism across vastly different domains of their lived lives; that is, from having a white friend tell a racist joke, to being racially profiled while shopping or driving, to being unfairly punished in school, or being denied a job because they are an African American. Thus, we argue that most, if not all, African Americans at some point in their lives are forced to deal with pejorative stereotypes, domain-specific stereotype threats, and being personally discriminated against because they are black.

Put simply, we hypothesize that the probability of African American offending increases as blacks become more aware of toxic stereotypes, encounter stereotype threats, and are discriminated against because of their race. Our theory additionally posits that these forms of racism impact offending because they undermine the ability of African Americans to develop strong ties with conventional institutions. The extant literature indicates that stereotype threats and personal experiences of racial discrimination negatively impact the strength of the bonds (attachment, involvement, commitment) that black students have with their schools (Smalls, White, Chavous, and Sellers, 2007; Thomas, Caldwell, Faison, and Jackson, 2009). And, the research is clear; weak social bonds increase the probability of black offending (Carswell, 2007). We additionally argue that these forms of racism can cause African Americans to experience negative emotions—hopelessness-depression and anger-defiance—which, in turn, increase their probability of offending.

We further assert that the strength of the relationship between these forms of racism and offending has been underestimated. As with perceived criminal justice injustices, we argue that researchers have underestimated the true extent to which negative stereotypes, stereotype threats, and personal experiences with racial discrimination negatively impact African Americans. We state that researchers should measure the *degree* to which African Americans experience these forms of racism similarly to how they measure the severity of child abuse.

Thus, we recommend that researchers, for example, ask at what age were African Americans exposed to the negative depictions of them and had personal experiences of being mistreated because of their race; who exposed the child to the toxic stereotypes and who discriminated against them because of their race (e.g., was it people in positions of trust and authority?); to what degree was the person socialized into believing negative depictions of them?; how often was the person exposed to pejorative stereotypes and to racial discrimination (e.g., did it happen in daily interactions, did it happen sporadically or chronically?); and, over what length of time was the person exposed to these deleterious racist behaviors (e.g., did it persist across their life span)? Our theory hypothesizes that offending increases with the *degree* to which African Americans experience these racial injustices.

White Collar Crime

Note that our theory asserts that stereotype threats and racial discrimination can weaken the bonds that African Americans have with white-dominated institutions. Thus, for example, we argue that African Americans who repeatedly encounter these forms of racism at their place of work are likely to have a tenuous relationship with their employment.[5] Deitch, Barsky, Butz, Chan, Brief, and Bradley (2003) found that "everyday racism" (mundane daily practices that intentionally or unintentionally convey disregard, disrespect or marginality [Banks, Kohn-Wood, and Spencer, 2006; Beagan, 2003; Swim, Hyers, Cohen, Fitzgerald, and Bylsma, 2003]) occurs in the workplace (e.g., "Set you up for failure," "Gave others privileges you didn't get") and that it is negatively related to measures of job satisfaction (e.g., pay and benefits, relationships with co-workers, and "the kind of work"). Noble (2006) contends that many African American men, particularly those seeking work in low-paying positions, encounter white employers who perceive them as "menacing" and threatening. Wingfield (2010:265) argues that African Americans who are in a minority at their place of work find that the normative "rules in professional workplaces are not neutral, but are in fact racialized in ways that deny them areas of emotional expression accessible to their white colleagues." He concludes that this racial subordination—that is, these racialized rules of conduct—results in African American professionals not only being scrutinized for what they do but also how they feel and that black professionals exhaust their emotional capital as they have to conceal their feelings (e.g., no anger at any costs) engendered by perceptions of racial injustice. Thus, the research indicates that middle- or working-class African Americans are not immune from the toxic consequences of experiencing criminal justice injustices, negative stereotypes, stereotype threats, and racial discrimination (Hirsh and Lyons, 2010). Thus, we argue that African Americans that chronically experience racism in their place of work are more likely to commit white collar crimes, such as embezzlement, especially if their workplace has few African Americans and it fails to explicitly embrace diversity (Gates and Steele, 2009).[6]

Gender and Crime

The research clearly indicates that racial stereotypes are pervasive; that is, no African American, regardless of their gender, is free from the negative emotions caused by being chronically devalued or "dissed." Studies also indicate that the vast majority of African Americans, regardless of their gender, perceive that they have been discriminated against because of their race. At face value, these findings suggest that African American males and females should be equally likely to offend. But, this is simply not the case. The data show that African American men disproportionately offend at higher rates than black women.

However, we argue that there are gendered differences in both perceptions of racial discrimination and stereotypes that can account for some of the gender disparities in African American offending. In general, the data indicate that African American men are more likely to report racial discrimination (Banks et al., 2006; Brondolo, Thompson, Brady, Appel, Cassells, Tobin, and Sweeney, 2005; Clark, 2004).

Our analysis of *The Washington Post*, Henry J. Kaiser Family Foundation, and Harvard University 2006 African American Survey support this hypothesis, which we report here. We find consistent significant gender differences related to perceived discrimination. We found that, because of their race, black males (26 percent) are significantly more likely than African American females (19 percent) to report being very worried about being a victim of racial discrimination; males (34 percent) are significantly more likely to report than females (22 percent) that they are very worried about being unfairly treated by the police; males (9 percent) are significantly more likely than females (5 percent) to report being "very often" treated with less respect; males (14 percent) are significantly more likely than females (9 percent) to report that "very often" people act as if they think they are not smart; males (13 percent) are significantly more likely than females (4 percent) to report that they "very often" have people act as if they are afraid of them; and, males (10 percent) are significantly more likely than females (5 percent) to report that people "very often" act as if they think they are dishonest.[7]

Notably, these data show that the greatest gender disparities are related to the toxic stereotyping of African American males as being "threatening," "menacing," and "criminal." African American males were three times more likely than females to perceive that people often act as if they are afraid of them and twice as likely as black females to report that people often act as if they are dishonest. These results suggest that black men are acutely sensitized to the prevailing acerbic stereotype of them being the *criminalblackman*. Indeed, our results indicate that few African American women are worried that society considers them as "threatening" or "dishonest," especially when compared with black men.

We hypothesize that this omnipresent labeling of African American men erodes their ability to build strong bonds with white-dominated institutions. For example, the data show that African American boys are disproportionately suspended by their schools for being "defiant." We further suggest that this stereotyping of African American men impacts their employability as they are likely to be prejudged to be dishonest or threatening (Wilson, 1996). Consequently, African American men, more so than black women, are asked to build strong bonds with white-dominated institutions—schools and places of work—that consider them as "menacing." In addition, these data tentatively suggest that the acute labeling of African American men as "criminal" increases their likelihood, more so than black women, of escalating into secondary deviance as they internalize and act out the label of being the *criminal-blackman*. Furthermore, these data confirm the results we presented in Chapter 3 that indicate that black men are more likely to perceive criminal justice injustices than females. Together, the data show that African American men are more likely to perceive criminal justice injustices, racial discrimination, and are more aware of being negatively stereotyped than black women.

There is research, although limited, that suggests that the gender disparity in offending may also result from African American women being able to more effectively cope with the deleterious consequences of racial injustices. Black females are significantly more likely than African American men to seek social support, talk with friends, and to address the perpetrator in coping with the toxic effects of racial discrimination (Swim et al., 2003; Utsey, Ponterotto, Reynolds, and Cancelli, 2000). We suggest that these differences in coping styles may also increase the likelihood that African American men will respond to racial injustices with anger-defiance, whereas black women will seek social support in order to dispel the negative feelings that arise from being "dissed."[8]

In sum, although limited, studies suggest that the acerbic and pervasive stereotyping of African American men may cause them to be more vigilant in perceiving racial biases. We suggest that their heightened concern with criminal justice injustices and racial discrimination coupled with their tendency to not seek social support may cause them to express greater anger-defiance when confronted with racial injustices. On the other hand, the data tentatively indicate that African American women are less worried about criminal justice injustices and being discriminated against and when confronted with these racial injustices, are able to more readily seek out social supports. We hypothesize that black women are less likely to offend than black men because, (1) they are less likely to perceive criminal justice injustices, (2) they are not targeted with the *criminalblackman* stereotype, (3) are less likely to perceive being discriminated against because of their race, (4) their healthier coping styles allow them to more effectively build strong bonds with white-dominated institutions, (5) their more effective coping skills protect them from internalizing pejorative labels, and

(6) their healthier coping styles lessen their likelihood of responding to racial injustices with hopelessness-depression and anger-defiance.

The Significance of Place

A critical question is whether African American perceptions of racism vary across characteristics of institutions and neighborhoods. Gay (2004) argues that a salient reason why there is homogeneity in African American opinions (e.g., their nearly universally held belief in criminal justice injustices) is that the historical segregation of African Americans has facilitated the transmission of group-based norms and collectively shared values and fates. However, she argues that the collective world-view of African Americans may weaken as blacks, relatively more affluent blacks, move from the inner city into suburban integrated areas. Consequently, it is possible that the place that African Americans live and work may be related to the degree to which they perceive and experience racial discrimination and pejorative stereotypes. This also implies that African American offending will increase if they live in areas where they are more likely to perceive and experience racial injustices.

The research on how context frames African American opinions is limited. McKown and Weinstein (2008) discuss two characteristics of schools-classrooms that may enhance the differential treatment of African Americans, that is, climate and inhabitants. Climate is the degree to which African Americans perceive whether teachers differentially treat students (i.e., whether the school has toxic race relations) and inhabitant is assessed by the school-classrooms demographic composition. They theorize that teachers may stereotype African Americans as their numbers increase, whereas teachers will view them as individuals and have the same expectations as white students if there are only a few black students. McKown and Weinstein (2008) found, analyzing two independent datasets with 1,872 elementary-aged children in 83 classrooms, that teacher bias increased in classrooms with more ethnic diversity and when teachers created climates characterized by high differential treatment of high and low achievers.

Relatedly, scholars note that the relationship between racially segregated schools and African American offending is complex. Eitle and

Eitle's (2010:440) macro study found that racial segregation within schools is *negatively* related to offending. They suggest that this negative relationship may indicate that racial conflicts arise in more integrated schools, especially if there are "anxious negative encounters," which are generated when African Americans and whites do not "share equal status, cooperative dependence, common goals, and have institutional and/or normative support." Goldsmith (2004:608) reports that interracial conflict across schools is related to the school's heterogeneity; that is, "school integration does increase interracial friendliness, but it appears to produce much more interracial conflict." In addition, Goldsmith (2004) reports that interracial conflict is related to the school's proportion of minority teachers; that is, as it increases racial conflict decreases. Also, Goldsmith argues that stereotype threats are less likely to negatively affect African Americans if the domain-specific institution explicitly embraces diversity and there are a substantial number of other blacks.

Together, this research tentatively suggests that the racial climate, that is, whether there are conflicted racial relations, is a key to assessing the degree to which African Americans identify with white-dominated institutions. A toxic racial climate can be characterized when an institution tolerates "everyday racism" (microaggressions) (e.g., whites stating that "some of my best friends are black") (Jean and Feagin, 1998; Swim et al., 2003). Scholars argue that toxic race relations can be minimized if the institution embraces and reinforces a climate of racial-ethnic diversity. A policy of embracing racial tolerance is evidenced when blacks are proportionately included in positions of authority-leadership (e.g., principals, managers, and teachers) and the workforce is proportionately African American. However, the research reveals that black identification does not necessarily increase as their percentage within the institution increases. Indeed, in the absence of African Americans in positions of leadership that promote and enforce a policy of racial tolerance, more blacks in the classroom-workforce may be perceived as "threatening." Thus, African Americans are more likely to identify with their institution (e.g., school)—that is, be less likely to offend—if it explicitly embraces and enforces a policy of racial tolerance, it has blacks in administrative positions, African Americans are proportionately represented in management positions (e.g., teachers), and there are enough blacks in the workforce (i.e., students) for individual African Americans not to feel isolated (Gates and Steele, 2009).[9]

Studies on whether neighborhood characteristics influence the perceptions of racism among African Americans are also limited. However, as previously discussed, the literature is unequivocally clear that perceptions of criminal justice injustices are most intensely felt in racially segregated, resource-depleted, neighborhoods. We, therefore, assume that African Americans residing in such neighborhoods are also more likely to report a greater awareness of being pejoratively stereotyped—that is, to be automatically thought of as being criminal—and to encounter personal instances of racial discrimination than those residing in more affluent racially integrated neighborhoods. We posit that the historical forces that created and now sustain "ghettos" are related to African Americans having more intense experiences with racism. That is, we assert that the macro-micro forces that created and now sustain "ghettos"—that is, racist stereotypes and racial discrimination (e.g., underfunded schools, "redlining," racial violence, negative stereotyping, white racism) have caused African Americans to reside in places where they will more likely encounter pejorative stereotypes, racial discrimination, and criminal justice injustices (Bass, 2001; Holmes and Smith, 2008; Massey, 1990; Robinson, 1981).

Gay's research (2004) supports the argument that African Americans' perceptions of racial injustices are framed within a context. She analyzed a multilevel dataset that merged the 1992–1994 Multi-City Survey of Urban Inequality with block-group-level demographic statistics from the 1990 Census. Gay (2004) found that her multivariate models predicted that 66 percent of African Americans who reside in the lowest-quality neighborhood (i.e., averaged scores on the extent to which, for example, blacks reported that their neighborhood had problems with neglected housing and property) expressed a strong belief in having a linked fate with other African Americans (e.g., "Do you think what happens generally to black people in this country will have something to do with what happens in your life?") and 67 percent were likely to view racial discrimination as a significant barrier to black socioeconomic attainment. In comparison, she found that when neighborhood quality was at its highest, the probability of holding these two views declined considerably, to 40 percent and 39 percent respectively. These results support our hypothesis that African Americans are likely to experience multiple racial injustices, including criminal justice injustices and racial discrimination, if they live in segregated poor areas.

Relatedly, studies show that context matters for the well-being of African Americans. Simons et al. (2002) examined whether African American youths residing in "highly discriminatory communities" (i.e., census blocks) were more likely to report depressive symptoms (a factor related to offending) regardless of whether they had personally reported being discriminated against. They measured whether the community was highly discriminatory by averaging across self-reported measures of racial discrimination within each community to obtain a measure of the incidence of racial discrimination for each of the 46 communities included in their data. These scholars report that African American youth, both boys and girls, were more likely to report symptoms of depression if they resided in highly discriminatory communities. Of interest, Simons et al. (2002) also found that African American youths experienced higher rates of depression if they resided in communities with high rates of criminal victimization but lower rates if they resided in areas that collectively expressed greater racial pride (averaged scores on items such as "you have a strong attachment toward your ethnic group" and "you feel good about your cultural or ethnic background"). These scholars conclude that community context is a strong predictor of the well-being of African American youth.

There is also research that shows that context matters in shaping the opinions that whites have about African Americans. Quillian and Pager (2001) found that the percentage of a neighborhood's black population, particularly the percentage of young black men, is significantly associated with perceptions of the severity of the neighborhood's crime problem, regardless of its actual rate of crime. This means that the majority of Americans stereotype an area as crime-ridden because it has a large percentage of young black men even if it in actuality has a low crime rate.

Quillian and Pager (2001) found that this relationship persisted after they controlled for official neighborhood crime rates and a variety of other individual and neighborhood characteristics. These scholars argue that whites (and perhaps blacks) perceive neighborhoods as less desirable that have larger percentages of young African American men because they associate race with crime, poverty, and disorder (see also Hipp, 2010; Sampson and Raudenbush, 2004). Thus, these data indicate that "ghettos" as a social construct have been "criminalized" as evidenced by the ascendancy of the acerbic stereotype of the *criminalblackman*. That is, the concept of a "ghetto" intensifies and consolidates the belief among whites that race and crime are inseparable.

Of interest, this is not a new insight. Du Bois (1903:104), over 100 years ago, noted that a consequence of racial segregation—the color line—is that "both whites and blacks see commonly the worst of each other." Renowned sociologist Herbert Blumer adds:

> The color line forced into being among [blacks] a posture of concealment of strong feelings of resentment and bitterness. The color line stood fundamentally for a denigration of Negroes as inferior and rejection of them as alien. Yet it was not wise for Negroes to express before whites their feelings as they experienced affronts, indignities, and the various forms of exploitation which went with their inferior and impotent status. It was precisely this area of feelings, and of the sentiments and thoughts built up in it, that was typically unknown to southern whites under the operation of the color line (1965:323–24).

Consequently, we contend that African Americans are aware that the rest of America thinks less of them because they happen to live in or near a stereotyped racialized-criminalized "ghetto" (Wacquant, 2001, 2008). In short, "ghettos" intensify the felt negative emotions that racial injustices provoke among African Americans.

Other studies show that the percentage of African American residents sharpens and intensifies anti-black sentiments among whites. Taylor (1998) found that the percentage of African Americans predicted anti-black prejudice (e.g., less intelligent, prone to violence, preference for living off of welfare), opposition to race-targeted policies (e.g., government should improve the conditions of blacks), and policy-related beliefs about blacks (e.g., the extent of discrimination faced by blacks) while controlling for other contextual (e.g., south) and individual factors (e.g., gender, employment status, occupational prestige). These data suggest that racially segregated neighborhoods intensify white racism and, therefore, increase the likelihood that African Americans who live in disadvantaged racially segregated neighborhoods will encounter racial biases.

Although limited, together, the research suggests that context shapes both the contours of African American and whites' opinions about race-related issues. Most importantly, studies show that racial segregation is a salient contextual factor. Racial segregation facilitates and consolidates the negative opinions that whites have about African Americans. More specifically, the existence of racialized "ghettos" increases the likelihood that whites will pejoratively stereotype African Americans as criminals. This intensification of white racial animus has two pragmatic outcomes; an increase of indifference toward African Americans and an increase in whites perpetrating injustices against blacks (Alexander, 2010). Racially segregated neighborhoods also intensify the likelihood that African Americans consensually believe that they will experience racial injustices. All told, these results present a disturbing reality. Racial segregation increases white racial animus, which in turn increases the likelihood that African Americans believe they are being discriminated against because of their race. We hypothesize that this self-reinforcing dynamic is a salient factor related to African American offending

Conclusions

Our theory states that the causes of African American offending must be located in their daily lived experiences. Unlike whites, we posit that African Americans are immersed in a worldview that has been formed in reaction to racist attitudes and behaviors over a long period of time. As noted scholar Glen Loury (2004:12) argues, these racist attitudes and behaviors have racially stigmatized African Americans, culminating in blacks having "spoiled collective identities." As Loury (2004:12) states:

> Moreover, and crucially, this stigmatization is not merely the drawing of a negative surmise about someone's productive attributes. *It entails doubting the person's worthiness and consigning him or her to a social netherworld* [emphasis in the original]. Indeed, although the language is somewhat hyperbolic, it means being skeptical about whether the person can be assumed to share a common humanity with the observer. Drawing on this observation, and calling to mind the legacy of racial dishonour engendered by the history of chattel slavery in the United States, I want to suggest that the idea of "racial stigma" can be used to gain insight into problems of perception, representation, and standing in contemporary American public life that adversely affect (some) blacks.

Our theory hypothesizes that these "spoiled collective identities" formed in reaction to racist stereotypes, stereotype threats, racial discrimination, and criminal justice injustices are related to why some African Americans offend.

5

RACIAL SOCIALIZATION AND AFRICAN AMERICAN OFFENDING

Introduction

In the previous chapters, we noted that nearly all African Americans, at some point in their lives, perceive criminal justice injustices, racial discrimination, and experience the negative consequences of being pejoratively stereotyped. We argue that these perceptions and experiences are related to African American offending because they weaken social bonds with conventional institutions and cause blacks to have heightened states of anger-defiance and depression. Yet, we also know that only a small percentage of African Americans offend. This, of course, means that the vast majority of African Americans somehow successfully negotiate the deleterious consequences of encountering racial injustices. In short, blacks are incredibly resilient (Brown, 2008; Keyes, 2009; Miller, 1999; Stevenson, Reed, Bodison, and Bishop, 1997). In fact, scholars argue that, in the absence of acknowledging this resiliency, there is a strong tendency to define African Americans in terms of the pathology associated with disproportionately living in resource-depleted neighborhoods (Nicolas, Helms, Jernigan, Sass, Skrzypek, and DeSilva, 2008). In this chapter, we argue that racial socialization experiences are a critical reason why so few African Americans respond to the damaging consequences of racial injustices by offending.

African Americans are faced with the reality of being black in a racist society. This means that they are confronted by racial discrimination, criminal justice injustices, and pejorative stereotypes that devalue them as being less than whites (Constantine and Blackmon, 2002). Scholars have revealed that many African American parents actively prepare their children to negotiate these perceptions of racial injustice (McHale, Crouter, Kim, Burton, Davis, Dotterer, and Swanson, 2006). They refer to this process as racial socialization.[1] Lesane-Brown (2006:400) defines racial socialization "as specific verbal and non-verbal messages transmitted to younger generations for the development of values, attitudes, behaviors, and beliefs regarding the meaning and significance of race and racial stratification, intergroup and intragroup interactions, and personal and group identity."

Ward (1996) adds that racial socialization involves passing on the knowledge needed to resist internalizing the prevailing pejorative images and evaluations of African Americans and to create a self-identity that includes blackness as positive and valued. Ward (1996:86) states:

> As agents of socialization, black families play an essential role in orienting their children to the existing social environment, teaching them what they need to know about the world and their place in it. African American parents socialize their children based on cultural and political interpretations and assumptions derived from their lived experience of being black in white America. The parenting of a black child is a political act. The psychological survival of a black child largely depends on the black family's ability to endure racial and economic discrimination and to negotiate conflicting and multiple role demands.

Thus, scholars of racial socialization detail how African American families experience and discuss racial inequalities and injustices and how they teach their children to manage them. More specifically, research recognizes that racial socialization is a multilayered phenomenon that "includes exposure to cultural practices and objects, efforts to instill pride in and knowledge about African Americans, discussions about discrimination and how to cope with it, and strategies for succeeding in mainstream society" (Hughes, Rodriguez, Smith, Johnson, Stevenson, and Spicer, 2006:748). Scholars argue that African American parents must racially socialize their children so that they understand: (1) African American culture and how to interact with other blacks; (2) how to get along with other racial groups; and (3) how to cope with their minority status (Lesane-Brown, 2006:401). Other scholars add that: "Race-specific barriers might include racial concerns, such as discrimination in the classroom, racial stereotyping, and issues of subordination. Effective racial socialization enables the youths to recognize the difference between these types of barriers and to cope with them effectively" (Nicolas et al., 2008:276). In short, racial socialization is the attempt by African American parents to provide their children with the skills to buffer the effects of having a "collective spoiled identity" (Goffman, 1963; Inzlicht, McKay, and Aronson, 2006; Loury, 2004).[2]

Scholars add that a critical component of racial socialization is inculcating African American youth with a critical consciousness:

> This critical consciousness enables blacks to resist internalizing the notion that the enemy resides within the psyche of the black individual, that is, that it is the black individual's lack of motivation, unsuccessful identity formation, internalized self-hatred, or learned helplessness that explains his or her lack of success. Undoubtedly, most black parents acknowledge the importance of personal effort and responsibility and do not wish to devalue their effect. However, many also recognize that a vital part of their child's socialization is to learn when to attribute lack of success to individual effort and when to attribute it to social forces. The refusal to allow oneself to become stifled by victimization or to accept an ideology of victim-blame entails the development of a critical perspective on the world—one that is informed by the particular knowledge gained from one's social and political position. Such knowledge, in mitigating self-abnegation while fostering self-esteem, enables blacks' resistance to oppression. It is one of the most powerful weapons

African American families have had throughout our history in the United States (Ward, 1996:89).

Researchers further argue that the development of a critical consciousness instills a healthy psychological resistance that allows African American youth to cope with, rather than repress, the negative emotions that are caused by experiencing racial injustices. Quite simply, it allows African Americans to address racism in an open and forthright manner (Ward, 1996).

Studies indicate that approximately two-thirds of African American parents proactively engage in at least one aspect of racial socialization (Bowman and Howard, 1985; Burt, Simons, and Gibbons, 2010; Lesane-Brown, 2006). Scholars note that African American parents feel compelled to racially socialize their children because their peers and teachers may give them misinformation or no information; that is, African American culture and history is generally ignored in most American schools (Thomas and Speight, 1999). The research also shows that there is considerable variation among African Americans in how they racially socialize their children. Shelton (2008:252) found that African Americans were more likely to racially socialize their children if they had a stronger sense of black pride, were attuned to African American culture, participated in African American organizations, were higher-income earners, and had white friends. Shelton (2008) also found that less educated African American parents were not as likely to teach their children to peacefully coexist with whites.

Furthermore, studies indicate that African American parents who do not racially socialize their children may cause them to be vulnerable and ill-prepared in race-related situations, inadequately prepared to deal with unanticipated racial circumstances, feel uncomfortable interacting with other African Americans, and be vulnerable to internalizing the negative images embedded within racial stereotypes (Lesane-Brown, 2006; Phinney and Rotheram, 1987; Thornton, Chatters, Taylor, and Allen, 1990). The research also shows that African American children who are not racially socialized are more likely to develop mental health problems if they encounter racial discrimination (Fischer and Shaw,

1999; Hughes et al., 2006). Ward (1996:93) states that: "In explicitly acknowledging the vulnerability of their children to discrimination and oppression, black parents hope that rather than being overwhelmed and disabled, their children will instead become empowered in the face of their condition and resist negative images." This empowerment allows African American youth to stand up in their own defense, preventing them from becoming psychologically and culturally alienated.

It is important to note that the worldview shared by the vast majority of African Americans includes the belief that "bad parenting" is related to why some African Americans and not others offend. Recall that Unnever (2008) found that African Americans are *more* likely than whites to report that black male imprisonment is related to African American parents failing to teach their children right from wrong. Indeed, his analysis of national survey data revealed that the majority of African Americans (55 percent) believe that a "big reason" why African Americans are disproportionately incarcerated is that "many black parents aren't teaching their children right from wrong" (of note, 23 percent reported that it was a "small reason"). These data clearly indicate that African Americans recognize that the problem of black offending results from forces largely outside of their control (e.g., criminal justice injustices) *and* from factors that they can control (e.g., more effective parenting).

Our theory of African American offending emphasizes the role that racial socialization has in offending. This focus does not diminish the unequivocal fact that offending is related to other deleterious forms of parenting (Edwards, Dodge, Latendresse, Lansford, Bates, Pettit, Budde, Goate, and Dick, 2010; Jungmeen and Cicchetti, 2010; Zahn, Agnew, Fishbein, Miller, Winn, Dakoff, Kruttschnitt, Giordano, Gottfredson, Payne, Feld, and Chesney-Lind, 2010). For example, the research clearly shows that authoritarian-abusive forms of parenting are related to aggressive behavior and offending, regardless of the race, ethnicity, or gender of the child (Roche, Ghazarian, Little, and Leventhal, 2010; Taylor, Manganello, Lee, and Rice, 2010). That is, children are significantly more likely to either self-report engaging in delinquency or have been arrested if their parents-guardians tried to control their behavior through the inconsistent use of violence or physical and emotional intimidation. Put most simply, the data show that children are more likely to engage in delinquent behaviors when their parents engage in or threaten to use physical violence to control their behavior (Dodge and Crick, 1990; Patterson, DeBaryshe, and Ramsey, 1989). In fact, the research indicates that this relationship occurs crossnationally. Gershoff, Grogan-Kaylor, Lansford, Chang, Zelli, Deater-Deckard, and Dodge (2010) found crossnationally that mothers' use of corporal punishment, expressing disappointment, and yelling at their children were significantly related to more childhood aggression. In addition, the research on parenting and crime indicates that another chief predictor of offending is how closely the parents monitor their children. That is, the more closely parents monitor their children (e.g., know where and who they are with) the less likely they are to offend regardless of their race-ethnicity. Other forms of parenting related to offending include insecure attachments, inconsistent discipline, and weak parent–child bonds (Fearon, Bakermans-Kranenburg, Ijzendoorn, Lapsley, and Roisman, 2010; Schroeder, Bulanda, Giordano, and Cernkovich, 2010; Schroeder, Giordano, and Cernkovich, 2010).

Our theory of offending complements the extant research on parenting and crime. In addition to the types of parenting outlined above, we argue that racial socialization experiences are specifically related to African American offending.[3] We further argue that the relationship between racial socialization and African American offending has not been fully developed or incorporated into the literature on crime, especially by scholars testing the general theories of crime. As a result of this unfortunate omission, the literature is not as pointed or as succinct as, for example, the research on racial discrimination and offending. However, despite these limitations, below we build a theoretical foundation that generates related hypotheses regarding the role that racial socialization has in explaining African American offending.

Our basic thesis is that racial socialization experiences can exacerbate the influences that criminal justice injustices, racial discrimination, pejorative stereotypes, and stereotype threats have on African American offending. We assert that there are three pathways through which racial socialization can increase the probability of individual African American offending. First, we argue that parents who do not racially socialize their children put them at greater risk for having the deleterious effects of racial injustices cause them to offend. Second, we assert that African Americans are more likely to offend if their parents inadvertently failed to fully prepare them to fend off the toxic effects of racial injustices. Third, we posit that African Americans are more likely to offend when exposed to criminal justice injustices, racial discrimination, and toxic stereotypes if their parents overly racially socialize them to be vigilantly distrustful of whites. We hypothesize that this aspect of racial socialization—the distrust of whites—intensifies the noxious effects of racial injustices. Below we review the relevant extant literature on racial socialization and then, at the end of the chapter, present our theory on racial socialization and African American offending.

The Different Dimensions of Racial Socialization

Researchers have only begun to assess the complexities of how African American parents prepare their children to live in a society that devalues them (Murry, Berkel, Brody, Miller, and Chen, 2009). As a result, scholars have not generated an agreed-upon definition that captures the full range of racial socialization experiences. Also, in the absence of a unifying definition, there is considerable variation in the way that researchers have measured racial socialization. It is also important to note that most scholars who research the racial socialization process focus on how it positively buffers the toxic effects of racial injustices. Consequently, there is a paucity of research that highlights and fully measures the negative qualities of racial socialization and how they are related to African American offending. However, scholars generally agree that racial socialization includes four dimensions: cultural socialization, preparation for bias, promotion of mistrust, and egalitarianism. The research shows that parents most often engage in cultural socialization followed by preparation for bias, egalitarianism, and the mistrust of whites (Hughes, Witherspoon, Rivas-Drake, and West-Bey, 2009).

Cultural Socialization

Nearly all the research on racial socialization includes measures of whether parents attempt to instill within their children a sense of racial pride. Scholars define racial pride as "the capacity of black youths to use racial identity and critical consciousness skills and resources to recognize racism and discriminatory experiences and to value themselves and resist personal and institutional racism in their lives and in environmental contexts" (Nicolas et al., 2008:270–271). Researchers generally assume that African Americans who are proud to be black will be significantly more likely to fend off the noxious effects of racial injustices. They define this process as "cultural socialization."

Cultural socialization involves African American parents emphasizing racial pride by teaching their children about black history, culture, and heritage (Hughes, Hagelskamp, Way, and Foust, 2009). Other examples of cultural socialization include exposing children to salient historical or cultural figures; exposing children to culturally relevant books, artifacts, music, and stories; and celebrating cultural holidays such as Kwanzaa (Hughes et al., 2006). Measures of cultural socialization include, "have you ever done things with your child to remember events in African American history?", "have you never been ashamed of your color?", "I've read or provided Black history books to my child," and "have your parents talked to you about being proud to be Black" (Caughy, O'Brien, O'Campo, Randolph, and Nickerson, 2002; Harris-Britt, Valrie, Kurtz-Costes, and Rowley, 2007; McHale et al., 2006).

In general, the research on cultural socialization shows that it buffers or moderates the debilitating consequences of perceived racial injustices. For example, Caughy, Nettles, O'Campo, and Lohrfink (2006) state that homes rich in African American culture are associated with fewer behavioral problems because they foster a positive racial identity and increase the child's self-esteem.[4] Hughes et al. (2006:764) comprehensively reviewed the research on racial socialization and they conclude that cultural socialization is associated with "fewer externalizing behaviors, lower fighting frequency and better anger management (especially among boys), higher self-esteem with peers, fewer internalizing problems, and better cognitive outcomes." Caughy et al. (2002) analyzed the influence of racial socialization practices (i.e., the Parent's Experience of Racial Socialization Scale) on behavioral problems (i.e., the Child Behavior Checklist) among a socioeconomically diverse sample of African American families who resided in an urban setting. Caughy et al. (2002) found that cultural socialization practices were associated with better problem-solving skills and fewer reported behavioral problems.

Preparation for Racial Bias

The research shows that African American parents are fully aware that their children, at some point, will encounter racial injustices. They are also fully aware that racial injustices can manifest themselves in a multitude of ways, from being pulled over by the police because they are black, to teachers "dissing" their children because of their race, to the negative stereotypes of blacks that are pervasively "in the air." Thus, African American parents are saddled with the burden of how to prepare their children to overcome the feelings of being devalued in a multitude of ways because they are black.

The research reveals that African American parents prepare their children for their encounters with racial injustices by promoting their child's coping skills. Measures used to assess preparation for bias include, "have you ever talked to your child about the fight for equality among African Americans?", "have you ever explained something to your child that she/ he saw on TV showing poor treatment of African Americans or warned the child that people might treat them badly because of their race?", and "racism is real and you have to understand it or it will hurt you" (Caughy et al., 2006; Hughes and Chen, 1997).

The following is an illustration of how African Americans prepare their children for potential encounters with racial injustices. An African American social worker reports that when her young son begins to drive, she will tell him:

> The police are supposed to be there to protect and to serve, but you being black and being male, you've got two strikes against you. Keep your hands on the steering wheel, and do not run, because

they will shoot you in your back. Let them do whatever they want to do. I know it's humiliating, but let them do whatever they want to do to make sure you get out of that situation alive. Deal with your emotions later. Your emotions are going to come second—or last (Harris, 1999:24).

Scholars argue that preparation of bias can both be a protective and risk factor for externalizing behavior. African American parents can decrease the odds that their children will engage in problem behaviors if they carefully instill within their child the social skills necessary to successfully negotiate perceptions of criminal justice injustices, the toxic consequences of being pejoratively stereotyped, and racial discrimination. On the other hand, research indicates that parents who are not skilled at preparing their children for bias may inadvertently instill within their children higher levels of anxiety, which can be expressed through higher rates of externalizing behavior (e.g., aggression) and internalizing behavior (e.g., depression) (Caughy et al., 2006). Indeed, based on their review of the literature, Hughes et al. (2006) conclude that a heightened awareness of persistent discrimination may undermine a child's self-esteem. Relatedly, Stevenson et al. (1997) found that boys who believed in the importance of emphasizing cultural pride and heritage (cultural socialization) reported higher levels of anger control than did those who endorsed a focus on discrimination against African Americans (preparation for bias).

Promotion of Mistrust

Promotion of mistrust is generally defined as practices that emphasize the need for wariness and distrust in interracial interactions (Hughes et al., 2006). Researchers have used a variety of measures to assess whether parents encourage their children to distrust whites, such as, "have you ever told your child that she/he should not trust Whites?", "whites make it hard to get ahead," and "African Americans should be suspicious of a white person who tries to be friendly" (Biafora, Taylor, Warheit, Zimmerman, and Vega, 1993; Caughy et al., 2006; Hughes and Chen, 1997:205). It is important to note that promotion of mistrust differs from preparation for bias as it includes no advice or inculcation of skills for coping with or managing discrimination.

Biafora et al. (1993) found that nearly a third of their sample of seventh-grade boys residing in Dade County, Florida, reported that they should be suspicious of a white person who tries to be friendly and that 28 percent believed that when a teacher talks to an African American student it is usually to get information that can be used against him or her. Hughes and Chen (1997) found that parents are particularly likely to encourage their children to mistrust whites when they perceived their children were being unfairly treated by adults and if their children reported that their peers or other adults were not treating them fairly. These scholars conclude that "parental perceptions of *some* unfair treatment may prompt Preparation for Bias, perceptions of *a lot* of unfair treatment may prompt Promotion of Mistrust" (Hughes and Chen, 1997:993).

There are a few studies that specifically examined whether the promotion of the distrust of whites can explain individual African American offending. Biafora et al. (1993:894) theorized that mistrust motivates African Americans to offend because they "act on their feelings by engaging in rebellious or reward seeking behaviors that deviate from the accepted norm of the dominant group." They collected data from African Americans (n=904), Haitians (n=168), and those from other Caribbean countries (n=171) in Miami, Florida's middle schools. More specifically, they analyzed whether self-report indices of minor (e.g., "take between $2 and $50" and "start a fist fight") and major delinquency (e.g., "break into/enter a home, store or building" and "use force to get money or expensive things from another person") were related to an index measuring racial distrust, the Cultural Mistrust Inventory (e.g., "Black parents should teach their children not to trust White teachers, Blacks should be suspicious of White persons who try to be friendly, when a White teacher talks to a Black student, it is usually to get information that can be used against him or her, and white teachers ask hard questions to Black students on purpose so they will fail") while holding constant the effects of socioeconomic status. Their multivariate analyses indicated that their indices of mistrust were the most robust predictor of both minor and serious offending.

Taylor, Biafora, Warheit (1994) extended the research by Biafora et al. (1993) by studying the potential deleterious consequences of a heightened state of racial mistrust on both self-reported delinquency and attitudes toward the law. Taylor et al. (1994:293) hypothesized that "mistrust may encourage both a dissatisfaction with the law and a disposition to deviance that runs counter to law-abiding expectations." These scholars created an index composed of five questions to measure the student's perceptions of the law—that is, legal cynicism (e.g., "it is important to follow rules and obey the law," "it is okay to sneak into a movie or ball game without paying"). Analyzing the same data as Biafora et al. (1993), Taylor et al. (1994) found that African American youth who distrusted whites were more likely to develop legal cynicism and to offend.

Caughy et al. (2006) collected data from African American first graders (241 children) and their families residing in 106 different Baltimore city neighborhoods. They analyzed whether child cognitive competence (i.e., the Peabody Picture Vocabulary Test—Revised and the Kaufman Brief Intelligence Test) and child behavioral competence (i.e., the Child Behavior Checklist, which yields scores for internalizing problems (e.g., anxiety, depression) and externalizing problems (e.g., aggression)) were related to racial socialization practices including preparation for bias and promotion of mistrust, while controlling for perceptions of the collective efficacy of the neighborhoods and their aggregate characteristics (e.g., percent below poverty). They found that preparation for bias and their measures of racial pride were associated with higher behavior problems for girls but not boys but that promotion of mistrust was associated with higher externalizing problems for boys.

Egalitarian Values

The fourth dimension of racial socialization is generally referred to as the promotion of egalitarian values. Researchers argue that many African American parents emphasize hard work, virtue, self-acceptance, and equality as their primary racial socialization strategy (Hughes et al., 2006). Lesane-Brown (2006:409) notes that egalitarian racial socialization practices tend to "deemphasize race but stress life skills and personal qualities, such as ambition and confidence in addition to emphasizing

Blacks' co-existence in mainstream society." Measures of egalitarianism include assessments of whether blacks agree with the statement that all people are basically and fundamentally the same. It must be noted, however, that the least amount of research has been conducted on this racial socialization practice. That is, most scholars who investigate the process of racial socialization include measures of cultural socialization, preparation of bias, and, to a lesser extent, the mistrust of whites. Thus, while some researchers argue that the promotion of egalitarian values is part of racial socialization, it has not received the same amount of empirical attention as the other three dimensions.

Of interest, Constantine and Blackmon (2002) found that African American children had less school-based self-esteem if their parents emphasized egalitarian values. They argued that the adoption of Eurocentric cultural values and behaviors can serve as a detriment to African American students' academic self-efficacy in the context of predominantly black school settings "because it may promote the misconception that Black is inferior to White" and "they are unable or unwilling to consider the possibility that racism or discrimination could be contributing to their suboptimal academic functioning in the context of some school environments" (Constantine and Blackmon, 2002:331–332). Of equal interest, scholars report that the more strongly African Americans believe in a just world and that any individual can get ahead regardless of group membership—that is, believe that the U.S. is a meritocracy—the less likely they are to report that they personally or members of their group are targets of racial discrimination, the less likely they are to blame discrimination when a member of a higher status group (e.g., a European American) rejects them for a desirable role, but blacks report lower self-esteem and feel more threatened when confronted with prejudice against themselves or their group (Major and O'Brien, 2005; Outten, Giguère, Schmitt, and Lalonde, 2010).

Racial Socialization and Racial Identity

The research on racial socialization overlaps with the equally complex study of how African Americans construct their racial identity.[5] Scholars note that the formation of a racial identity is a dynamic development process that begins during early adolescence and continues across the lifespan and is shaped by the group interests of African Americans (Burton, Bonilla-Silva, Ray, Buckelew, and Freeman, 2010; Mandara, Gaylord-Harden, Richards, and Ragsdale, 2009; Scott, 2003). Scholars argue that "a positive Black racial identity requires the capacity to hold on to the positive aspects of one's own racial group (e.g., history, accomplishments), while adapting to what is utilitarian from White society" (Nicolas et al., 2008:272).

Oyserman and Yoon (2009:67) add that an African American's racial identity is multifaceted and that it includes a "sense of membership, valued goals, norms, and behaviors perceived to be shared by in-group members and beliefs about how the in-group is perceived by others." They further elaborate that: "First, membership in racial and ethnic groups matter for how individuals make sense of themselves and others. Second, membership in racial and ethnic groups is associated with beliefs about commonalities in experience (including shared history, language, and traditions). Third, membership in racial and ethnic groups is associated with beliefs about possible future outcomes" (Oyserman and Yoon, 2009:68).

Researchers also argue that an African American's racial identity may be "riddled with confusion, alienation, negativity, and lack of coherence" if they internalize the negative stereotypes, messages, and images of black people and African American culture (Cross and Fhagen-Smith, 2001:254). However, Phinney and Chavira (1995:36) argue "through a developmental process of questioning, learning about, and coming to appreciate their own ethnicity and culture, most minority youths achieve a secure and confident ethnic identity."

There is not a single definitive scale or index that measures the complexity of how African Americans construct their racial identity (Pieterse and Carter, 2010). Indeed, DeCuir-Gunby (2009) notes that there are over 40 survey instruments that explore various aspects of an African American's racial identity (currently, the most widely used are versions of the Racial Identity Attitude Scale [RIAS] and the Scale of Racial Socialization for African American Adolescents [SORS-A] [Stevenson, 1994]).

In general, the research argues that an African American's racial identity has, at least, the following three salient dimensions: race centrality, private regard, and public regard. Outten et al. (2010) define race centrality as the degree to which African Americans define themselves in terms of their race, private regard as the attitudes that blacks have toward African Americans and about being black and public regard is the extent to which African Americans believe that the broader society views them positively or negatively.

Arnett and Brody (2008:291) add "that identity issues are more complicated and difficult for young African American adults than for other young minorities because they must overcome the negative assumptions that others have about them as young Black people." Accordingly, some scholars theorize that a strong positive racial identity can buffer African Americans from the deleterious effects of racial injustices. And, the data show that a positive racial identity increases both physical and mental health (Caldwell, Kohn-Wood, Schmeelk-Cone, Chavous, and Zimmerman, 2004; Oyserman and Yoon, 2009).

Smith and Brookings (1997) found that a positive racial identity facilitates the likelihood of African American youths interacting with members of other races and ethnicities. Research also shows that a positive racial identity tends to be related to lower levels of depressive and anxiety symptoms (note that the effects were larger for depressive than anxiety symptoms) among African American adolescents as they transitioned between seventh and eighth grade (Mandara et al., 2009). However, there is research that indicates that a positive racial identity can both increase the likelihood that African Americans will perceive racial discrimination and that it can intensify its deleterious consequences and that the dimensions of a black's racial identity (i.e., public and private regard) may differentially impact their level of emotional distress (Brondolo, ver Halen, Pencille, Beatty, and Contrada, 2009; Sellers, Copeland-Linder, Martin, and Lewis, 2006).

Scholars recognize that parental socialization experiences have a salient role in the social construction of an African American's racial identity. In fact, the research shows that positive racial socialization experiences, especially the promotion of racial pride (race centrality) via cultural socialization, are the foundation upon which African Americans construct a positive racial identity (Hughes et al., 2009; Thomas and Speight, 1999). Scholars also have found that positive racial social experiences are related to children developing a resilient self-empowering racial identity that protects them from the negative consequences of criminal justice injustices, racial discrimination, and stereotype threats (Caldwell et al., 2004; Lesane-Brown, 2006; Stevenson, 1995; Rivas-Drake, Hughes, and Way, 2009). However, we note that the relationship between racial socialization experiences and a positive racial identity is complex; that is, increasing the awareness among blacks that they may be targeted for racism may help them "gather the strength they need to avoid being denied rights or misjudging their own competence, but this awareness can also be exhausting, elicit distress and anger, and erode some relationships" (Brondolo et al., 2009:75).

Racial Identity and Offending

We found two studies that investigated the relationship between children's racial identity and their propensity to embrace aggressive attitudes—a factor related to offending (Dodge and Crick, 1990; Unnever, Cullen, Mathers, McClure, and Allison, 2009). Arbona, Jackson, McCoy, and Blakely (1999) collected data over a three-year period on 142 African American middle school peer-nominated leaders. They examined whether aggressive attitudes were related to the strength of the child's racial identity (e.g., "I have a lot of pride in my ethnic group and its accomplishments, I am happy that I am a member of the racial/ethnic group I belong to, and I have spent time trying to learn about my ethnic group, such as its history, traditions, and customs"). Arbona et al. (1999) found that African Americans who had a positive racial identity were significantly less likely to embrace aggressive attitudes while controlling for parental involvement (e.g., "My parent(s) know who my friends are") and peer negative behaviors (e.g., "my friends destroyed or damaged property that did not belong to them"). They concluded that "together with other known predictors (e.g., parental control and positive peer influences), feelings of pride and commitment to one's ethnicity are related to these adolescents' self-reported attitudes and skills in resolving conflicts with peers in nonviolent ways" (Arbona et al., 1999:336).

McMahon and Watts (2002) surveyed 209 fifth- through eighth-grade students in two schools located in a public housing development community in Chicago. They assessed whether a positive racial identity (using the Multi-Group Ethnic Identity Scale) was associated with depression (i.e., the Children's Depression Inventory [CDI]), anxiety (i.e., the Revised Children's Manifest Anxiety Scale [RCMAS]), coping (e.g., direct problem-solving), normative beliefs about aggression (e.g., "is it generally wrong to get into physical fights with others?"), and an aggressive behavior scale (e.g., an 11-item scale that measured the frequency of self-reported aggressive behaviors). McMahon and Watts (2002) found that a more positive racial identity predicted depression and more active coping but did not predict higher anxiety scores. Most importantly, they report that a positive racial identity reduced the likelihood of endorsing and engaging in aggressive behaviors among African American youths.[6]

Racial Socialization and Gender

Thus far, we have presented data that show that African American males are substantially more likely to offend than black females. We also have presented data that clearly indicate that African American males and females share the same worldview and that it includes perceptions of criminal justice injustices, racial discrimination, and stereotype threats. Thus, we are confronted by the fact that African American females are substantially less likely to offend yet they share the same worldview as their male counterparts.

Zahn et al. (2010), as part of the Girls Study Group convened by the Office of Juvenile Justice and Delinquency Prevention, reviewed over 1,600 articles and book chapters and concluded that boys and girls share many of the same correlates of offending. However, they report that there are factors that girls are more likely to experience that are related to offending, including sexual abuse and rape, depression, anxiety, post-traumatic stress disorder, early maturation, and affiliation with older males. In addition, research clearly indicates that parents do not socialize their daughters in the same way as their sons and that these differences are related to less offending among girls (Brown, Linver, and Evans, 2010). For example, the research indicates that parents are significantly more likely to monitor the behavior of their daughters than their sons, which is a robust predictor of delinquency. Thus, we assume that a large portion of the differences between male and female offending among African Americans can be explained by differences in non-race-based socialization practices such as the fact that parents more closely monitor their daughters than their sons.

We were not able to locate any research that examines whether there are any gender-based differences in how African American parents racially socialize their sons and daughters and whether these differences are specifically related to male-female offending. However, scholars have identified that there are gender differences in how African American parents racially socialize their daughters and sons, although the findings are equivocal and based on a limited number of studies.

Brown et al. (2010) analyzed data collected from 218 native-born African American adolescents attending a diverse public high school in the northeastern United States. They examined the patterns of racial socialization messages provided to African American adolescents by their primary female and male caregivers in order to investigate whether socialization messages differ for adolescent girls and boys. Brown et al. (2010) examined three dimensions of racial socialization: (1) racial barrier awareness (e.g., "my female/male caregiver teaches me that racism is present in America"); (2) coping with racism and discrimination (e.g., "My female/male caregiver teaches me what to do if I'm called a racist name"); and (3) the promotion of crossracial relationships (e.g., "my female/male caregiver encourages me to have White friends"). And, they included measures of cultural socialization (e.g., "my female/male caregiver teaches me that knowing about African history is important").

Brown et al. (2010) found that adolescent girls and boys perceived their maternal caregivers as providing higher levels of racial socialization across all of the measured dimensions than their male caregivers and that female adolescents reported receiving higher levels of racial socialization and ethnic socialization than male adolescents while controlling for age, family structure of each adolescent's family, and the employment and education status of the adolescents' maternal and paternal caregivers.

Thomas and Speight (1999) report that African American parents emphasized negative stereotypes and strategies for coping with racism for their sons, whereas parents emphasized achievement and racial pride for their daughters. More specifically, they found that "both boys and girls get messages on racial pride, self-pride, the importance of achievement, negative societal messages, overcoming racism, moral values, and the importance of the family. Boys, however, were given more messages on overcoming racism, whereas girls are more encouraged to pursue a good education. Although boys and girls were given an equal percentage of messages on self-pride, girls tended to receive more messages on racial pride" (Thomas and Speight, 1999:165).

Hughes et al. (2009:608) conclude in their review of the racial socialization literature, that when "gender differences in ethnic-racial socialization have been found, they indicate that boys are more likely to report messages regarding racial barriers, whereas girls are more likely to report messages regarding racial pride." These scholars argue that these gender differences emerge because parents anticipate race-based differences in external contexts such as neighborhoods and schools with boys more likely to encounter pejorative stereotypes (e.g., the violent angry young predator) and racial discrimination.

Scholars have also found gendered patterns in parents' racial socialization; that is, African American mothers and fathers differ in how they racially socialize their children. In a comprehensive analysis, McHale et al. (2006) analyzed data collected from fathers, mothers, and two offspring in 162 families that were participating in the first phase of a short-term longitudinal study of gender socialization and development in two-parent, black/African American families who resided in the northeast. They focused on two dimensions of racial socialization: cultural (e.g., "I've read or provided Black history books to my child") and preparation for bias (e.g., "I've talked to my children about racism") and assessed whether they were related to parental warmth (e.g., "I am a person who makes my child feel better after talking over his/her worries with me"), racial identity (e.g., "I am happy that I am African American/Black"), youth locus of control (e.g., "Most problems will solve themselves if I just don't fool with them"), and depression (e.g., "I am sad once in a while"), while controlling for the age of the family members, levels of education, information about the couple's relationship (i.e., marital status, duration of co-residence), information about youth's relationship to each parent and to one another, and information about parents' employment (i.e., status, occupation, income).

They found that parental warmth and racial socialization were positively related; that is, the more nurturing African American parents were the more likely they were to racially socialize their children. They also report that "mothers, but not fathers, engaged in more preparation for bias and cultural socialization with older as compared with younger offspring. In contrast, fathers' but not mothers' socialization practices varied by offspring gender, with fathers engaging in more racial socialization with sons than with daughters" (McHale et al., 2006:1398). In addition, these scholars found that lower self-control and depression occurred more often when mothers were highly involved in the child's racial socialization (both cultural socialization and bias preparation) but fathers were not.

In general, these studies indicate that the gender of the parent as well as the gender of the child matters in relation to racial socialization. Although equivocal, the research suggests that African American mothers are more likely to racially socialize their children, particularly in terms of inculcating them with a sense of racial pride. The data also suggest that when fathers engage in the racial socialization of their children they tend to prepare them for racial bias. Furthermore, the data indicate that African American parents are more likely to culturally socialize their daughters and prepare their sons for potential encounters with racism. Lastly, the data suggest that African American youths may be more likely to experience low self-control and depression if their father is not as actively engaged in their racial socialization as is their mother.

Racial Socialization and Social Bonds

In our previous chapter, we discussed how perceived racial discrimination and stereotype threats cause African American adolescents to become disidentified with their schools (and possibly place of employment), which results in higher rates of offending, particularly if these youths associate with other disenfranchised peers. However, not all blacks who perceive racial injustices disidentify with their schools or place of employment and subsequently offend (Osborne, 1997).

Our theory argues that racial socialization experiences can mitigate the relationship between perceptions of racial injustices and weak social bonds. That is, African Americans who have positive racial socialization experiences will not offend even if they perceive racial injustices. We recognize that this assumption places a great deal of emphasis on the role that parenting has in African American offending. Therefore, we proceed with one caveat. That is, we also assume that in some cases the degree to which African Americans experience racial injustices might exceed the capacity of the mitigating effects of even the best racial socialization practices. Thus, our theory of offending allows for racial injustices to directly impact offending but only when they substantially exceed what most African Americans normally experience. Below, we review the literature that examines how positive racial socialization experiences allow African Americans to build strong bonds with conventional institutions even when they perceive that they are biased against blacks.

Murry et al. (2009) analyzed two waves of a longitudinal study of 671 rural African American families to examine the relationship between racial socialization and the development of a positive orientation to education. More specifically, they hypothesized that racial socialization would be indirectly linked to youths' academic outcomes over time through youth self-pride, defined as positive racial identity, and self-esteem. They found that adaptive racial socialization (i.e., preparation for bias and cultural socialization) promoted a positive racial identity, which in turn reduced the use of negative academic self-presentation strategies (i.e., minimizing their school achievements; for example, "I could probably do better in school, but I don't try because I don't want to be called a nerd"). Murry et al. (2009) further found that African American youths who did not minimize their academic achievements were more likely to be evaluated by their mothers and teachers as being academically competent (e.g., "This child is very good at his or her schoolwork" and "She/he does well in class"). They conclude that: "Teaching youths about both racial and ethnic issues facilitates high academic achievement by encouraging them to be strong and to work hard, which in turn fosters a sense of empowerment, confidence, and pride" (Murry et al., 2009:7).

Similarly, Smalls, White, Chavous, and, Sellers (2007) studied 390 self-identified African American middle and high school students (grades 7 to 10) residing in a large midwestern school district to assess the relationship between engagement in school, a positive racial identity, and racial discrimination. More specifically, these scholars analyzed whether African American adolescents' beliefs about the meaning of being black (racial ideological beliefs) and their experiences of racial discrimination predicted school engagement (i.e., linking one's personal identity to the roles of student and learner, showing sustained interest in class, and displaying intense efforts in learning tasks and academic performance).

Smalls et al. (2007:323) found that perceptions of racial discrimination were related to academic disengagement and that "regardless of their level of experiences with racial discrimination, adolescents endorsing an ideology that Blacks should emphasize their ethnic minority group status in the context of a shared experience and history of oppression with other ethnic minority groups (minority ideology) reported being less fearful of being viewed as academically oriented and more academically persistent in the face of challenges." Smalls et al. (2007:323) concluded that a positive racial identity "may provide African American adolescents with a worldview in which oppression is recognized and is possibly to be expected. Such a worldview may motivate some African American students to achieve even in the face of racial obstacles to their academic achievement."

The research by Byrd and Chavous (2009), using 564 African American adolescents who were included in a longitudinal study being conducted in Maryland, also shows that a positive racial identity is related to developing strong bonds. They found that African American youths who had a positive racial identity tended to value school more, spend more time on their homework, miss school less, and had a higher GPA, particularly in racially segregated areas. In fact, Byrd and Chavous (2009:557) argue that living in predominantly white neighborhoods may place the formation of a positive racial identity at risk as "African Americans may be less valued as a group in those neighborhoods; subsequently African American adolescents may have experiences that lead them to identify less strongly with or feel less proud of their group." These scholars argue that youths attending racially mixed schools may be also more vulnerable to internalizing pejorative stereotypes; that is, more vulnerable to the toxic effects of stereotype threats and secondary deviance. Byrd and Chavous (2009:557) conclude that: "Youth who remain highly identified or proud in such negative settings may feel stigmatized in ways that lead to school disengagement or avoidance." In short, their research confirms the assertions made by Steele and Aronson (1995) that African Americans are particularly susceptible to the deleterious consequences of stereotype threats when they are a limited minority.

Note that other studies confirm that positive racial socialization experiences or relatedly a positive racial identity are associated with African American youths developing strong school-related bonds (Altschul, Oyserman, and Bybee, 2006). For example, Dotterer, McHale, and Crouter (2009) found that preparation for bias was a significant and positive predictor of school self-esteem. Of interest, however, they did not find that racial socialization experiences could significantly buffer the deleterious effects of perceived racial discrimination. Chavous, Bernat, Schmeelk-Cone, Caldwell, Kohn-Wood, and Zimmerman (2003) found that having high race-centrality, strong group pride (private regard), and positive beliefs about society's views of blacks (public regard) were related to more positive academic beliefs and that African American youths who perceived positive societal views about African Americans showed a stronger attachment to their school. Of interest, researchers have found that the effect of these measures on school bonds may vary across gender, although this research is very limited. For example, a study found that racial pride (race centrality) may more effectively buffer the effect of racial discrimination on school bonds for boys than girls (Chavous, Rivas-Drake, Smalls, Griffin, and Cogburn, 2008).

Thus far, the research indicates that positive racial socialization practices and a positive racial identity can buffer the negative effects of perceived racial discrimination on bonds with schools. However, studies suggest that they may not be as effective in protecting African Americans from experiencing the deleterious consequences of stereotype threats. Ho and Sidanius (2010) studied 40 African Americans and whites attending Harvard University to assess the degree to which two components of racial identity could either enhance or diminish stereotype threats: public regard (i.e., judgments concerning how others view them: "I feel that Blacks have made major accomplishments and advancements") and private regard (i.e., how college students view other African Americans and feel about being themselves: "In general, others respect Black people"). These college students were given a test consisting of questions from the verbal section of the Graduate Record Examination (GRE). One group was exposed to a stereotype threat; that is, these students were told that the test assessed their cognitive and verbal reasoning abilities and were asked to identify their race-ethnicity. Students in the no-threat condition were asked to help with the development of a new test, were told it had no diagnostic ability, and were not asked to self-identify their race-ethnicity.

Ho and Sidanius (2010) found that African American students attending Harvard who were threatened with a stereotype did less well on the standardized test compared with those who were not threatened and less well than white participants. Most importantly, they report that the African American students who felt positive about the perception that others have of African Americans (public regard) were more susceptible to the stereotype threat effect and that the black students who felt positively about being an African American (private regard) were also more susceptible to the effect. Ho and Sidanius (2010) argue that African Americans who are high in public or private regard are particularly susceptible to the toxic effects of stereotype threats because they "have the most to lose by confirming negative stereotypes (and thus are more susceptible to stereotype threat), those who believe that Blacks have a positive identity have more to lose in potentially confirming a negative stereotype than those who already believe that Blacks are viewed negatively." In other words, African Americans are more aware of and susceptible to stereotype threats if they strongly identify with being black and perceive that others devalue them because they are black.

Racial Socialization and the Black Church

Our theory hypothesizes that African Americans who have a greater involvement with the *black church* should be less likely to offend (Johnson, Jang, Li, and Larson, 2000). Du Bois (1899b, 1903) was among the earliest scholars to document the important role that the black church has in the African American community. Indeed, Wortham (2009:167) asserts that Du Bois is "one of the founding figures in the sociology of the Black Church and in the sociological study of religion." In his ethnographic research of Philadelphia in the last decade of the 19th century, Du Bois (1899b:207) observed that all the efforts for social betterment in the city were centered in the black church and that it was the place where "the race problem in all its phases is continually being discussed." In fact, scholars unequivocally recognize that the black church has long been a place where strategies to deal with racial subordination have been crafted and everyday racial injustices challenged (Genovese, 1974; Lincoln and Mamiya, 1990; Lincoln, 1999; Taylor, Thornton, and Chatters, 1987). The clearest illustration of this is the prominent role that southern black churches had in the civil rights movement (Sherkat and Ellison, 2009; Swain, 2008). In short, the black church is a core institution within the African American community for inculcating resiliency and prosocial behaviors (Johnson et al., 2000).

Scholars argue that the black church has a unique worldview that is based on blacks' African heritage and their collective experience in America. This unique worldview makes the black church a place where African Americans "come together and to find strength in their unity as a group" (McRae, Carey, and Anderson-Scott, 1998:782). Barnes (2009:180) asserts that "the collective represents one of three primary repositories of Black culture and is central to the maintenance of Black heritage" and "that church involvement provides a buffer and coping strategies to combat problems such as racism, discrimination, and poverty. Furthermore, such involvement can increase self-regard and self-esteem, create an emotional cushion for participants, and foster overall positivity." Thus, scholars argue that the unity found in the black church fosters racial pride and provides a base of social support as African Americans negotiate their everyday encounters with racial injustices. In short, we hypothesize that the more African Americans are exposed to the positive racial socialization experiences within the black church the less likely they will offend.

Racial Socialization, Racial Discrimination, Hostility, Depression, and Offending

We highlight the research by Burt, Simons, and Gibbons (2010) because it addresses some of the core hypothesis of our theory of African American offending that we have thus far outlined. They analyzed whether racial socialization experiences mediate the influence of perceived racial discrimination on delinquency. They analyzed two waves of the longitudinal Family and Community Health Study (FACHS), a survey of African Americans from Iowa and Georgia that included 867 families. Their self-report measures of crime included offenses such as shoplifting, physical assault, setting fires, cruelty to animals, vandalism, burglary, and robbery. Their measure of racial discrimination assessed the frequency during the past year that the respondents experienced specific discriminatory behaviors because of their race that included racially based slurs and insults, physical threats, false accusations from law enforcement officials, and disrespectful treatment from others. They measured racial socialization experiences by asking questions related to their cultural socialization experiences (e.g., how often during the past 12 months did their parents take them places that reflected their racial heritage and encouraged them to read books about their racial heritage) and whether their parents prepared them for encountering racial bias (e.g., people might limit you because of your race and people might treat you badly or unfairly because of your race).

They also assessed whether hostile attitudes (e.g., some people oppose you for no good reason), depression (e.g., feelings of sadness, irritability, worthlessness), and rejection of conventional norms—legal cynicism— (e.g., how wrong the children considered various deviant behaviors, such as physical assault, selling marijuana, or shoplifting) intervened between racial discrimination and delinquency. Their analysis controlled for authoritative parenting (e.g., the extent to which caregivers displayed warmth and support, avoided harsh and hostile parenting, and engaged in problem-solving, inductive reasoning, and positive reinforcement), the youth's age, and previous delinquent involvement. Unfortunately, their analysis was limited to males.

These scholars found that: (1) racial discrimination substantially increases the likelihood of individual black offending; (2) that perceived racial discrimination increases feelings of hostility, depression, and legal cynicism; (3) offending is related to heightened states of hostility, depression, and legal cynicism. Notably, Burt et al. (2010) also found that cultural socialization and preparation for bias were not strong direct predictors of offending. The effect that cultural socialization had on offending was indirect; it reduced the level of legal cynicism among the African American youth. Of particular interest, they found that preparation of bias can both increase and decrease the likelihood that African Americans will offend. Preparing African American youths for their encounters with racial bias decreases their likelihood of offending because it lessens the likelihood that African Americans will reject the legitimacy of conventional norms and it substantially decreased the relationship between offending and hostility and depression. Then again, they found that preparation for bias can amplify the potential of offending because it increases the likelihood of African American youths to develop a hostile-mistrustful orientation in their interactions with others, which in turn increases their probability of offending. Thus, preparation for bias can minimize the noxious consequences of racial discrimination but can also cause African Americans to be more wary in their interactions with others.

Of note, they also explored whether quality supportive parenting moderates the effects of preparation for bias on hostile views of relationships. They hypothesize that African American children may become particularly distrustful if their parents' attempts to prepare them for racial injustices are accompanied with harsh parenting techniques. Conversely, they suggest that children may be especially likely to learn healthy coping skills if their parents are more generally supportive and caring. In other words, parents will be particularly ineffective if they are yelling at their children while telling them that they will be discriminated against because of their race. Burt et al. (2010) found that African American children are most likely to learn healthy skills to cope with racial injustices if their parents are supportive and caring.

Coping with Racism

It is clear that African Americans racially socialize their children to prepare them to successfully resist their racial subordination. This includes African American parents teaching their children how to successfully cope with both acute and chronic encounters with racial injustices. Utsey, Ponterotto, Reynolds, and Cancelli (2000:73) define coping as "the process whereby an individual attempts to manage, through cognitive and behavioral efforts, external or internal demands that are assessed as exceeding one's resources." The research on how African Americans cope with racism is limited but is attracting greater attention, especially as scholars continue to document the deleterious health consequences of racial subordination. We also note that the research on how African Americans cope with general stress (e.g., relationship problems) may not generalize to how they respond to racial discrimination. Research indicates that African Americans are less likely to engage in problem-solving and seek social support in racially stressful situations than in more general stressful situations (Plummer and Slane, 1996). In part, this reluctance stems from the power differentials that are intrinsic to experiences with racial injustices.

We encourage scholars to study the many nuanced ways that African Americans provide specific guidance as to how their children can best resist their racial subordination. This research should detail the connections between specific coping strategies and racial socialization experiences.

Along these lines, we could only find two articles that examined the complex relationship between racial socialization and specific coping strategies. These studies showed that African American adolescents who reported receiving frequent messages concerning racism from their parents or guardians were more likely to use a problem-solving coping strategy—attempts to change the dynamics of the encounter—and to seek social supports (Scott, 2003, 2004). Thus, these findings indicate that African American parents can decrease their children's likelihood of offending if the content of their racial socialization includes providing their children with effective coping skills to fend off the toxic effects of racial discrimination. Indeed, Scott (2004:134) concludes that "racial socialization serves a protective function for African American adolescents. African American adolescents who are not prepared for the multiple racial assaults they may encounter in everyday interactions may be more at risk for internalizing racial oppression and utilizing ineffective coping strategies." Below we review the limited research on the different coping strategies African Americans use to resist their racial subordination.

Brondolo et al.'s (2009) excellent review of the coping literature outlines the substantial demands placed on African Americans as they try to effectively resist their racial subordination. They contend that the choice and effectiveness of the coping strategy must be related to the intensity and nature of the racial injustice, the perceived degree of intentionality of the perpetrator, the potential consequences of the racist act, and the availability of resources to assist in their resistance. In addition, different types of coping may be needed at the time of exposure, following the episode, and in coping with the long-term consequences. That is, African Americans need to have coping mechanisms that allow them to immediately resist acts of racial injustice and long-term strategies that allow them to effectively ameliorate their emotional sequelae (Scott, 2004). Brondolo et al. (2009:66) conclude that:

> Consequently, one of the most serious challenges facing minority group members is the need to develop a broad range of racism-related

coping responses to permit them to respond to different types of situations and to adjust the response depending on factors that might influence the effectiveness of any particular coping strategy. Targets must also develop the cognitive flexibility to implement an appropriate and effective strategy in each of the wide range of situations in which they may be exposed to discrimination, judge the relative costs and benefits of these strategies, and deploy them as needed over prolonged periods of time. This level of coping flexibility is beneficial, but difficult to achieve.

Brondolo et al. (2009) also reviewed the various means by which African Americans cope with their exposures to racial injustices. They note that a positive racial identity may have some buffering effects but the research is equivocal (see also Scott, 2003). Brondolo et al. (2009) also assert that an often used coping mechanism is seeking out social supports or "leaning on the shoulders of others." Research generally concludes that social supports buffer stressors because it "can help people solve problems, provide them with a way to express or vent their emotions, help them redefine the stressful event, or distract them from the event" (Miller and Kaiser, 2001:87).

Scott and House (2005) analyzed 71 blacks youths of relative affluence and report that greater self-reports of perceived control over discriminatory experiences are related to seeking social support. However, Brondolo et al. (2009) conclude that the research is equivocal as to the degree to which seeking out social supports minimizes the deleterious effects of experiencing racial discrimination. In general, they conclude that the inconsistency of the results may largely be a result of the methodological difficulties in assessing the degree to which African Americans seek social support (and the quality of the support) and the degree to which they experienced racial discrimination.

Central to our theory is how African Americans cope with the anger that arises from their encounters with racial injustices. Our theory recognizes that the anger that surfaces from perceiving racial injustices provides African Americans with the agency—energy—to resist their racial subordination. This resistance can manifest itself both in individual and collective actions (e.g., joining protest marches). In general, scholars argue that "confrontation coping"—using the anger to do something about being discriminated against—or problem-solving coping minimizes the injurious consequences of personally experiencing racial injustices. Scott (2004) argues that coping with perceived discriminatory experiences by directly confronting the situation or perpetrator alleviates feelings of powerlessness and victimization. Scholars also assert that problem-solving coping is related to emotional regulation (Miller and Kaiser, 2001; Scott and House, 2005). The more control that African Americans feel they have over discriminatory experiences, the more likely they are to use problem-solving coping strategies (Scott, 2004). Concomitantly, African Americans feel that when they gain greater control over the experience of being discriminated against they are in more control of their own emotions.

On the other hand, while limited, the research indicates that avoidance coping—repressing and ruminating about the anger—can have deleterious consequences including depression, externalizing behavioral problems, and negative psychobiological effects. Miller and Kaiser (2001:85) stipulate that African Americans "who cannot free themselves from thoughts about prejudice-inspired mistreatment or who worry about confirming stereotypes may be less resilient with respect to their stigmatized status than are those who do not have these involuntary engagement responses." Scott (2004:134) argues that internalizing or avoidance coping strategies increase distress and that: "A possible negative consequence of daily encounters with prejudice and discrimination include the internalization of or identification with negative attitudes and hostilities directed at one's ethnic/racial group [Akbar, 1991; Baldwin, Brown, and Hopkins, 1999]. Hence, the use of internalizing strategies cannot be considered adaptive or conducive for the psychological well-being of African American adolescents under any circumstance."

Avoidance coping can also result in African Americans physically and socially avoiding situations in which they are likely to experience racial injustices (Plummer and Slane, 1996). In addition, African Americans may resolve their feelings of being discriminated against—that is, feeling sorry for themselves—by devaluing the gains that they could have accrued if they remained strongly bonded to the situations-institutions in which they perceived racial discrimination. Together, these findings indicate that an avoidance coping strategy compounds the likelihood that African Americans will disidentify with white-dominated institutions, which in turn decreases their likelihood of having positive racial socialization experiences with whites. It also suggests that avoidance coping is likely to increase offending as it exacerbates the negative feelings that arise from experiencing racial injustices such as anger (Noble, 2006).

It must be noted that the coping mechanisms that African Americans employ and, perhaps, their efficaciousness are situationally determined (Brondolo et al., 2005; Clark, 2004; Feagin, 1991; Scott, 2004; Utsey et al., 2000). That is, for example, in the workplace the best strategy may be for African Americans to not confront a racist perpetrator if it will result in the loss of their job. It is also possible that under acute exposure to an injustice—for example, a criminal justice injustice—a problem-solving confrontational strategy may be misperceived by racist whites as aggressive "insolent" behavior, thus adding more fuel to a potentially combustible situation. Acute racial injustices may also overtax the problem-coping abilities of African Americans, increasing their likelihood of impulsively responding to their racial subordination (Clark, 2003). Likewise, it also might be efficacious for some African Americans to avoid places of chronic exposure to racial injustices as they can be devastatingly debilitating over the long term. In addition, scholars stipulate that resources that African Americans bring into their encounters with racial injustices can impact the coping mechanisms they employ. Scott (2004) reports that African American adolescents from homes with greater resources in terms of their guardian's professional status and education were less likely to use externalizing coping strategies.

Our Theory on Racial Socialization and Offending

African Americans are immersed in a worldview that includes the perceptions of criminal justice injustices, racial discrimination, and the awareness that they are being pejoratively stereotyped. Our theory of offending argues that these crime-causing forces undermine the willingness of African Americans to develop strong bonds with institutions that they

believe are biased against blacks and it causes them to either react defiantly or to retreat into a state of hopelessness as they experience racial
injustices. We further argue that offending is related to these heightened
emotional states. Yet, the data show, remarkably, that only a minority of
African Americans offend. We assert that a reason why the majority of
African Americans do not offend, despite the racist hardships they
confront, is the ability of African American parents to instill within their
children coping skills that allow them to effectively interact with individuals and institutions that they perceive are biased against blacks.

On the other hand, our theory posits that there are racial socialization experiences that can exacerbate the likelihood that African
Americans will offend. The data show that not all parents assertively
instill within their children the social coping skills required to feel positive about institutions and individuals that they perceive to be biased
against blacks. Surveys indicate that between 20 and 50 percent of
African American parents do not engage in any racial socialization of
their children (Hughes et al., 2006). Studies also show that the African
American parents who are the least likely to racially socialize their children are poorer and have less education.

We assert that African American parents place their children at risk
for offending if they do not positively racially socialize their children.
These children are left on their own to construct their racial identity
and to come to terms with how they feel toward individuals and institutions that they perceive to be biased against blacks. We hypothesize
that these children are likely to construct their racial identity and their
feelings about racial injustices by interacting with their peers and other
individuals in their neighborhood. That is, we stipulate that African
American children who are not positively racially socialized by their
parents are more exposed to constructing a racial identity by interacting
with the "street."

Oliver (2006) defines this racial socialization process as "street
socialization":

> The phrase "the streets" is used here to refer to the network of
> public and semipublic social settings (e.g., street corners, vacant

lots, bars, clubs, after-hours joints, convenience stores, drug houses, pool rooms, parks and public recreational places, etc.) in which primarily lower and working-class Black males tend to congregate. Hence, a major assumption guiding this discussion is that for many marginalized Black males, "the streets" is a socialization institution that is as important as the family, the church, and the educational system in terms of its influence on their psychosocial development and life course trajectories and transitions (Oliver, 2006:919).

Thus, we posit that, in the absence of parents proactively racially socializing their children, African American youths are more likely to interact with other disidentified youths and adults who reside in their neighborhoods. We additionally assert that it is likely, especially in isolated disadvantaged racially segregated neighborhoods, that the individuals that they will most likely interact with will be disidentified blacks. We further hypothesize that it is likely that these disidentified individuals will have developed deep resentments toward individual whites and perceived racist institutions such as the criminal justice system. Indeed, Payne (2008) found that the longer black men lived on the streets, the more negative their attitudes became toward white-dominated institutions. Consequently, we posit that African American youths who are not proactively and positively racially socialized by their parents will inculcate the attitudes and values that they are exposed to on the "streets."

This means that these disidentified youths will be more likely to construct a racial identity that includes resentments toward racial injustices (Noble, 2006). We argue that these resentments can, over time, manifest themselves in oscillating feelings of anger-defiance-hopelessness-depression. We also hypothesize that youths who are racially socialized on the "street" are more likely to develop weak social bonds with conventional institutions, such as their schools or places of employment. Oliver (2006) argues that these feelings of rage coupled with weak ties to white-dominated institutions often manifest themselves in African American offending. Thus, we posit that African Americans are more likely to offend if their "street" racial identity includes deep resentments toward racial injustices and race-based rationalizations to weaken their attachments to white-dominated institutions.[7]

Our theory of offending also recognizes that there are variations in how African Americans racially socialize their children. That is, it is possible for African American parents to proactively racially socialize their children but inadvertently instill within them attitudes that actually increase their likelihood of offending. Accordingly, we assert that there are specific racial socialization experiences that can increase the likelihood of African American offending.

The research indicates that African American offending increases when parents overly emphasize a mistrust of whites and white-dominated institutions. Scholars further note that the more African Americans believe that other groups (e.g., whites) devalue them—that is, have a low public regard—the more likely they are to perceive racial injustices (Outten et al., 2010; Sellers, Caldwell, Schmeelk-Cone, and Zimmerman, 2003). The research additionally shows that racial attitudes can negatively relate to the quality of their contact experiences with whites regardless of whether this contact is voluntary (close friends), involuntary (first-year roommates), or with strangers. That is, the more African Americans perceive that whites are prejudiced, the less they want to have contact with them, the more they try to avoid them, and it diminishes the quality of their interactions (Shelton and Richeson, 2006). Thus, we hypothesize that African Americans who perceive racial injustices are more likely to offend if their parents taught them, either purposefully or implicitly—that is, verbally or nonverbally—to distrust whites, white-dominated institutions, and that whites hold them in contempt (Brown et al., 2010).

We further argue that researchers need to more expansively understand how the inculcation of the mistrust of whites leads to African American offending. We suggest that scholars assess the *degree* to which African Americans are socialized to mistrust whites and white-dominated institutions. We posit that African American offending increases as the degree to which they mistrust whites and white-dominated institutions deepens. We also posit that institutions can exacerbate this tendency. For example, research on educational achievement clearly reveals that the more blacks distrust their teachers, the weaker the bonds they have with their schools (Noguera, 2003). Thus, researchers should assess the age at which African American youths were first socialized to distrust whites and white-dominated institutions, the frequency and chronicity of the exposure, and how extensive was their exposure (e.g., was this distrust reinforced by parents, relatives, teachers, and peers). We hypothesize that African American offending should most likely occur among those who were socialized at an early age to distrust whites and who had this belief frequently reinforced over a long period of time by significant socialization agents (parents, relatives, and peers).

We posit that African Americans raised by parents that overly emphasize the mistrust of whites and encourage their children to become defiant in the presence of racism are likely to develop a stigma sensitivity and stigma consciousness.[8] Scholars define stigma sensitivity as race-based rejection sensitivity or an African American's "tendency to anxiously expect, readily perceive, and strongly react to rejection due to race" (Inzlicht et al., 2006:263), and stigma consciousness as a chronic self-conscious awareness of having a stigmatized status (Brown and Pinel, 2003).[9]

African Americans with these sensitivities are more likely to personally perceive discrimination directed at them, interpret ambiguous situations as identity threatening, can provide more concrete examples of instances of racial discrimination, are less likely to want to prove the stereotype wrong, and are more vulnerable to the toxic effects of stereotype threats (Brown and Pinel, 2003; Inzlicht et al., 2006; Pinel, 1999). Link and Phelan (2001) add that people who have been stigmatized— that is, African Americans—may act less confidently and more defensively, may avoid potentially threatening social interactions, will have strained and uncomfortable interactions with whites, more constricted social networks, a compromised quality of life, depressive symptoms, and unemployment and income loss.

Most notably, scholars have found that these heightened states of sensitivity may cause African Americans to have less self-control, a factor that is unequivocally related to offending (Gottfredson and Hirschi, 1990; Pratt and Cullen, 2000; Unnever, 2005; Unnever and

Cornell, 2003; Unnever, Cullen, and Pratt, 2003; Unnever, Cullen, and Agnew, 2006).

In a series of experiments involving African American college students, Inzlicht et al. (2006) found that blacks high in stigma sensitivity (as measured by the Race-Based Rejection Sensitivity Scale) scored lower on a scale measuring their self-control (as measured by the Self-Regulated Learning Scale). These scholars conclude that African Americans chronically exposed to negative stereotypes use and deplete their self-control as they attempt to manage their spoiled collective social identity, "thus leaving them less able than their nonstigmatized counterparts to engage in self-control for other things" (Inzlicht et al., 2006:263). Consequently, African Americans are confronted by noxious situations—experiences of racial injustices—that can consume their cognitive resources, create anxiety, engender automatic vigilance to racial discrimination, undermine trust in whites and white-dominated institutions, and lessen their ability to self-regulate their response to perceptions of racial discrimination, pejorative stereotypes, and criminal justice injustices (Major and O'Brien, 2005). In short, exposure to racial injustices can impair the ability of African Americans to control and regulate their behavior.

We also argue that scholars need to more closely examine the possible link between preparation for bias and African American offending. The research has generated equivocal findings, with some research suggesting that preparation for bias ameliorates the toxic consequences of racial injustices while other studies indicate that it may increase African American offending. We suggest that these equivocal findings principally result from the way that researchers have measured preparation for bias. Most often, scholars use a list of events-questions assessing whether African American parents engaged in the preparation for bias, such as, "have you talked to your children about racism?" While informative, we argue that these measures of preparation for bias do not assess its most important dimensions; that is, the content and effectiveness of how parents prepare their children for their encounters with racial injustice.

Scholars argue that the key to positive racial socialization is the transmission of effective skills to fend off the noxious consequences of racial injustices, such as teaching children to report racist acts to appropriate authorities and affirmatively, but not angrily, standing up to the perpetrators. In addition, scholars have found that African Americans can more effectively cope with racial injustices if they can control important resources (e.g., access to lawyers), limit their exposure to "toxic" others, have a strong racial identity, or a dispositional optimism (Major and O'Brien, 2005). In the absence of these personal skills and extraneous resources, there is the tendency for African Americans to disidentify or emotionally withdraw. Scholars argue that withdrawal may serve immediate purposes, such as: "Black boys are socialized to suppress their anger at being treated unfairly by police officers as a means of living through such encounters. Withdrawal in such cases might better be called defusing potentially explosive situations and having the skills to do so might be called strengths" (Nicolas et al., 2008:273). However, we argue that, in the long term, withdrawal can generate negative emotions related to offending. African Americans "who use passive withdrawal as a coping strategy, may exhibit increased anger, aggression, and irritability" and "decreased energy often associated with depression" (Nicolas et al., 2008:273).[10]

Consequently, we argue that the key component in assessing whether African American parents have effectively prepared their children for encounters with racism is determining the specific coping skills that are proffered. We suggest that most of the research on racial socialization has not empirically assessed which coping skills most African Americans teach their children. Thus, our theory argues that African American parents will inadvertently increase their children's probability of offending if they: (1) fail to racially socialize their children; (2) teach their children ineffective coping skills; (3) only partially transmit effective coping skills; or (4) prepare them to respond to racial injustices with emotions, such as anger and hostility, or behaviors—aggression— that are related to offending.

Note that our theory of African American offending recognizes that racial socialization experiences will vary across the lifespan, vary across situations, be susceptible to period effects (e.g., the election of Barack Obama), may vary across generations, and can be individually altered by changes in patterns of interactions (e.g., having positive or negative interactions with whites) (Brown and Lesane-Brown, 2006; Lesane-Brown, 2006; Major and O'Brien, 2005).

Racial Socialization and Weak Bonds

In the previous chapter, we outlined how racial discrimination and the awareness of pejorative stereotypes weaken the bonds African Americans develop with their schools and places of work, which in turn increases their probability of offending. Our theory of offending posits racial socialization experiences can further weaken the bonds that individual African Americans attain. More specifically, we hypothesize that African Americans will be more likely to develop weak bonds with their schools or place of employment if their parents: (1) did not culturally socialize them, that is, instill within them a positive racial identity; (2) ill-prepared them for racially biased encounters; (3) encouraged them to mistrust whites; and (4) underemphasized the teaching of egalitarian values.

Our theory recognizes that other forms of parenting can modify the relationships among racial socialization, weak social bonds, negative emotions, and offending. Research shows, for example, that poor parenting (e.g., authoritative parenting) increases the detrimental effects of inadequate racial socialization experiences (Simons, Simons, Burt, Stewart, Brody, Gibbons, and Cutrona, 2006).

In sum, our theory places parenting as a core factor in African American offending. We argue that African American parents can substantially reduce their children's likelihood of offending if they competently prepare them for their encounters with racial injustices. On the other hand, we stipulate that African American parents can inadvertently increase their children's probability of offending if they do not adequately prepare them for their encounters with criminal justice injustices, racial discrimination, and the deleterious consequences of being pejoratively stereotyped. Consequently, we assert that the highest incidences of offending should occur among those African Americans who are poorly parented, have been ill-prepared by their parents to develop strong bonds with white-dominated institutions, and inadequately prepared to fend off the noxious effects of racial injustices. In short, we specifically hypothesize that youths who are inadequately racially socialized will be more likely to offend because they are: (1) more likely to perceive racial injustices; (2) more likely to respond to perceptions of racial injustice with anger-defiance or depression-hopelessness, and, therefore, engage in impulsive behaviors; and (3) less likely to forge strong bonds with white-dominated institutions, especially if they are perceived to be biased against blacks.

Hip hop artist Schoolly D ('Don't call me nigger', from the album *Am I black enough for you*) expresses his frustration, anger-defiance, and hopelessness toward racial injustices:

> Don't call me nigger . . . WHITEY! (2X)
> Don't call me nigger (nigger) WHITEY! (2X)
>
> The whitey my man, you say you're my fan
> I look into your face and I gots to say damn
> I feel a lot of pain, the money you gain
> because I'm black you think it's come out of 'caine
> I'll put you on a level, same as the devil
> Stole my bass then you steal all my treble
> Line to the eye, a bullet to the head
> For all those lies, motherfucker you said
> No you can't face this, so you disgrace it
> I'm Schoolly School boy, and I will lace it
>
> Don't call me nigger . . . WHITEY! (2X)
> Don't call me nigger (nigger) WHITEY! (2X)

Gender and African American Offending

The data show that black women are less likely to offend than black men but have higher rates of crime than white women. Interestingly, it could be argued that African American women should have higher rates of offending than black men because they encounter what scholars refer to as "gendered racism." Essed (1991:31), in her seminal work on black women in the United States and the Netherlands, describes "how sexism and racism narrowly intertwine and combine under certain conditions into one, hybrid phenomenon." Thomas, Witherspoon, and Speight (2008:307) add that "the oppression African American women experience is structured by racist perceptions of gender roles. Gendered racism suggests that African American women are subject to unique forms of oppression due to their simultaneous 'Blackness' and 'female-ness.' For some African American women, the experiences of being both a woman and an African American cannot be easily separated, and they may perceive discrimination due to being an African American woman in combination."

The data show that the lifetime prevalence of gendered racism is high, with at least 90 percent of African American women reporting that as a *black woman* they have experienced racial discrimination with service professionals (e.g., waiters and sale clerks) and from strangers. The data also show that gendered racism has a pervasive effect on the psychological distress of African American women (Thomas et al., 2008). Thus, the effects of gendered racism can add to the explanation of why African American women are more likely to offend than white women. But, it obviously does not explain why African American women are substantially less likely to offend than black men.

Our theory recognizes that the everyday encounters that African American women have with their racial subordination overlap but also are uniquely different than those experienced by black men. In our last chapter, we detailed how African American men report higher levels of racial discrimination than black women, especially in terms of their encounters with criminal justice injustices. We also highlighted that there are gendered stereotypes and that these negative images are more likely to cause African American men to offend. This is particularly the case as gendered stereotypes of African American men mostly depict them as the *criminalblackman*, whereas the pejorative stereotypes of black women portray them "as Mammy-figures, promiscuous, and emasculating" (Thomas et al., 2008:307). Thus, we hypothesize that African American men disproportionately offend because their encoun-ters with racial discrimination are more pervasive and that they are more likely to encounter gendered racial stereotypes that are linked directly and indirectly to their offending.

Our theory also identifies that African American women encounter different racial socialization experiences than black men. Research shows that the relationship between perceived racial discrimination and conduct problems including delinquency is stronger for African American boys than for girls (Brody et al., 2006). These authors argue that this relation occurs because African American boys are more likely than girls to respond to racial discrimination by losing inhibitory controls and expressing anger and frustration through their behavior. We assert that gendered differences in racial socialization can add to the explanation of why African American men who are exposed to racial injustices are more likely to offend than black females.

Our theory asserts that there are three gendered variations in racial socialization experiences that add to explanations of gender differences in African American offending. First, research indicates that African American parents are more likely to socialize their daughters with a greater sense of racial pride than their sons.[11] The research shows that a strong positive racial identity decreases the likelihood of offending and enhances academic commitment and performance. Second, studies indicate that African American parents are more likely to emphasize egalitarian values with their daughters, especially encouraging them to build stronger bonds with their schools through hard work. The data show that offending is more likely among those who have weak bonds with institutions. Third, studies indicate that African American parents are significantly more likely to prepare their sons than their daughters for encounters with racial discrimination. However, we hypothesize that African American parents are more likely to overemphasize to their sons the likelihood that they will encounter racial injustices, to respond to those injustices with hostility-anger, and to mistrust whites. Scholars argue that this overemphasis stems from the recognition among African American parents that their sons are "endangered." That is, African American parents are fully aware that black men are disproportionately incarcerated and that the dominant society has constructed gendered stereotypes depicting young African American men as angry crime-prone "superpredators" (DiIulio, 1994). In sum, we hypothesize that African American parents, particularly those residing in "apartheid neighborhoods," prepare their daughters to better cope with racial injustices than their sons (Population Studies Center, 2010).

We also hypothesize that African American women are less likely to offend because of their higher rates of church involvement and, thus, their greater exposure to the positive racial socialization experiences that the *black church* promotes (Levin and Taylor, 1993; Reese and Brown, 1995; Taylor, Chatters, and Jackson, 2007). In general, scholars find that black church attendance reduces crime among African American youth, both males and females, even if they live in disadvantaged neighborhoods (Johnson et al., 2000; Johnson, Larson, De Li, and Jang, 2000). The data also show that African American females are more likely to attend church than black males (Nunnally, 2010; Taylor, 1988). Research also indicates that African American females are significantly more likely than black males to use religious coping responses to perceived racial discrimination (Clark, 2004).

In addition, scholars have found that black women significantly exceed African American men in levels of religiosity at all ages, even when controlling for the effects of education, marital and employment status, region, residing in an urban area, and health satisfaction (Levin and Taylor, 1993). We argue that their higher rates in church attendance should predict lower levels of offending because religiosity/ spirituality has been found to be an effective mechanism for dealing with racism (Shorter-Gooden, 2004), stigmatization (Brega and Coleman, 1999), and recovery from drug abuse (Chu and Sung, 2009). More specifically, we hypothesize that African American women should have lower rates of offending than black men because their greater church involvement inculcates them with a greater sense of pride in their racial identity and provides them with a base of social support that they can lean on as they cope with everyday racism.

Although the research is limited and equivocal, we further hypothesize that the different racial socialization experiences encountered by African American women cause them to have a more powerful and flexible inventory of coping mechanisms that they routinely employ across situations as they resist their everyday encounters with racial injustices. More specifically, we stipulate that African American women are more likely than black men to resist their racial subordination by using problem-solving coping strategies rather than avoidance coping, are more likely to seek out social supports, and to use religious coping (Clark, 2004; Scott, 2004; Swim, Hyers, Cohen, Fitzgerald, and Bylsma, 2003; Utsey et al., 2000).

Ward's (1996:91) interviews with African American girls reveal how racial socialization and sharing the negative feelings associated with racial injustice ameliorates the likelihood of having their anger result in offending. April, an African American girl, states: "I don't want to say I accept it, but I don't have the hostility that might be there if I hadn't been taught about it before. I can't say I get rid of the hostility and the frustration all completely, but that always helps—to be able to talk about it." We hypothesize that this greater facility with a problem-solving coping strategy and seeking out social supports lessens the likelihood that African American women will internalize or externalize their anger, which in turn should increase their ability to bond with white-dominated institutions.

In addition, we contend that African American men are particularly constrained in their resistance to racial injustices by the *criminal-blackman* pejorative stereotype. African American men are fully aware of how this toxic stereotype constrains their behavior:

> Keith Borders tries hard not to scare people. He's 6-foot-7, a garrulous lawyer who talks with his hands. And he's black. Many people find him threatening. He works hard to prove otherwise. "I have a very keen sense of my size and how I communicate," says Borders of Mason, Ohio. "I end up putting my hands in my pockets or behind me. I stand with my feet closer together. With my feet spread out, it looks like I'm taking a stance. And I use a softer voice."
>
> Every day, African-American men consciously work to offset stereotypes about them—that they are dangerous, aggressive, angry. Some smile a lot, dress conservatively and speak with

deference: "Yes, sir," or "No, ma'am." They are mindful of their bodies, careful not to dart into closing elevators or stand too close in grocery stores (Associated Press, 2006).

We assert that the awareness of this pejorative stereotype restrains the ability of African American men to use the healthier confrontational problem-solving coping strategy when faced with racial injustices, particularly criminal justice injustices. That is, as mentioned earlier, African Americans are keenly aware that out-group members perceive them as threatening—prone to violence. We contend that this pejorative stereotype, which is always "in the air," overly taxes black men as they experience acute and chronic forms of racial injustices.

African American men know that they should confront the perpetrators of their racial subordination. But, yet, they recognize that there are real costs for doing so. Any display of assertiveness could be readily interpreted as aggression, "insolence," or violence. Black men further recognize that this racist interpretation of their healthy response to the interaction could intensely escalate the costs involved. For example, their use of a confrontation problem-solving coping strategy could result in their arrest if it is a perceived criminal justice injustice that caused the interaction. As a result, we hypothesize that African American men are more likely than black women to "swallow their anger-humiliation" when they are confronted with their racial subordination. We further argue that this inability among some African American men to successfully defend themselves from the toxic consequences of their everyday encounters with racial injustices is a source for the maintenance and perpetuation of the "reservoir of bad will" or a "sea of hostility" that we argue is related to their disproportionate offending (Noble, 2006; Tyler, 1990). In sum, we hypothesize that the greater and more flexible inventory of coping mechanisms that African American women have allows them to more efficaciously resist their racial subordination, thus allowing them to more positively process the negative emotions that are caused by experiencing racial injustices than black men.

Drugs, Gender, and Crime

Our theory asserts that the gender disparities in racial discrimination, being pejoratively stereotyped, racial socialization, and in coping mechanisms leaves African American men with a larger reservoir of internalized anger than black women. We hypothesize that African Americans who internalize their anger are more likely to self-medicate their feelings (including depression) through substance abuse. However, we more specifically stipulate that African American men are more likely to internalize their anger than black women, and, therefore are more likely than black women to abuse alcohol and drugs (Clark, 2004).

In general, the research indicates that perceived racial discrimination is related to substance abuse (Martin, Tuch, and Roman, 2003; Minior, Galea, Stuber, Ahern, and Ompad, 2003; Simons et al., 2006). Borrell, Jacobs, Williams, Pletcher, Houston, and Kiefe (2007) analyzed the Coronary Artery Risk Development in Young Adults dataset and found that African Americans who perceived racial discrimination were more likely to consume alcohol in the past year and to use marijuana and cocaine over their lifetime. Terrell, Miller, Foster, and Watkins (2006) analyzed survey data collected from 134 black adolescents (ages 14 to 18) and report that racial discrimination-induced anger was a significant predictor of drinking.

Gibbons, Etcheverry, Stock, Gerrard, Weng, Kiviniemi, and O'Hara (2010) analyzed a longitudinal dataset, the Family and Community Health Study (FACHS), and found that African American parents and their children were more likely to report higher levels of hostility and anger if they perceived racial discrimination. In addition, they revealed that adolescents who reported more anger and African American parents who became more hostile because they were discriminated against were substantially more likely to engage in substance abuse while controlling for their risk-taking tendencies, their neighborhood risk, and their parents' use. It is also of significance that Gibbons et al. (2004) found that perceived racial discrimination was associated with a greater (and increased) tendency to affiliate with other substance abusers. Also of note, scholars report that the relationship between substance abuse and racial discrimination may be buffered by supportive parenting. That is, black adolescents who had more supportive parents were less likely to report feeling angry and to report drug and drinking willingness if they had experienced discrimination (Gibbons et al., 2004, 2010). These studies indicate that substance abuse is an unhealthy mechanism used by African Americans to cope with racial discrimination.

Related to gender, the research indicates that African American males are more likely to use alcohol and drugs. Terrell et al. (2006) report that African American males were significantly more likely to report drinking behavior. Martin, Tuch, and Roman (2003) studied whether African Americans are more likely to adopt a set of beliefs that support alcohol consumption and to drink if they perceive racial discrimination. Their analysis of the National Survey of Black Workers (N=2,638) found that black men were significantly more likely to report problematic drinking patterns than African American women and that blacks who perceived racial discrimination were significantly more likely to both endorse attitudes that support drinking and to be a problem drinker. Martin et al. (2003) found that perceived racial discrimination predicted problem drinking while controlling for other covariates, including the respondent's socioeconomic status.

Thus, the research indicates that the internalization of the negative feelings associated with encountering racial injustices can have debilitating consequences. It causes African Americans, especially black men, to engage in "escapist' behaviors as they self-medicate, through the use of illegal drugs and alcohol, the negative feelings that result from their racial subordination. We argue that this avoidance coping strategy becomes a particularly acute problem for African American men (and, to a lesser extent, black women) when it involves the use of illegal drugs and it becomes a chronic problem if it results in an addiction (e.g., heroin). Our theory contends that African American men who self-medicate by using illegal drugs are more likely to offend because it potentially immerses them in risk-taking behavior as they are overexposed to the drug street culture as need to procure illegal drugs to maintain their addiction (Gibbons et al., 2010). In addition, these African American men are confronted by the debilitating consequences of being stereotyped as being a black male and a drug addict (Minior et al., 2003). Thus, we stipulate that African American men are more likely to offend than black women because they self-medicate (e.g., by using illegal substances) the anger and depression that results from their disproportionate exposure to the humiliating experiences associated with their racial subordination. In short, our theory asserts that gender differences in African American offending are related to male–female differences in experiences with criminal justice injustices, racial discrimination, being pejoratively stereotyped, and their ability to cope with these racial injustices.

Racial Socialization, Place, and Offending

In our previous chapter, we hypothesized that place matters because it can increase the likelihood that African Americans will experience racial injustices. Below we discuss how place can increase the likelihood of African American offending because it alters the ability of black parents to effectively racially socialize their children.

We recognize that there is tremendous variation within neighborhoods (Martin, 2010). Put more simply, even in the most crime-ridden neighborhoods, most African Americans do not offend. This fact triumphs the resiliency of most African Americans to overcome the deleterious effects of chronic exposure to criminal justice injustices, being pejoratively stereotyped, and racial discrimination. Thus, even in pockets of legal cynicism—areas of concentrated disadvantages—some African American parents are able to competently protect their children from the negative effects of personal or vicarious experiences with repeated racial injustices. Indeed, some African American parents are able to transform these injustices into challenges that they encourage their children to overcome. Research shows that the deleterious consequences of stereotype threats are eradicated when they are reframed as challenges (Alter, Aronson, Darley, Rodriguez, and Ruble, 2010). Other scholars argue that the ability of parents to effectively racially socialize their children empowers them to have a critical race-consciousness.[13] This, in turn, allows black youths to "analyze situations for race-related power imbalances" and to negotiate these racial barriers "from a position of pride in oneself, self-esteem, and affirmative self-agency (i.e., a belief that one can make a positive difference)" across their lifespan (Nicolas et al., 2008:265). For example, a critical racial conscious self-agency allows African Americans to reject stereotypes because they evaluate them as being racist and recognize the perpetrators as having a racist agenda. Therefore, African American parents can be highly effective when they equate a sense of racial pride with the challenge of overcoming racial injustices (Murry et al., 2009; Stevenson, Reed, and Bodison, 1996). Ward (1996) adds that this critical race-consciousness allows African American adolescents to reject "victimhood," gain self-determination, achieve personal and racial affirmation, and to resist racial oppression.

Our theory of African American offending celebrates this resiliency. However, the data on offending clearly indicates that while the majority of African Americans living in "ghettos" overcome the deleterious consequences of racial injustices, this is not the case for all. Consequently, the data indicate that place of residence matters. We stipulate that place indirectly impacts African American offending because of its relationship with the ability of black parents to effectively racially socialize their children. That is, residing in areas of concentrated disadvantages impacts the ability of African American parents to competently racially socialize their children, which in turn increases their individual probabilities of offending. The research shows that there are specific attributes of concentrated disadvantage that negatively impact the ability of African American parents to effectively racially socialize their children (Caughy et al., 2006).

Why Place Matters

Below we outline five reasons why place alters the relationship between racial socialization and African American offending.

First, Oyserman and Yoon (2009) examined whether aggregate neighborhood characteristics (e.g., percentage of adults with less than a high school education, percentage of households living below the poverty line, percentage of individuals aged 16 and over in the labor force, and the degree of segregation as measured by the Neighborhood

Diversity Index) are related to whether African Americans develop a positive racial identity (e.g., connectedness, awareness of racism, and embedded achievement). Interestingly, they found that concentrated poverty and unemployment did not have an impact on the person's racial identity. However, they report that *racially segregated* neighborhoods were negatively related to the likelihood that African Americans developed a positive racial identity. That is, race trumps class.

Oyserman and Yoon (2009) argue that isolated racially segregated neighborhoods negatively impact the racial identity of African Americans because they reduce opportunities for blacks to perceive members of their own race in a positive light. Isolated racial segregation can also decrease the probability that African Americans will develop close friendships with whites. Research shows that parents are more likely to encourage their children to mistrust whites if they do not have any close white friends (Shelton, 2008). In addition, isolated racial segregation decreases the likelihood that African American children will see their parents positively interacting with whites. In the absence of observing these positive black–white interactions, it becomes less likely that African American youths will be positively socialized toward whites through direct modeling, reinforcement, and imitation of behaviors (Bandura, 1977; Lesane-Brown, 2006).

Other scholars have found that African Americans residing in areas of concentrated disadvantage will racially socialize their children differently than those living in more affluent neighborhoods. For example, Caughy et al. (2006) report that parental racial socialization practices differed by neighborhood context, measuring both individual perceptions of neighborhood disorder and aggregate characteristics (e.g., percent living in poverty). They report that African American parents were more likely to emphasize racism and mistrust if they resided in neighborhoods characterized by physical disorder, a fear of retaliation, and a fear of victimization. And, importantly, they found that racial socialization messages associated with promotion of mistrust were more common among African American parents living in primarily black neighborhoods (Caughy et al., 2006). They further found that disorganized neighborhoods increased the positive association between promotion of racial mistrust and internalizing problems such as anxiety and depression and that parental racial socialization strategies were associated with higher rates of aggressive behavior in neighborhoods with a low negative social climate but unrelated in neighborhoods with a highly negative social climate. Smith, Atkins, and Connell (2003) report that impoverished neighborhoods enhance mistrust in whites. Relatedly, Hughes and Chen (1997) found that African American parents were more likely to promote the mistrust of whites if they perceived institutional-level discrimination in their place of employment.

Thus, in areas of concentrated disadvantages—especially in isolated racially segregated places—African American parents may implicitly or explicitly socialize their children to be overly mistrustful of whites, minimize their children's cultural socialization, or inadequately prepare them for overcoming the challenges of experiencing racial injustices. We further posit that in the areas of concentrated disadvantage, African American parents' experiences with racial injustices will cause them to either underemphasize or to skeptically teach their children egalitarian values, including the beliefs that all people are basically and fundamentally the same and that the United States is truly a "color blind" society. Consequently, we hypothesize that in areas of concentrated disadvantage—particularly in isolated racially segregated areas—it is more likely that African Americans will overemphasize the mistrust of whites, ineffectively prepare their children for their encounters with bias, underemphasize the development of a prosocial racial identity, and underemphasize teaching their children egalitarian values such as that the United States is truly a "color blind" society (Outten et al., 2010).

Second, the data show that areas of concentrated disadvantage are characterized by African American families that are female-dominated—that is, female-headed single-parent households. According to the U.S. Census Bureau's 2008 American Community Survey, 67 percent of African American households whose income in the past 12 months was below the poverty line were headed by a female with related children under 18 years of age. The data also show that 75 percent of poor black children are in a female-headed household (Anna, 1987;

Sampson, 1987). Alexander (2010) adds that a principal reason for the concentration of female-headed households among African Americans is the war on drugs; that is, the war on drugs has been nearly universally waged against blacks resulting in the mass imprisonment of approximately 1 million black men. Research indicates that single parents are less likely to racially socialize their children than married parents (Thornton et al., 1990). Consequently, disadvantaged neighborhoods increase the likelihood that African Americans will not be racially socialized because they are more likely to have female-headed households and single parents are less likely to racially socialize their children. Thus, we hypothesize that in areas of intense poverty and racial segregation, a greater number of youths will be racially socialized in the streets.

Third, areas of concentrated disadvantage have a larger number of African Americans residing within them with fewer years of education than those residing in more middle to upper class neighborhoods. The research shows that the more education African American parents have the more likely they are to both racially socialize their children and to provide them with competent coping strategies to overcome experiences with racial injustices (Caughy et al., 2002; Thornton et al., 1990). Thus, the data indicate that areas of concentrated disadvantage will have more African American youth who will either not be racially socialized or less competently socialized because their parents are less educated.

Fourth, our theory of offending posits that areas of concentrated disadvantage—especially areas of isolated racial segregation—are characterized by widely and intensely embraced perceptions of criminal justice injustices, racial discrimination, and pejorative stereotypes. Thus, African American parents residing in these isolated areas will be continuously exposed to racial injustices. Our theory argues that this constant exposure to racial injustices profoundly impairs the ability of African American parents to successfully racially socialize their children.

Brody, Chen, Murry, Ge, Simons, Gibbons, Gerrard, and Cutrona (2006) found that perceptions of racial injustices negatively impact the ability of African American mothers to competently racially socialize their children because they undermine their own emotional stability. That is, exposure to racial discrimination increases the likelihood that African

American parents will become depressed and angry. Cumulatively, these perceptions place their entire family system under undue stress as the parents-guardians try to come to terms with their own negative feelings brought on by experiences with criminal justice injustices, racial discrimination, and being negatively stereotyped. Thus, African American youths who offend are more likely to be racially socialized by parents who have been rendered emotionally unstable—parents whose feelings oscillate between anger, irritability, and depression—because of their own confrontations with concentrated racial injustices.

Fifth, and finally, we hypothesize that place may interact with other parenting practices that can alter the relationship between racial socialization practices and offending.[14] That is, African American children are unlikely to learn healthy coping skills if their parents are teaching them when they are experiencing undue stress (i.e., when the parents are angry and irritable). Indeed, studies show that the negative consequences of inadequate racial socialization (e.g., overly emphasizing mistrust) are compounded when African American parents are hostile or indifferent (Burt et al., 2010; McHale et al., 2006). The research also shows that African Americans socialized by uninvolved parents are particularly likely (i.e., more so than whites) to internalize an angry identity, which in turn increases the likelihood of offending across the lifespan (Schroeder, Bulanda, Giordano, and Cernkovich, 2010). Thus, in areas of extreme disadvantage it is likely that African American parents will be under considerable stress, which should decrease their ability to be effective parents. In turn, it is unlikely that African American children will be effectively racially or otherwise socialized if their parents are unduly experiencing a range of negative emotions.

In closing, it could be argued that the United States is fortunate that the crime rate among African Americans is not higher. Nearly every African American, at some point in their lives, will experience a form of racial injustice and the research shows that these debilitating experiences increase offending. Yet, the data show that despite these lived experiences, only a minority of African Americans offend. Our theory argues that this lower than expected amount of crime is powerful evidence of the resiliency of individual blacks and the power of the

African American family to overcome their racial subordination. Thus, our theory, as do the majority of African Americans (55 percent), stipulates that the African American family plays a pivotal role in whether individual blacks will offend. But, unfortunately, and not of their choosing, African American families are confronted by the dual tasks of overcoming the consequences of their own experiences with racial injustices while simultaneously providing their children with the coping skills they need to ward off the negative effects of racial discrimination, criminal justice injustices, and being pejoratively stereotyped. We celebrate their resiliency while acknowledging that African Americans have no choice but to contend with crime-causing forces outside of their own control; that is, racial injustices.

6

A THEORETICAL MODEL OF AFRICAN AMERICAN OFFENDING

In this chapter, we fully present our theory of African American offending. We locate the motivation for African Americans to offend in their unique worldview. We assert that this worldview has been and continues to be forged as African Americans are confronted by racial injustices in their lived experiences. There are a multitude of racial injustices that persistently shape the collective memories of African Americans. Chief among them are criminal justice injustices, the many variegated forms of racial discrimination, and the deleterious consequences of being pejoratively stereotyped. We note that nearly all African Americans have either directly or vicariously experienced these forms of racial subordination. In short, our theory posits that African American offending must be situated in the reactions that African Americans have to being racially subjugated; that is, perceiving and experiencing profound and nuanced racial injustices.

The Unique Worldview of African Americans

We have presented data that unequivocally show that African Americans have an inimitable worldview. This worldview is distinct from those that inform the attitudes and behaviors of other racial groups (e.g., whites, Native Americans) and other ethnic minorities (e.g., Hispanics). We argue that this worldview has been shaped by racial dynamics largely outside of the control of African Americans. That is, there is a "long history of public dishonor and ritualized humiliation of African Americans by Euro-Americans" that has caused blacks to develop their peerless worldview (Hagan, Shedd, and Payne, 2005:382). Hence, our theory assumes that African Americans, unlike any other racial group or other ethnic minority, have a unique racial lens that informs their beliefs and behaviors, especially as they relate to the salience of race and how racism impacts their lives in the U.S. It is important to note that this collective memory also includes the history of their survival—their resistance to racial subordination. Therefore, we contend that the unique worldview shared by African Americans provides the majority of African Americans with the impetus to fend off the deleterious consequences of racial injustices. However, we argue it also can provide the impetus for a minority of blacks to offend.

Our theory of African American offending identifies the aspects of their worldview that heighten their probability of offending; that is, their perceptions and experiences with criminal justice injustices, racial discrimination, and the deleterious consequences of being injuriously stereotyped. The genesis of this worldview, of course, was the forceful removal of African Americans from Africa and their subsequent enslavement in the United States. This worldview was further solidified through the humiliating oppression of the "Jim Crow" racial apartheid that followed the formal dismantling of slavery.

This racial apartheid persists as African Americans reside in the most disadvantaged neighborhoods. This purposeful racial segregation of African Americans caused them to rebel throughout the U.S. during the 1960s. As a result, African Americans witnessed the National Guard patrolling their neighborhoods, often with armed vehicles. A federal study of these urban unrests—the Kerner Commission—concluded that America was "moving toward two societies, one black, one white—separate and unequal" (Kerner, 1968). Notably, these urban unrests were, in part, the impetus for the passage of major civil reforms, such as the Fair Housing Act of 1968, which were specifically designed to ameliorate the multifaceted forms of discrimination that African Americans encounter.

Despite these gains, the data indicate that severe racial segregation and its concomitant problems continue to disproportionately impact African Americans (Charles, 2001, 2003; Massey, 2005). These problems are evidenced in the fact that civil unrests continue to plague the U.S. For example, the 1980 Miami, Florida, unrest, the 1992 Los Angeles civil unrest, and the 2001 Cincinnati urban disorder (see also Hacker, 2003). Similar to other urban unrests, these disruptions were triggered by perceived criminal justice injustices—in Miami the acquittal of four police officers for the murder of Arthur McDuffie, an unarmed African American man who had been a U.S. marine and a military police officer, in LA the acquittal of four Los Angeles police officers who were accused of the beating of the unarmed African American motorist, Rodney King, and in Cincinnati the fatal shooting of an unarmed 19-year-old black male, Timothy Thomas, by a white police officer during an on-foot pursuit.

African American Offending and Criminal Justice Injustices

Our theory asserts that a cause of African American offending is their perceptions and experiences with criminal justice injustices. We argue that these perceptions and experiences must be situated or contextualized within their collective worldview. That is, the worldview shared by African Americans was largely formed as a result of the collective negative experiences blacks have had with the criminal justice system. Most notably, for example, agents of the criminal justice system aided and abetted the lynching of countless African Americans. A quote in Silberman's (1978:168) *Criminal Violence, Criminal Justice* captures how racist attitudes have been embedded within the criminal justice system and how it has tacitly encouraged crime among blacks:

> Southern police departments had three classes of homicide. "If a nigger kills a white man, that's murder," . . . "If a white man kills a nigger, that's justifiable homicide. If a nigger kills another nigger, that's one less nigger."

Thus, our theory of African American offending argues that African Americans are fully aware that the criminal justice system has purposefully, with the consent of white power structures, humiliated them through systemic, and, at times, murderous acts of criminal justice injustices. In short, this awareness is a core belief shared by African Americans living in the United States.

We further stipulate that this core belief is resurrected and reaffirmed among African Americans living in the 21st century when they personally or vicariously experience criminal justice injustices. Thus, we assert that the well-earned distrust that African Americans have toward the criminal justice system is further crystallized when the media displays the aftermath of a black man who was brutally sexually assaulted by a gang of white New York City police officers (i.e., Abner Louima), or a gang of white Los Angeles police officers beating an unarmed African American man (i.e., Rodney King), or a white police officer arresting a black Harvard professor for resisting arrest who was trying to enter his own home (i.e., Henry Louis Gates) (Holmes and Smith, 2008; Ogletree, 2010). These feelings are further compounded when they personally experience their own criminal justice injustices as when, for example, they are a victim of racial profiling (DWB—driving while black or shopping while black).

Notably, the research reveals that these perceptions of racial bias are not instances of African Americans "playing the race card." That is, their perceptions are grounded in their "real conditions" (DuBois, 1899b, Ogletree, 2010). For example, Ayres and Borowsky (2008) analyzed more than 810,000 field data reports collected by the Los Angeles Police Department (LAPD) from July 1, 2003 through June 30, 2004 and found, after controlling for violent and property crime rates in specific LAPD reporting districts, as well as a range of other variables, that:

- Per 10,000 residents, the black stop rate is 3,400 stops *higher* than the white stop rate.
- Relative to stopped whites, stopped blacks are 127 percent *more* likely to be frisked.
- Relative to stopped whites, stopped blacks are 76 percent *more* likely to be searched.

- Relative to stopped whites, stopped blacks are 29 percent *more* likely to be arrested.

Their research further found that the racial profiling of African Americans is counterproductive as it does not result in enhanced public safety. That is, Ayres and Borowsky (2008) report that:

- Frisked African Americans are 42.3 percent *less* likely to be found with a weapon than frisked whites.
- Consensual searches of blacks are 37.0 percent *less* likely to uncover weapons than consensual searches of whites.
- Consensual searches of blacks are 23.7 percent *less* likely to uncover drugs than consensual searches of whites.
- Consensual searches of blacks are 25.4 percent *less* likely to uncover anything else than consensual searches of whites.

Ayres and Borowsky (2008:i) conclude that their data are "prima facie evidence that African Americans and Hispanics are over-stopped, over-frisked, over-searched, and over-arrested."

Note, that these racial disparities are replicated in other places. Geller and Fagan (2010) found substantial racial disparities in the implementation of marijuana enforcement activity; that is, street stops for marijuana are more prevalent in New York City precincts with large black populations, as are combined marijuana stop and arrest totals and they report that this disparity holds up across neighborhoods after controlling for local crime and socioeconomic conditions. Thus, our theory of African American offending asserts (and the data confirm) that the vast majority of African Americans, through either personal or vicarious experiences, believe that the criminal justice system treats them less fairly than other races and ethnicities. In short, this perception is a core belief firmly embedded within the worldview shared by nearly all African Americans.

Criminal Justice Injustices and Weakening the Restraints of the Rule of Law

A core value of our American democracy is the belief that people are governed by the rule of law. The legitimacy of this belief rests on the fundamental premise that no one is above the law. This means that the poor and the rich, whites and blacks, the rulers and the ruled are all equally subject to the law. Thus, the "rule of law" is in opposition to the possibility that the law can be applied in a discriminatory manner by the "rule of men." Scholars argue that the legitimacy of these beliefs is the first line of defense from a possible onslaught of chaos and crime. In short, people obey the law because they believe in its legitimacy; that is, they believe that the law is of, by, and for the people, and that everyone regardless of their class, race, or gender will be treated the same by the criminal justice system.

Our theory assumes that people, regardless of their race-ethnicity, are less likely to offend if they respect the law; that is, believe in its legitimacy. However, the data indicate that nearly all African Americans believe that laws and the criminal justice system systematically treat them unfairly because of their race. In addition, the research unequivocally reveals that the vast majority of African Americans believe that the salient reason why so many blacks are imprisoned is that the police and courts discriminate against blacks. Moreover, the research clearly shows that the majority of African Americans perceive that the police engage in a variety of racist behaviors that communicate their disrespect for them. Thus, researchers consistently find that there are serious "rifts" between African American communities and the police. In fact, scholars find that poor African American youth have "virtually *no* conception of the police as guardians" and considered them as "bullies in uniform" (Brunson and Weitzer, 2009:879).

Our theory argues that these perceptions of the law and the criminal justice system are core components of the legal socialization of African Americans. This means that African Americans are raised within a worldview—a reservoir of bad will—that includes an emphasis on negative experiences with the criminal justice system. This socialization is reinforced as African Americans share among themselves their personal or vicarious experiences with criminal justice injustices. Thus, this belief becomes a shared common understanding that is continuously reinforced through daily interactions with other African Americans. In short, a significant component of the African American racial identity is the belief that laws and the criminal justice system are racist; that is, most African Americans believe that to be black in the United States means that they will, at some point in their life, be disrespectfully and unfairly treated by the criminal justice system.

We posit that the belief that the criminal justice system is racist heightens the tendency for African Americans to perceive criminal justice injustices and to react to them with shame, anger, hostility, and defiance. Noble (2006) describes how perceived injustices may evoke "dual levels of anger." That is, on one level, African Americans become angered as a result of the perceived injustice and, on the other level, "there is residual anger brought on by the cognitive connection between the racist act and historical racism. With a higher degree of anger, the propensity towards aggression significantly increases" (Noble, 2006:133). It is also likely that some African Americans will experience bouts of depression as a result of being chronically exposed to criminal justice injustices. We additionally theorize that chronic exposure to criminal justice injustices will cause some African Americans to oscillate between depression and anger-defiance. In short, we hypothesize that these emotive responses substantially undermine the potential of the law to restrain offending behavior. That is, it is difficult for African Americans to believe that they should obey the law when they see it as a racist means to disrespect, harass, humiliate, bully, and unfairly imprison them.

African American Offending and Racial Discrimination

Our theory additionally posits that another core component of being black in a conflicted racially stratified society is the worldview—shared belief—that they will, at some point in their lives, be discriminated against because of their race. The survey data show that nearly every African American in the United States believes that they have been discriminated against because they are black. Our theory does not differentiate among the endless ways in which African Americans can experience racial discrimination, from "shopping while black" to being denied housing and employment because of their race. Our point is quite simple. Nearly all African Americans share the worldview that they have been or will be racially discriminated.

Research shows that the vast majority of African Americans experience some form of racial discrimination. These experiences can range from the profound (e.g., being excluded from social networks, being denied housing, or not being hired because they are black) to "everyday racism"—racial microaggressions—microinjustices—that include subtle degradations and putdowns (Essed, 1991, 2002; Jean and Feagin, 1998; Smith, Allen, and Danley, 2007; Swim, Hyers, Cohen, Fitzgerald, and Bylsma, 2003). These cumulative events can be experienced directly or vicariously and can include being "ignored or overlooked while waiting in line, being mistaken for someone who serves others (e.g., maid, bellboy), and being followed or observed while in public."

Scholars note that these experiences can "feel demoralizing, dehumanizing, disrespectful, or objectifying (i.e., being treated as a stereotype)" and "the accumulation of these experiences contributes to the overall stress load of the individual" (Harrell, 2000:46). In addition, scholars argue that these "mundane" events are profound in their consequences because they continually trigger memories embedded within the African American worldview, similar incidents that they personally experienced, and are exhausting as they demand the need to cognitively resolve the emotional costs of everyday racism (Essed, 2002; Feagin and Sikes, 1995).

Indeed, Essed (2002) asserts that everyday racism produces three mutually reinforcing consequences. These three compounding consequences are the *marginalization* of blacks, the *problematization* of African American culture and identities, and the symbolic and physical *repression* of their resistance through humiliation or violence (e.g., accusations of oversensitivity about discrimination, racist jokes, ridicule in front of others, patronizing, rudeness) (Essed, 2002). Our theory emphasizes that offending is related to the cumulative consequences of racial discrimination. Thus, we are not arguing that African Americans offend because they experience a single isolated form of racial discrimination, such as being denied housing because of their race (see also Du Bois, 1899b:351). Rather, we argue that African American offending is related to the total cumulative consequences of being black in a racially stratified society with conflicted race relations.

Studies indicate that the experience of racial discrimination has pervasive deleterious consequences for the health and well-being of African Americans. The research shows that racial discrimination is related to increases in stress, high blood pressure, substance abuse, depression, hypertension, and diminished mental health and that these toxic effects generalize to the young and old, rich and poor, and across gender. In short, the research unequivocally shows that "discrimination ranks in significance with major stressful life events such as divorce, job loss, and death of a loved one" (Sellers, Bonham, Neighbors, and Amell, 2009:33).

A core hypothesis of our theory is that racial discrimination increases the probability of African American offending. That is, the more African Americans encounter racial discrimination, the more likely they are to offend. More specifically we hypothesize that offending increases with the *degree* to which African Americans report being discriminated against because of their race.

An accumulating body of research supports our core hypothesis. This research shows that African Americans are likely to offend the more often they report perceiving racial discrimination. Importantly, the research shows that this positive relationship persists even after controlling for the core measures of "general theories" of crime such as control theory (i.e., weak social bonds), differential association-social learning theory (i.e., delinquent peers), and general strain theory (i.e., stressors such as divorce or victimization) (Brody, Chen, Murry, Ge, Simons, Gibbons, Gerrard, and Cutrona 2006; Gibbons, Gerrard, Cleveland, Wills, and Brody 2004; Simons, Chen, Stewart, and Brody 2003; Simons, Simons, Burt, Drummund, Stewart, Brody, Gibbons, and Cutrona 2006; Stewart, Schreck, and Simons 2006; Stewart and Simons 2006). Of note, our theory asserts that the toxic effects of discrimination on African American offending generalize across class and gender.

Our theory also specifies why racial discrimination should predict higher rates of African American offending. We assert that racial discrimination increases the probability of black offending in two ways. First, it undermines the ability of African Americans to develop strong bonds with white-dominated institutions. Second, we contend that

African Americans who experience racial discrimination are more likely to express oscillating feelings of anger-defiance-hopelessness-depression.[1] Our theory hypothesizes that the ability of African Americans to build strong bonds with white-dominated institutions (especially schools and their place of employment) and to positively resist racial injustices decreases with the *degree* to which African Americans report being discriminated against because of their race.

For example, the data show that the ability of African American youth to feel a strong sense of commitment to their education is significantly compromised when they report that they are being discriminated against in their schools. There are a multitude of ways that African Americans can encounter racial discrimination within their schools, including, but not limited to, knowing that their school is inferior to other schools that have more whites, their white peers rejecting them because of their race (e.g., not allowed access to the "in-group"), being called racist epithets (e.g., the "N" word), being told racist jokes, being bullied because of their race, being physically attacked, teachers only calling on white students, teachers belittling black students, teachers assuming that they are "lazy" or prone to violence (i.e., invoking a stereotype threat), incidents of hate crimes targeting African Americans (e.g., a display of a white doll dressed in a Ku Klux Klan robe and a black doll with a noose around its neck), racially biased texts and curricula, racial tracking, discriminatory penalties (e.g., whites get detention while blacks get suspended from school for the same incident), lowered teacher expectations, less encouragement to take advanced courses, a hostile racial climate, and the school authorities' denial and refusal to acknowledge that there is racism within their schools (Alliman-Brissett and Turner, 2010; Donaldson, 1996; Goldsmith, 2004; Mattison and Aber, 2007; Rosenbloom and Way, 2004; Wong, Eccles, and Sameroff, 2003). Also, note that scholars have found that schools with a greater proportion of African American students are more likely to respond to misbehavior in a punitive manner and less likely to respond in a restorative manner (Payne and Welch, 2010).

Although limited, the research shows that reported instances of racial discrimination within the school negatively impact a variety of education-related outcomes for African Americans (Massey and Probasco, 2010). The research shows that experiences with racial discrimination are related to declines in school self-esteem, school bonding, grades, academic ability, self-concepts, academic task values, and increases in school detentions and suspensions. Most notably, scholars have found that the more African American students perceive their school's racial climate as a "toxic environment," the weaker their attachment and commitment to their school and the more likely they are to report higher rates of offending. Thus, we assert that racial discrimination indirectly increases African American offending by undermining their ability to build strong ties with conventional institutions. In short, it is difficult for African Americans to build strong ties with institutions that disrespect them and unfairly discriminate against them because of their race.[2]

Negative Stereotypes

Our theory hypothesizes that there is another form of racial discrimination that profoundly affects the likelihood that African Americans will offend; that is, the deleterious consequences of being pejoratively stereotyped. Since blacks were forcefully removed from Africa and enslaved in the United States, whites have constructed derogatory stereotypes of African Americans. Indeed, even the "founding fathers", many of whom were slave owners, perpetuated horrific stereotypes of African Americans.[3] Thomas Jefferson (1785/1999:266), for example, in his book *Notes on the State of Virginia*, proposed, even though he had a sexual relationship with one of his slaves, Sally Hemmings, that blacks "are inferior to the whites in the endowments of both body and mind" and "that in imagination they are dull, tasteless, and anomalous." Further, based on his direct observations, Jefferson noted the childlike simplicity of blacks, their wild imaginations, their incapacity to reason, their inability to create serious art, their very strong and "disagreeable odor," their tolerance for heat, their low cognitive abilities ("But never yet could I find that a black had uttered a thought above the level of plain narration" [Jefferson, 1785/1999:266]), and the sexual desire of African American men for white women.

Jefferson (1785/1999:266) also perpetuated the stereotype that African Americans are rhythmic: "In music they are more generally gifted than the whites ... Whether they will be equal to the composition of a more extensive run of melody, or of complicated harmony, is yet to be proved" and that African Americans had sex with orangutans as the "preference of the orangutan for the black women" (Jefferson, 1785/1999:265). In the end, Thomas Jefferson speculated that African Americans were of a distinct race that was inferior to the white race.

The data are unequivocally clear that these pejorative stereotypes of African Americans have persisted into the 21st century. Devine and Elliot (1995) found that the top nine list of adjectives that whites checked to describe African Americans were, in order: athletic, rhythmic, low in intelligence, lazy and poor (these were tied), loud, criminal, hostile, and ignorant. In contrast, no whites checked, for example, that African Americans are ambitious, tradition loving, sensitive, or gregarious. Other research shows that, in 2000, whites thought blacks were 5 times more violent than whites (Unnever and Cullen, 2010). It is important to note that the stereotypes that whites have constructed are gendered. Research shows that a prevailing racialized gendered stereotype is that of the *criminalblackman*—the angry, young, male, urban, black superpredator that has no remorse (Russell-Brown, 2009). The research further notes that by 3–4 years of age children can sort people by race and that between the ages of 6 and 10, African Americans have developed "stereotype consciousness." (Parker et al., 2010) That is, African American children are fully aware of the pejorative stereotypes that systematically devalue them. In short, scholars argue that persistent and prevailing pejorative stereotypes of African Americans are a reason why blacks have a "collective spoiled identity" (Loury, 2004).

Our theory of offending outlines three pathways through which pejorative stereotypes can increase the likelihood of African American offending. First, we argue that some African Americans internalize the negative depictions that are embedded in racist stereotypes—more specifically, the stereotype that they are criminal—and take on that label as their self-identity (Harrell, 2000). This proposition is consistent with the secondary deviance thesis within labeling theory. The secondary deviance hypothesis posits that some African Americans will internalize the widespread belief that they are a criminal and adjust their behavior to make it consistent with how others define them, particularly when those who are applying the label have a higher status (e.g., whites, particularly whites in positions of power such as teachers). Thus, we hypothesize that some African Americans, especially young black men, internalize and act out the pejorative gendered racialized stereotype that African American males are remorseless superpredators.

Second, we hypothesize that pejorative stereotypes negatively impact African Americans in many of the same ways as racial discrimination. Thus, our theory stipulates that pejorative stereotypes of African Americans—particularly when there is chronic exposure—are debilitating. That is, they deplete ego resources as African Americans are continually confronted with the negative emotions that arise from being "dissed" or insulted by stereotypes that "put them down." We assert that the negative emotions that arise can oscillate between depression-humiliation and anger-defiance. Brezina (2010) argues that anger is related to offending because it strengthens aggressive attitudes, weakens the belief that crime is wrong by fostering the belief that offending is justifiable, and increases the likelihood that individuals will associate with criminal peers. Burt, Simons, and Gibbons (2010) state that depression is related to offending as it increases impatience, irritability, reduces inhibitions and self-regulation, reduces empathy, and decreases a person's stake in conformity. Thus, African Americans who respond to racial stereotypes with humiliation-depression and anger-defiance should have higher rates of offending because it energizes them to action, lowers their inhibitions, increases their felt injury, increases their likelihood of associating with other disidentified individuals, and creates desires for retaliation and revenge (Agnew, 1992; Brezina, 2010). In short, our theory hypothesizes that offending becomes an ill-fated attempt by some African Americans to reestablish a sense of control and status in their life, which is lost when they are confronted by toxic racist stereotypes (Miller, 2001).

Third, we assert that negative depictions of African Americans increase the probability of black offending because they diminish the strength of the social bonds that blacks develop with white-dominated institutions (e.g., schools and their place of employment). Scholars recognize that "stereotype threats" directly undermine the ability of African Americans to develop strong bonds with white-dominated institutions (Steele, 1997). Stereotype threats are toxic because they heighten African Americans' anxieties that they will be judged stereotypically or that they may conform to the validity of the relevant stereotype through their behavior. That is, African Americans have to contend with the experience that anything they say or do can confirm the pejorative stereotypes that others have about them because they are black. The threats that stereotypes have undermine the ability of African Americans to generate strong bonds or to excel because they heighten vigilance, self-doubt, create greater stress and anxiety, and deplete emotional resources. As a result, some African Americans avoid situations where they will acutely experience stereotype threats.

Our theory hypothesizes that stereotype threats profoundly affect African American offending by weakening their belief, attachment, commitment, and involvement in their education (Noble, 2006). The research is clear that stereotype threats (e.g., that African Americans are low in intelligence and prone to violence-crime) significantly undermine the ability of African Americans to build strong bonds within their schools. Steele (1997) argues that strong school-related bonds emerge when African Americans feel good about themselves as a result of positive outcomes at their schools (e.g., performing well academically). This process is reinforcing as positive school outcomes strengthen a positive self-identity, which in turn further enhances the African American student's sense of academic self-worth. The data are clear that stereotype threats short-circuit this positive reinforcing process.

We posit that African Americans who eventually offend initially enter their schools with the intent of doing well. However, two factors intervene that heighten their probability of offending. First, they personally experience some form of racial discrimination. This discrimination can originate from multiple sources, including from their peers or their teachers. The research shows that experiences with racial discrimination weaken the African American student's bonds with their schools and increases their probability of experiencing anger-hostility-defiance-depression.

Second, African Americans who offend are more likely to experience the injurious consequences of stereotype threats, which in turn triggers the disidentification process. Steele (1997) argues that disidentified students initially want to do well in school but the invidious consequences of stereotype threats undermine their efforts. Disidentified students underperform because stereotype threats trigger a heightened state of vigilance, self-doubt, increased stress and anxiety levels, and exhaust their limited developmental emotional resources. As a result, a feedback process unfolds whereby underperforming African American students reconceptualize their self-identity by removing school-based achievements as a basis for positive self-evaluation. This, in turn, leads to further school-based failures. In the end, disidentified students emotionally withdraw from their schools. We additionally assert that disidentified African American youths who have not reached developmental maturation are more likely to experience the intense mood-swings associated with racial discrimination and stereotype threats. Research shows that impulsivity is corollary of oscillating bouts of depression, anger, and defiance and that impulsivity is a robust predictor of offending.

We further contend that the reciprocal disidentification process is related to African American offending because it knifes off students from prosocial protective bonds. Rather, disidentified students, who are more likely to experience bouts of anger-hostility-defiance-aggression and depression, find themselves associating with other disidentified peers. We assert that one of the domains that these groups of disidentified black youths are likely to choose is delinquency, a behavior that most often does not demand a high level of competence (Gottfredson and Hirschi, 1990). Thus, delinquent behavior offers an opportunity for disidentified black youth to gain a sense of self-importance; that is, an identity that is not diminished by their tenuous relationship with white-dominated institutions, such as their schools (Owens-Sabir, 2007). Alexander (2010:166) adds that some African Americans embrace the stigma of criminality because it is "an attempt to carve out a positive identity in a society that offers them little more than scorn, contempt, and constant surveillance." In short, "up in the air" derogatory stereotypes weaken social bonds, are ego-depleting, and increase the likelihood that African Americans will injuriously express anger-hostility-defiance-depression.

Lastly, studies show that perceptions of injustice—unfairness—undermine the motivation of disadvantaged groups such as African Americans (also the economically disadvantaged) to achieve success. Laurin, Fitzsimons, and Kay (2010) found consistent evidence, across five studies, that beliefs in societal unfairness diminished the motivation to pursue long-term goals and that this effect was stronger among members of socially disadvantaged groups. More specifically, they report that "members of disadvantaged groups are more likely than members of advantaged groups to calibrate their pursuit of long-term goals to their beliefs about societal fairness" (Laurin et al., 2010:182). These findings indicate that perceptions of discrimination—that is, perceptions of being treated unfairly—cause African Americans to lessen their willingness or commitment to work hard because they believe that their earnest efforts will not result in the same rewards that whites routinely achieve. Thus, the more African Americans perceive that success is unfairly distributed the less motivated they are to invest their time and energy in achieving long term goals such as academic and financial achievements.

Individual Offending

We are fully aware that theories of racial oppression overpredict African American offending. Our theory could be particularly susceptible to this criticism. We have argued that the worldview shared by nearly all African Americans causes offending, yet, only a minority of blacks engage in crime. Thus, we need to explain why African Americans who report experiences with criminal justice injustices, racial discrimination, and being injuriously stereotyped do not offend. We address this issue in two ways.

Variations in Experiences with Racial Injustices

We argue that a key to understanding offending resides in the *degree* to which African Americans experience criminal justice injustices, racial discrimination, and being negatively stereotyped. We theorize that not all African Americans equally experience these crime-causing social forces. That is, all African Americans may report that they have experienced these events but we argue that there is tremendous variation in the *degree* to which they are experienced.

Therefore, we argue that the degree of exposure to racial injustices should be measured across multiple dimensions including, but not limited to: age of onset (i.e., at what age did the individual first encounter racial injustices); who committed the racial injustice (e.g., was it a person in authority such as a school teacher or a police officer), the frequency of the exposure (i.e., how often was the individual exposed; was it daily, weekly, or monthly), and the duration of the exposure (i.e., did it persist across the person's life course). We further posit that scholars should assess the degree to which the individual is embedded in networks that both sensitize and reinforce perceptions of racial injustices. In short, our theory hypothesizes that individual differences in African American offending are related to variations in the *degree* that blacks experience racial injustices.

Variations in Racial Socialization

We assert that individual differences in African American offending are related to variations in racial socialization practices. Lesane-Brown (2006:400) defines racial socialization "as specific verbal and non-verbal messages transmitted to younger generations for the development of values, attitudes, behaviors, and beliefs regarding the meaning and significance of race and racial stratification, intergroup and intragroup interactions, and personal and group identity." The data show that about two-thirds of African American parents racially socialize their children. In general, these parents proactively attempt to prepare their children for encounters with criminal justice injustices, racial discrimination, and the invidious consequences of being depreciatively stereotyped.

Our theory argues that racial socialization experiences can mitigate the relationship between perceptions of racial injustices, weak social bonds and offending. Thus, our theory posits that African Americans who have positive racial socialization experiences will not offend even if they perceive racial injustices.

We recognize that this assumption places a great deal of emphasis on the role that parenting has in African American offending. Therefore, we proceed with one caveat. That is, we also assume that in some cases the degree to which African Americans experience racial injustices might exceed the capacity of the mitigating effects of even the best racial socialization practices. Thus, our theory of offending allows for racial injustices to directly impact offending but only when they substantially exceed what most African Americans normally experience and when they overwhelm the mitigating experiences of prosocial racial socialization experiences. Our basic thesis is that variations in racial socialization can exacerbate the influences that racial injustices have on the likelihood that blacks will engage in crime. We assert that there are four pathways through which racial socialization can increase the probability of individual African American offending.

First, we argue that parents who do not racially socialize their children put them at greater risk for experiencing the deleterious consequences of racial injustices that are related to offending (e.g., anger-hostility-defiance-depression and weak social bonds). Our theory posits that in the absence of parental-guardian racial socialization experiences, African American youth are more likely to construct their racial identity and their feelings about racial injustices by interacting with their peers and other individuals in their neighborhood; that is, on the "streets" (Oliver, 2006; Sharkey, 2006; Stewart and Simons, 2006; Stewart, Schreck, and Simons, 2006; Stewart and Simons, 2010). We additionally assert that it is likely, especially in disadvantaged isolated racially segregated neighborhoods, that the individuals that they will most likely interact with will be disidentified African Americans. We further hypothesize that it is likely that these disidentified individuals will have developed deep resentments toward individual whites and white-dominated institutions such as the criminal justice system. Consequently, we contend that African American youths who are not proactively and positively racially socialized by their parents will inculcate the attitudes that they are exposed to on the "streets" (Sharkey, 2006).[4] We also hypothesize that youths who are racially socialized on the "street" are more likely to develop weak social bonds with institutions, such as their schools.

Therefore, we stipulate that African Americans are more likely to offend if their "street" racial identity includes deep resentments toward racial injustices and race-based rationalizations that function to weaken their attachments to white-dominated institutions.

Second, we hypothesize that African Americans who are chronically exposed to criminal justice injustices, being pejoratively stereotyped, and racial discrimination are more likely to offend if their parents taught them, either purposefully or implicitly—verbally or nonverbally—to distrust individual whites, white-dominated institutions, and that whites hold them in contempt (Brown, Linver, and Evans, 2010). We posit that African Americans raised by parents that overly emphasize the mistrust of whites and encourage their children to become overly defiant in the presence of racism are likely to develop a stigma sensitivity and stigma consciousness. The research shows that African Americans with these sensitivities are more likely to perceive discrimination directed at them personally, interpret ambiguous situations as identity threatening, are less likely to want to prove the stereotype wrong, are more vulnerable to the toxic effects of stereotype threats, and can provide more concrete examples of instances of racial discrimination (Brown and Pinel, 2003; Inzlicht, McKay, and Aronson, 2006; Pinel, 1999).[5] In addition, researchers have found that these heightened states of sensitivity may cause African Americans to have less self-control, a factor that is unequivocally related to offending. Thus, our theory stipulates that an overemphasis on the mistrust of whites causes African American offending because it heightens their sensitivity to recognizing racial injustices, increases their likelihood of negatively reacting to racial injustices with anger-defiance-depression-hopelessness, enhances their likelihood of engaging in impulsive behaviors, and it weakens their ability to develop strong bonds with white-dominated institutions.

Third, our theory hypothesizes that African American parents may increase their children's probability of offending if they inadequately prepare them for their encounters with racial injustices. This aspect of racial socialization is referred to as "preparation for bias." We suggest that there are two aspects of preparation for bias that may lead to higher individual rates of offending. First, African American parents may stress inappropriate responses to racial injustices, such as defiance and aggression. Second, African American parents may not provide their children with effective coping skills, such as encouraging them to seek social supports (e.g., to talk with them or other positive role models), reporting racist acts to appropriate authorities, and affirmatively, but not angrily-aggressively, standing up to the perpetrators. In the absence of these effective resistant skills, we argue that African American youth will become more vulnerable to developing stigma sensitivity and stigma consciousness, which in turn predict higher rates of offending.

Fourth, our theory hypothesizes that certain racial socialization experiences should weaken the ability of African American youth to develop strong bonds with white-dominated institutions. More specifically, we hypothesize that African American youths will develop weak bonds with their schools or place of employment if their parents: (1) did not culturally socialize them, that is, instill within them a positive racial identity; (2) ill-prepared them for racially-biased encounters; (3) encouraged them to mistrust whites; and (4) underemphasized the teaching of egalitarian values. Note that our theory recognizes that other forms of parenting, such as authoritarianism, can exacerbate or attenuate the relationships among racial socialization practices, weak social bonds, and offending. Consequently, we hypothesize that the highest incidences of offending should occur among those African Americans who are poorly parented, have been ill-prepared by their parents to develop strong bonds with white-dominated institutions, and ill-prepared to fend off the noxious effects of racial injustices.

Our theory recognizes that racial socialization experiences will vary across the lifespan, vary across situations, be susceptible to period effects (e.g., the election of Barack Obama), may vary across generations, and can be individually altered by changes in patterns of interactions (e.g., having positive or negative interactions with whites) (Brown and Lesane-Brown, 2006; Lesane-Brown, 2006; Major and O'Brien, 2005; Nunnally, 2010).

Our Theoretical Model of African American Offending

Below, we present a heuristic model that explicates our theory of African American offending. What separates our theory from the more general explanations of crime is that we contend that African American offending emerges from their unique worldview—that is, their peerless racialized daily experience. This unique worldview is only shared by African Americans and arose because of their inimitable racial oppression. In short, our theory of African American offending is race-centered; that is, it locates the cause of offending in the lived experiences of blacks residing in a conflicted racially stratified society—the United States.

Figure 1 indicates that the unique worldview shared by African Americans is reciprocally related to three core concepts of our theory: perceptions of criminal justice injustices, perceptions of racial discrimination and the effects of being negatively stereotyped, and racial socialization practices. Note that these are reciprocal relationships (i.e., two-headed arrows). This means that these three concepts are salient components of the unique worldview shared by African Americans but, at the same time, their worldview is reinforced each time an African American experiences these racial injustices and is racially socialized. For example, our theory argues that the inimitable worldview shared by African Americans causes them to engage in the racial socialization of their children while, simultaneously, the racial socialization of African American youth further reinforces and sustains their unique worldview. This same process equally unfolds for the experiences that African Americans have with criminal justice injustices and different forms of racial discrimination. In the end, African Americans have a unique worldview that is reinforced when they encounter racial injustices and are embedded in social networks that reinforce the beliefs that emerge from their lived experiences with racial subordination.

Figure 1 highlights the importance that we assign to racial socialization experiences as we assert that it is the key factor that mediates the effects of criminal justice injustices, racial discrimination, and being noxiously stereotyped on whether African Americans express injurious negative emotions and develop weak bonds, which in turn directly impact offending. Thus, the model indicates that, as a result of experiencing racial injustices, inadequate racial socialization experiences will increase the likelihood that African Americans will express negative emotions and develop weak social bonds. Note that there are reciprocal

Figure 1 Our Theory of African American Offending.

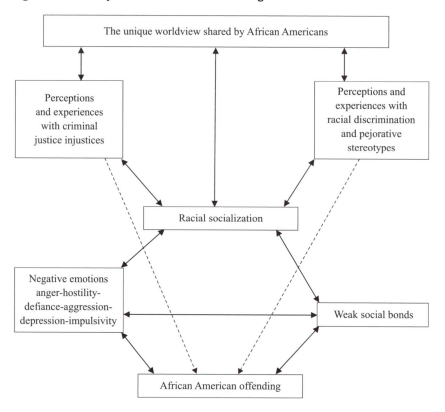

arrows between racial socialization and perceptions and experiences with both criminal justice injustices and racial discrimination-pejorative stereotypes. Our model stipulates that some African Americans are racially socialized to be more vigilant in perceiving both of these racial injustices and, therefore, are more likely to react to these injustices with negative emotions and will have less ability to develop strong bonds with institutions. Our model also allows for there to be "child-effects" (Keijsers, Branje, VanderValk, and Meeus, 2010; Zadeh, Jenkins, and Pepler, 2010). These transactional child-effects are represented by the reciprocal causal arrows between racial socialization and both negative emotions and weak social bonds. These reciprocal relationships model the likelihood that African American parents will alter their racial socialization practices based on whether their children are overly expressing negative emotions or are having trouble developing strong bonds with conventional institutions.

Figure 1 reveals that the African Americans who are the least likely to offend are those that peripherally perceive criminal justice injustices, racial discrimination, and being negatively stereotyped and experience positive racial socialization practices that provide them with the ability to cope with their encounters with racial injustices by engaging in prosocial behaviors (e.g., reporting the perpetrator of racist acts to the appropriate authorities). It further indicates that African Americans who are unlikely to offend are those whose parents inculcated them with the ability to develop strong bonds with white-dominated institutions, even if they personally perceive them to be racist.

Our model indicates that the African Americans who are most likely to offend are those that intensely perceive or experience criminal justice injustices, racial discrimination, and being derogatorily stereotyped, and experience racial socialization practices over time that increase their likelihood of developing weak bonds with institutions, such as with their schools and places of employment, and are socialized to react to racial injustices with negative emotions (i.e., anger-hostility-defiance-aggression-depression-impulsivity). Figure 1 additionally indicates that there is a reciprocal relationship between the negative emotions that flow from racial injustices and developing weak bonds with conventional institutions. Our model predicts that African Americans who manifest negative emotions—anger-defiance-depression—will be more likely to develop weak bonds and that blacks who are unable to bond to white-dominated institutions will be more likely to express anger-defiance-depression. Note that Figure 1 also has two broken line causal arrows. These indicate that it is possible for criminal justice injustices, racial discrimination, and being pejoratively stereotyped to directly impact offending. We argue that these direct relationships occur when these experiences are so intense that they overwhelm positive prosocial racial socialization experiences.

Finally, our model includes reciprocal arrows between African American offending and negative emotions and weak bonds. These arrows indicate that African Americans are more likely to offend if they express negative emotions and have weak social bonds. They also indicate that African Americans who offend are likely to have encounters with the criminal justice system that will cause their feelings of hostility-defiance-depression to intensify and to develop even weaker social bonds with conventional institutions as they become disenfranchised because of their arrest record (Alexander, 2010). Our theory posits that these more intense feelings and weaker social bonds increase the probability that African American offenders will have further encounters across their lifespan with the criminal justice system.

Gender and African American Offending

Our theory predicts that African American females should engage in less crime than black men but they should also have higher rates than comparable white females. We recognize that gender disparities in offending can be largely explained by differences in parenting, especially by the fact that parents more closely monitor the behavior of their daughters than their sons. We also recognize that there are gendered pathways to crime and gendered roles within crime (Johansson and Kempf-Leonard, 2009; Miller and Mullins, 2006; Salisbury and Van Voorhis, 2009). However, we stipulate that there are gender differences in experiences with criminal justice injustices, stereotype threats, racial discrimination, and racial socialization experiences that are related to gender differences among African Americans in offending.

Our explanation of gender differences in offending begins with the recognition that whites have persistently perpetuated gendered racist stereotypes that most pointedly negatively target African American men. That is, throughout the racist history of the United States, whites have constructed gendered stereotypes of African American males as "threatening" (Gabbidon, 2010; Russell-Brown, 2009; Sampson and Laub, 1993). For example, Feagin (2001:113) states that: "Another common white stereotype is that of the dangerous black man. This seems to be the staple of white thinking, including the thinking of white leaders and intellectuals speaking or writing about the black 'underclass.' A majority of whites seem to view the generic street criminal as a black man . . ." Feagin (2001:113) adds that this perception of black men runs deep in American culture as "during the first centuries of American development, whites constructed a view of enslaved black men as dangerous 'beasts,' a stereotyped view that has rationalized much discrimination over the centuries, including bloody lynchings." Research further indicates that "the criminalization of the black man"—the *criminalblackman*—permeates the criminal justice system resulting in racist practices that are reflected in the brutalization of African American men, such as Rodney King (Holmes and Smith, 2008).

Our theory argues that these pervasive toxic gendered stereotypes profoundly impact the probability that black males will offend at higher rates than African American females in a multitude of ways. We contend that the unparalleled pejorative stereotyping of black males underlies the likelihood that they are more likely than African American women to encounter criminal justice injustices and the many variegated forms of racial discrimination. Researchers report that African American boys are more likely to report experiences of racial discrimination (Hughes, Rodriguez, Smith, Johnson, Stevenson, and Spicer, 2006). Scholars report that these gender differences are most pronounced when African Americans were asked whether they were "accused or suspected of doing something wrong" or whether "people misunderstood your intentions and motives" (Fischer and Shaw, 1999:404). Seventy-one percent of African American males in comparison with 35 percent of females reported that they were unfairly accused of doing something wrong and 74 percent of males compared with 53 percent of females reported that their intentions and motives were unfairly understood.

In addition, our research (reported in Chapter 4) shows that across six domains (e.g., treated with less respect, people act as if they think you are not smart, act as if they think you are dishonest), African American men report higher perceptions of racial discrimination than black women. Indeed, our research shows that the greatest gender disparities are related to the toxic stereotyping of African American males as being "threatening," "menacing," and "criminal." African American males were three times more likely than females to perceive that people often act as if they are afraid of them and twice as likely as black females to report that people often act as if they are dishonest.

Most notably, our data reveal that black men are more likely to report than African American females that they are very worried about being unfairly treated by the police. This latter finding indicates that black men are more likely to experience the particularly debilitating consequences of experiencing criminal justice injustices.

Thus, our theory hypothesizes that gender differences in offending are related to gender disparities in the *degree* to which African American males and females encounter criminal justice injustices and racial injustices. More specifically, we assert that African American males are significantly more likely to encounter criminal justice injustices, racial discrimination, and prejorative stereotypes than black females and are, therefore, more likely to experience their deleterious effects (e.g., anger-defiance-depression), which in turn are related to offending.

We also contend that because racist stereotypes most stridently target African American males, black men are particularly susceptible to the injurious consequences of stereotype threats. We assert that these stereotype threats permeate the interactions that African American men have within their schools and the interactions black males have within their place of employment. Thus, we argue that it is especially difficult for African American men to build strong bonds with white-dominated institutions when they have to be continuously vigilant to avoid engaging in behaviors that might be interpreted as them being "insolent," "loud," or "violent." A black male at a historically white university expresses this frustration after being confronted by the police:

> And, we're saying at that same time, we're feeling restricted because if we act in a way that we want to react—number one, we're going to jail; number two, it's just going to feed into the stereotype that they think we're supposed to be violent or whatever (quoted in Smith et al., 2007:566).

Together, these findings indicate that black men are acutely sensitized to the prevailing acerbic stereotype of them being the *criminal-blackman* (Gibbs, 1988; Kunjufu, 2004). Importantly, the research shows that African Americans become fully consciously aware of the stereotypes that poisonously depict them by the time they are 10 years old. Thus, we argue that African Americans, particularly black men, have to contend with the debilitating consequences of being pejoratively stereotyped across their lifespan.

Our theory argues that the awareness that black men have of being chronically considered a "criminal" is emotionally depleting; it exhausts their emotional capital. Consequently, we stipulate that African American men are more likely than black women to experience oscillating feelings of anger-defiance-rage and depression (Noble, 2006; Smith et al., 2007).[6,7] We further hypothesize that African American men with depleted emotional capital are more likely to engage in impulsive-related offending. In addition, our theory hypothesizes that the acute labeling of African American men as "criminal" increases their likelihood, more so than black women, of escalating into secondary deviance as they internalize and act out the label of being the *criminalblackman*.

Our theory stipulates that there are also gender differences in racial socialization practices that increase the likelihood that African American males will offend. Our theory asserts that there are four gendered variations in racial socialization experiences that contribute to male-female differences in offending (Brown, Linver, and Evans, 2010; Fischer and Shaw, 1999; Hughes et al., 2006; Hughes, Hagelskamp, Way, and Foust, 2009; McHale, Crouter, Kim, Burton, Davis, Dotterer, and Swanson, 2006; Thomas and Speight, 1999). First, we hypothesize that females are less likely to offend because African American parents are more likely to socialize their daughters with a greater sense of racial pride than their sons. The research shows that a strong positive racial identity decreases the likelihood of offending and enhances academic commitment and performance. Second, we stipulate that African American women are likely to be inculcated with positive racial socialization experiences because they attend church services more often than black males. Research indicates that the black church assertively promotes the positive racial socialization of their parishioners by, for example, encouraging a greater sense of racial pride and providing them with the support to actively resist their racial subordination. Third, we contend that African

American parents are more likely to emphasize egalitarian values with their daughters, especially encouraging them to build stronger bonds with their schools through hard work. Fourth, we posit that African American parents are significantly less likely to positively prepare their sons than their daughters for encounters with racial discrimination.

Our theory contends that these gendered differences in racial socialization experiences result in gender disparities in how African American males and females respond to their encounters with racial injustices. Research indicates that a proactive confrontation with racial discrimination is to use the anger that flows from being insulted—dissed—to resist the racist actions of the perpetrator. Thus, African Americans who are positively racially socialized assertively resist their racial subordination by confronting their abusers. This assertive, but not angry-aggressive, resistance clearly informs the racist perpetrators that their behaviors are unacceptable and intolerable. Our theory asserts that African American men are less likely to proactively and prosocially respond to racial injustices than black women.

We hypothesize that two factors mitigate African American men taking a more positive proactive resistance to their gendered enhanced racial subordination: the gendered disparities in their early racial socialization experiences and the constraints of being negatively gender stereotyped as being prone to anger, "insolence," and violence. We argue that these two factors exponentially increase the likelihood that African American men adopt an avoidance-coping style when confronted by a racial injustice. This coping style has deleterious and debilitating consequences. It substantially increases the likelihood that African American men will internalize their anger and deleteriously ruminate about it or episodically externalize it in acts of offending (Noble, 2006). On the other hand, the research shows that black women are more likely to seek social supports when confronted with racial injustices. This coping style allows black women to dissipate the anger caused by their racial subordination.

We further hypothesize that African American men who internalize their anger are more likely to self-medicate their feelings (including depression) through substance abuse-drug addiction. This consequence has especially debilitating consequences. It causes African American men to become immersed in the drug-street culture as they are forced every day to procure illegal drugs to maintain their addictions. Thus, we stipulate that African American men are more likely to offend than black women because they self-medicate (i.e., by using illegal substances) the anger and depression that results from their disproportionate exposure to the humiliating experiences associated with their racial subordination. In short, our theory asserts that male-female differences in African American offending are related to gender differences in experiences with criminal justice injustices, racial discrimination, being pejoratively stereotyped, and racial socialization practices.

Place Matters

Our theory explains African American offending regardless of their place of residence. However, we recognize that African Americans who reside in racially hypersegregated urban isolated "ghettos" will have a higher probability of engaging in violent crimes than, for example, blacks living in relatively more affluent neighborhoods. The data indicate that a plurality of African Americans—over 40 percent—reside in metropolitan areas and that violent crime is disproportionately an urban phenomenon (Charles, 2003). This means that our theory must explain why the happenstance of where an African American was born—that is, the neighborhood in which they reside—will increase their individual probability of offending. Thus our theory recognizes that structural disadvantage fosters violence as a general rule but we concur with scholars who argue that the exact nature of the impact of structural disadvantage on offending will "depend on the history, organization, and culture of particular groups" (Steffensmeier, Ulmer, Feldmeyer, and Harris, 2010:1161).

We begin our explanation for why African Americans are more likely to offend if they live in a disadvantaged segregated neighborhood with the stipulation that racist whites purposefully constructed "ghettos" as a means of subordinating, isolating, and containing African Americans (Bass, 2001). That is, contemporary "ghettos" are not accidents or were not solely created because of the structural transformation of the inner-city economy, such as jobs being shipped overseas or the decline of the manufacturing sector. We further assert that African Americans did not exercise their free-will and purposefully choose to create or live in segregated resource-depleted neighborhoods. In fact, the data show that African Americans overwhelmingly prefer mixed neighborhoods; that is, areas that have the same percentage of white and black residents—a density that is far too high for most whites. That is, whites prefer neighborhoods where no more than 30 percent of the population is black (Quillian and Pager, 2001). Thus, African Americans do not live in segregated neighborhoods because they may only want to live with other blacks or a neutral ethnocentrism but by fears of white hostility.

Notably, the data show that even relatively affluent African Americans live in less advantaged neighborhoods in comparison to their white counterparts. Scholars report that after controlling for socioeconomic status and wealth, black Americans live in neighborhoods that are less affluent and more segregated than those occupied by whites of similar status (Sharkey, 2008). Studies further indicate that whites *and* Latinos are likely to move if they live in neighborhoods where African Americans have a growing presence, further isolating blacks in the worst places (Sampson and Sharkey, 2008). In addition, research finds that more than 70 percent of African American children who are raised in the poorest quarter of American neighborhoods will continue to live in the poorest quarter of neighborhoods as adults and that since "the 1970s, more than half of black families have lived in the poorest quarter of neighborhoods *in consecutive generations*, compared to just 7% of white families" (Sharkey, 2008:933, emphasis in original). These findings indicate that it is nearly impossible to examine whether place matters more for African American than white offending because cross-generation "white ghettos" simply do not exist (Peterson and Krivo, 2010).

The data further show that almost all blacks are willing to move into largely white areas if there is a visible black presence. However, white preferences play a key role in racial segregation because whites are reluctant to move into neighborhoods with more than a few African Americans (Krysan and Farley, 2002; Sampson and Sharkey, 2008). In fact, scholars conclude that "negative racial stereotypes and perceptions of group threat from blacks are the strongest predictors of whites' resistance to integration" (Charles, 2003:185). Indeed, the data on racial attitudes reveals that there is a distinct ranking among Americans for which minority they would most desire to have as a neighbor, with Asians ranked as the most, African-Americans as the least desirable, and Hispanics falling in the middle (Crowder and Downey, 2010).

Therefore, we stipulate that centralized racist policies (i.e., racial covenants, racial zoning, violence or threats of violence, preemptive purchases, harassments, or collusion by realtors, banks, and mortgage lenders) and decentralized racist policies (i.e., racist whites pay more to live in white communities) created and maintain racially segregated neighborhoods (Glaeser, Hanushek, and Quigley, 2004; Robinson, 1981). In other words, hypersegregation "is best understood as emanating from structural forces tied to racial prejudice and discrimination that preserve the relative status advantages of whites" (Charles, 2003:182). Put more plainly, "ghettos" were purposefully constructed by racist whites for the containment of African Americans (Sharkey, 2008; Wacquant, 2001).

Thus, the basic premise of our theory is that the same racist forces that created and sustain American "ghettos" are the reasons why they have little collective efficacy; that is, less formal and informal controls. We assert that the macro-micro forces that sustain "ghettos"—that is, racist stereotypes and racial discrimination—have caused African Americans to reside in places where they will more likely encounter pejorative stereotypes, racial discrimination, and criminal justice injustices (Massey, 1990; Massey and Denton, 1993; Robinson, 1981). Indeed, Holmes and Smith (2008) report that the police disproportionately use excessive force against African Americans and that the police are more likely to use coercive force against black suspects in segregated African American neighborhoods. They conclude that "police brutality is a grim symptom of intractable intergroup dynamics" involving African Americans and the police who patrol their neighborhoods (Holmes and Smith, 2008:5).

In addition, studies suggest that urban hypersegregation combined with perceived racial injustices is so combustible that it fuels massive outbreaks of African American defiance. Olzak, Shanahan, and McEneaney (1996) found that urban hypersegregation is systematically related to large-scale urban disorders by African Americans even after controlling for population size, poverty levels, unemployment, and proportions of minorities. Therefore, we concur with Massey and Denton's (1993:8) conclusion that: "residential segregation is the institutional apparatus that supports other racially discriminatory processes and binds them together into a coherent and uniquely effective system of racial subordination."[8]

Our theory recognizes that place matters but we also emphasize that it is not deterministic. Certainly, imposed environments enhance the likelihood that African Americans choose to offend. However, as we have noted, only a minority of African Americans living in "ghettos" engage in crime. Indeed, Sharkey (2006) found analyzing the Project on Human Development in Chicago Neighborhoods, which is a longitudinal study of children and families living in a diverse set of Chicago neighborhoods, that only 6 percent of the African American adolescents' street efficacy—that is, their perceived ability to avoid violent confrontations and to feel safe in their neighborhood—is explained by neighborhood characteristics (e.g., concentrated disadvantage, collective efficacy, and neighborhood violence). This relatively small percentage clearly reveals that "agency matters in any context"; that is, people still choose to engage in crime wherever they live (Sharkey, 2006:828).

However, we assert that place matters because it directly and indirectly is related to choosing to offend. We hypothesize that in severely disadvantaged neighborhoods place directly matters because it disproportionately exposes African Americans to racial discrimination, stereotypes that "put them down," and, most profoundly, criminal justice injustices. Our theory stipulates that each of these racial injustices increases the likelihood that African Americans will offend.

We also hypothesize that place can indirectly increase the probability of African American offending by altering racial socialization practices. Our theory hypothesizes that there are four reasons why places of extreme poverty and hypersegregation impair the ability of parents to effectively racially socialize their children. First, we argue in areas of concentrated disadvantages—especially in isolated racially segregated places—African American parents may implicitly or explicitly racially socialize their children to be overly mistrustful of whites, minimize their children's cultural socialization, or inadequately prepare them for overcoming the challenges of experiencing racial injustices. We further posit that in the areas of concentrated disadvantage, African American parents' experiences with racial injustices will cause them to either underemphasize or to skeptically teach their children egalitarian values, including the beliefs that all people are basically and fundamentally the same and that the United States is truly a "color blind" society. Consequently, we hypothesize that in areas of concentrated disadvantage—particularly in isolated racially segregated areas—it is more likely that African Americans will overemphasize the mistrust of whites, ineffectively prepare their children for their encounters with racial bias, underemphasize the development of a prosocial racial identity, and underemphasize teaching their children egalitarian values such as that the United States is truly a "color blind" society.

Second, we posit that economically disadvantaged neighborhoods decrease the likelihood that African Americans will racially socialize their children. The research shows that urban poor areas disproportionately have higher rates of female-headed households and single parents are less likely to racially socialize their children. Thus, we hypothesize that in areas of intense poverty and racial segregation, a greater number of youths will be racially socialized in the streets. Third, studies show that these areas are disproportionately populated with African Americans with less years of education. Thus, our theory posits that areas of concentrated disadvantage will have more African American youth who will either not be racially socialized or less competently socialized because their parents are less educated.

Fourth, we stipulate that severely segregated poor neighborhoods disproportionately expose African American parents to the stressors associated with poverty (e.g., higher rates of victimization) and the toxic effects associated with criminal justice injustices, racial discrimination, and being pejoratively stereotyped. We contend that the experience of these racial injustices coupled with stressors related to poverty deplete the emotional resources of African American parents. Therefore, African American youths will be more likely raised in households where their parents-guardians are themselves experiencing the invidious consequences of poverty, racial discrimination, criminal justice injustices, and being negatively stereotyped. Thus, we hypothesize that African American youths who offend are more likely to be racially socialized by parents who have been rendered emotionally unstable—parents whose feelings oscillate between anger, irritability, and depression—because of their own confrontations with concentrated racial injustices.[9]

In addition, we hypothesize that African American offending should be related to the degree to which neighborhoods are racially segregated even after taking into account the extent to which it is economically disadvantaged. Research shows that a chief factor related to the degree to which African American parents emphasize the mistrust of whites is whether they associate with whites (Shelton, 2008). Racial segregation, therefore, decreases the likelihood that African American children will view their parents positively interacting with whites. Thus, it is less likely that African American youths will be positively socialized toward whites through direct modeling, reinforcement, and imitation of behaviors if they live in racially segregated areas.

More specifically, we assert that African American parents are most likely to ineffectively racially socialize their children in areas of *isolated* and *centralized concentrations* of racial segregation—that is, in the most severely racially segregated urban areas (see Massey, 1990; Massey and Denton, 1993; Xie, 2010). In these areas, we hypothesize that African American youth will be more likely to be racially socialized to have a heightened vigilant distrust of whites and white-dominated institutions. These heightened states should cause African Americans to develop weaker ties with white-dominated institutions and they should cause blacks to more readily react to racial injustices with anger-defiance-depression, which in turn should increase their offending.[10]

Lastly, we contend that segregated social exclusion coupled with poverty has an additional deleterious consequence for African Americans. Research shows that social exclusion heightens the desire to affiliate with others and that people who feel rejected seek new ways to satisfy their need to belong. It also reveals socially excluded individuals' attempt to assuage their feelings of exclusion by engaging in conspicuous risky consumption even if it subverts their personal tastes and desires. Mead, Baumeister, Stillman, Rawn, and Vohs (2011:915) conclude that "rejected and socially excluded persons may desire money in part so they can spend it on future occasions to enhance their interpersonal appeal." Thus, we hypothesize that the emphasis on conspicuous consumption found among some poor African American offenders, especially young blacks residing in segregated neighborhoods, arises from their greater exposure to more intense racial injustices (which in turn, produce feelings of social exclusion) and their desire to affiliate as equals with others (Lamont and Molnár, 2001).

Ethnic Differences in African American Offending

Ethnicity and Immigration Status

Our theory acknowledges that differences among blacks based on their ethnicity and immigration status should influence their rates of offending. For example, Biafora, Taylor, Warheit, Zimmerman, and Vega (1993) found that Haitians had higher levels of mistrust of whites than native-born African Americans and those with a Caribbean island background had the lowest levels of mistrust. In addition, Ruck and Wortley (2002) found that the longer black students (and other minorities) had lived in Canada, the more likely they were to perceive bias toward members of their racial/ethnic group.

Deaux, Bikmen, Gilkes, Ventuneac, Joseph, Payne, and Steele (2007) report that the performance under conditions of stereotype threat among second generation West Indian immigrants (Caribbean countries originally colonized by the British) were similar to those reported by native-born African Americans, whereas the first generation's performance increased. These scholars also found that the strength of racial identity diminishes across generations. That is, second-generation West Indian immigrants were significantly less likely to identify as West Indian. Gates and Steele (2009) add that the impact of stereotype threats on performance is minimal on first generation black immigrant children. "You get very little stereotype threats effects among the first generation immigrants, but you get them in second generation immigrants" as they become "Americanized" (Gates and Steele, 2009).

Thus, we hypothesize that less offending should occur among first generation foreign-born blacks who have immigrated to the United States. That is, we posit that blacks born outside the U.S., such as in Jamaica or Africa, who have immigrated to the U.S., will have lower rates of offending than indigenous African Americans. We argue that these differences, which should be significant, occur because first generation African Americans do not fully embrace the worldview that nearly all U.S.-born African Americans share. That is, "the lived experiences of being black in America and of being black American are distinct" (Broman, Torres, Canady, Neighbors, and Jackson, 2010:89).

Therefore, we assert that the degree to which different ethnic groups (e.g., Jamaicans, Ethiopians) embrace the worldview shared by native-born African Americans has profound consequences. Indeed, Hughes et al. (2006:757) report that "immigrant West Indian, Caribbean, and Dominican parents express strong convictions that their children should distinguish themselves from native-born African Americans because of African Americans' low social status. These convictions are typically accompanied by cautions and warnings to children about African Americans' undesirable characteristics [Pessar, 1995; Waters, 1994, 1999]. This type of promotion of mistrust—aimed at protecting children from affiliations with groups who are negatively stereotyped—may be substantively different from cautions about closeness to Whites, which have been described among African Americans."[11]

Together, these findings indicate that first generation non-native blacks resist embracing the worldview that recognizes the racial injustices African Americans encounter in their daily lives. We hypothesize that this resistance alters the way in which these first generation parents racially socialize their children. Our theory stipulates that first generation parents are more likely to emphasize egalitarian values rather than emphasizing other dimensions of racial socialization, such as the mistrust of whites and the preparation of bias. However, we posit that this imbalance of egalitarian values at the expense of preparing their children for living in a society with conflicted race relations can place their children at risk for offending. That is, the second generation will be ill prepared to fend off the debilitating consequences when they confront criminal justice injustices, racial discrimination, and being derogatorily stereotyped because they are black. Accordingly, we hypothesize that second generation blacks will approach the same level of offending as native-born African Americans, everything else being equal. In short, our theory assumes that there should be ethnic-immigrant variations in African American offending.

Colorism

We further recognize that skin tone or color—colorism—may accent differences in offending among African Americans (Harrell, 2000). Burton, Bonilla-Silva, Ray, Buckelew, and Freeman (2010) argue that there is strong evidence indicating that colorism—racialized and color-conscious hierarchies—affects both psychological and socioeconomic outcomes, with darker-skinned African Americans being more likely to grow up in poverty, more likely to abuse drugs and alcohol, and less likely to marry. More specifically, scholars report that darker-skinned African Americans are more likely to have less than a high school diploma (9.9 percent) and have lower income (18.4 percent) than their lighter-skinned counterparts (4.4 percent and 13.8 percent, respectively), regardless of their gender (Borrell, Kiefe, Williams, Diez-Roux, and Gordon-Larsen, 2006).

Burton et al. (2010) additionally argue that racial socialization processes may vary according to children's skin tone, just as they do for birth order, gender, and other individual traits. In addition, research indicates that the harshness of white stereotyping of African Americans is conditioned by their skin tone. Clark (2004:509) reports that more positive traits were used to characterize lighter-skinned blacks compared to negative traits. For instance, relative to darker-skinned black males, lighter-skinned black men were described as being less criminal, more intelligent, less poor, less aggressive, and wealthier. Compared with darker-skinned females, lighter-skinned women were characterized as being more intelligent, less lazy, more motivated, less poor, more self-assured, and less unattractive.

In addition, Clark (2004) found that African Americans contribute approximately 15 percent of problematic life experiences to *intragroup* racism. Consequently, we hypothesize that lighter-skin African Americans are less likely to encounter the same intensity of racial subordination—criminal justice injustices, racial discrimination, and the deleterious consequences of being negatively stereotyped—as those with darker skin. In addition, we suggest that darker-skinned African Americans are more likely to encounter both intergroup and intragroup racism. Therefore, we stipulate that these cumulative disadvantages should produce higher levels of offending among darker-skinned African Americans, especially if they are not proactively and positively racially socialized.

Conclusion

Our theory recognizes that African Americans, just like other races (e.g., whites) or ethnicities (e.g., Hispanics), are more likely to offend if they experience other stressors, such as divorce and victimization (i.e., general strain theory), associate with delinquent peers (i.e., differential association), have weak social bonds (i.e., control theory), are impulsive (i.e., Gottfredson and Hirschi's general theory), and live in economically disadvantaged neighborhoods with little collective efficacy (i.e., theories of social disorganization). Indeed, we have integrated many of these insights into our own theory. However, we argue that the causal relationship between each of these general theory concepts and African American offending only can be fully understood if they are situated within the racial dynamics of a conflicted racially stratified society.

Our theory of African American offending centers its analysis on the lived experiences of African Americans in a conflicted racially stratified society. We argue that African Americans have a unique worldview that has been and continues to be shaped by experiences with criminal justice injustices, racial discrimination, and pejorative stereotypes. Our theory contends that these experiences have deleterious consequences that are related to offending. They cause African Americans to experience negative emotions that are related to offending, including anger, hostility, aggression, defiance, and depression. Together, these debilitating feelings exhaust their emotional capital, leaving them vulnerable to engaging in impulsive behaviors, which is a chief factor related to offending. Experiencing racial injustices also causes African Americans to offend because they undermine their capacity to build strong bonds with conventional white-dominated institutions. That is, African Americans are confronted with the paradoxical task of building strong bonds with "conventional" white-dominated institutions that many of them perceive to be racist, such as the criminal justice system.

Our theory additionally stipulates that African American parents can attenuate the deleterious consequences of racial injustices. Indeed, the research shows the brilliance of African American parents as some reframe these injustices as challenges that their children must overcome. This resiliency is reflected in the fact that only a minority of African Americans offend, even those residing in areas purposefully constructed to racially subordinate blacks, that is, urban ghettos. Thus, the data indicate that the vast majority of African Americans rise to the challenge. The rage that flows from their racial subordination is transformed into a healthy resistance (Noble, 2006). It provides them with the energy—the agency—that they have channeled into dismantling many of the institutionalized forms of their repression, such as the legacies of Jim Crow.

Our theory further recognizes that the U.S. remains a conflicted racially stratified society. Consequently, African Americans are confronted with the reality that they will encounter criminal justice injustices, racial discrimination, and the consequences of being injuriously stereotyped. These debilitating racial injustices place inimitable burdens on the black family. African American parents are confronted with having to deal with their own anger-defiance-rage-depression as they are assaulted by these injustices while simultaneously preparing their children so that they not falter from their own awareness of how their race and racism will negatively impact their lives. Put more simply, it is emotionally exhausting to continually have to fend off the deleterious consequences of racial injustices.

Consequently, a minority of African American parents fail to fully provide their children with the skills that they need to fend off their own encounters with racial stices. Therefore, the cumulative consequences of these experiences place African American youth—especially African American males—at risk of offending. Those who offend do so because they do not have the emotional capital to successfully negotiate their encounters with racial injustices. As a result, their offending will be fueled by their overwhelming emotions of anger-depression and their inability to bond with the institutions that have discriminated against them because they are black. In the end, our theory posits that the American dilemma of race and racism that Du Bois pointed out over 100 years ago will not be resolved—especially as they are related to black offending—until African Americans can live their daily lives free from the experience and perception of being racially subjugated.

Epilogue: Environmental Racism and African American Offending

Introduction

The research conducted by environmental sociologists, physicians, public health researchers, psychologists and others unequivocally shows that environmental toxins have poisonous effects on a person's physical and mental health. This expansive literature also reveals the profound and nuanced ways that exposure to environmental toxins is related to criminal behavior. In this Epilogue, we argue that environmental racism—the disproportionate exposure of African Americans to environmental toxins—is another aspect of their daily lived experiences that contributes to their probability of offending. Chavis (1993:3) defines environmental racism as:

> Environmental racism is racial discrimination in environmental policymaking. It is racial discrimination in the enforcement of regulations and laws. It is racial discrimination in the deliberate targeting of communities of color for toxic waste disposal and the siting of polluting industries. It is racial discrimination in the official sanctioning of the life-threatening presence of poisons and pollutants in communities of color. And, it is racial discrimination in the history of excluding people of color from the mainstream

environmental groups, decision-making boards, commissions, and regulatory bodies.

We hypothesize that environmental racism is related to African American offending in four ways. First, we consider environmental racism as another form of racial discrimination. Consequently, we stipulate that known environmental racist practices should trigger the same processes that we have previously outlined that increase the probability of African American offending. Second, we assert that disproportionate exposure to environmental toxins can impair the cognitive development abilities of African Americans. We hypothesize that African Americans with impaired cognitive functioning will be less effective in fending off the deleterious consequences of their racial subordination. Third, we contend that these cognitive deficits impede the ability of African American parents to efficaciously racially socialize their children, again, causing them to be more vulnerable to the noxious consequences of criminal justice injustices, racial discrimination, and being pejoratively stereotyped. Fourth, we hypothesize that African Americans who are disproportionately exposed to environmental toxins will be less likely to bond, because of the cognitive impairments and lack of effective racial socialization, to white-dominated institutions, such as their schools.

Environmental Racism

Rachel Carson's *Silent Spring* (1962) has been credited with instigating the modern environmental movement in America. In fact, scholars argue that there have been two powerful mass movements within the U.S. since the 1960s: the civil rights movement (including extending the rights of women) and the environmental justice movement. Indeed, the years from 1970 to 1980—on the heels of Carson's powerful book— have been identified as the "environmental decade." This environmental justice mass movement is responsible for producing sweeping landmark legislation such as the Clean Air Act of 1970 (Zilney, McGurrin, and Zahran, 2006). It also caused researchers to acknowledge the fact that environmental hazards are unevenly located near or even in poor minority communities. Robert Bullard (1983) was one of the first researchers to recognize this disconcerting reality. Bullard studied waste disposal in Houston and found that most of the municipal landfills and garbage incinerators were located in African American communities (see also GAO, 1983). Bullard's research was among the earliest studies to identify what is now uniformly referred to as "environmental racism."

The United Church of Christ's (UCC) landmark 1987 report, *Toxic Wastes and Race in the United States*, provided further evidence of the reality of environmental racism. The report found that race was "the most potent variable in predicting where commercial hazardous waste facilities were located in the U.S., more powerful than household income, the value of homes and the estimated amount of waste generated by industry" (Bullard, Mohai, Saha, and Wright, 2007:x). Additional evidence mounted showing a clear connection between environmental hazards and their disproportionate siting in close proximity to minority communities (Adeola, 1994; Bullard, 1990, 1993; Bryant and Mohai, 1992; Cutter, 1995; Downey, 1998; Maher, 1998; Mitchell, 1993; Szaz and Meuser, 1997; Stretesky and Hogan, 1998). As a result of accumulating evidence, the United Church of Christ produced a 20-year follow-up to their seminal study and concluded that:

> Twenty years after the release of *Toxic Wastes and Race*, significant racial and socioeconomic disparities persist in the distribution of the nation's commercial hazardous waste facilities. Although the current assessment uses newer methods that better match where people and hazardous waste facilities are located, the conclusions are very much the same as they were in 1987. In fact, people of color are found to be more concentrated around hazardous waste facilities than previously shown (Bullard et al., 2007:170).

Downey and Van Willigen (2005:290) conclude that "people of color communities are disproportionately exposed to environmental pollutants, are angry about their disproportionate exposure, and want the burden of exposure to be distributed more equitably throughout society."

This anger is evidenced by the fact that between 1992 and 2000, the number of environmental justice organizations listed in the People of Color Environmental Groups Directory increased from 200 to over 400 (Downey and Van Willigen, 2005).

The Empirical Research on Environmental Racism

Race and Proximity to Environmental Toxins

The empirical research on environmental racism details the nuanced and complex ways in which African Americans are being unequally exposed to environmental toxins. For example, Pastor, Sadd, and Hipp (2001) investigated whether storage and disposal facilities (TSDFs) are located within racial/ethnic minority communities or whether minorities *move into* areas where environmental hazards already exist. Using data from Los Angeles County, their research found that minorities are more likely to be overly exposed to these facilities because they are *built* in their communities. Pastor et al. (2001:19) conclude that: "Demographics reflecting political weakness—including a higher presence of minorities, a lower presence of home owners, or a significant degree of ethnic churning [the replacing of one racial/ethnic group by another]—seems to be attractors of TSDFs."

Crowder and Downey (2010:1118) examined whether "blacks will be less likely [than whites] to leave and more likely to enter polluted areas, thereby increasing their overall proximity and exposure to environmental hazards." These scholars found that African Americans are more likely to reside in areas with industrial pollution than other racial and ethnic (e.g., Hispanics) groups even after controlling for individual income and educational level. Their results also revealed that blacks were less likely to move out of highly polluted areas and they tended to relocate "to destinations with higher levels of proximate industrial pollution than those experienced by mobile white households" (Crowder and Downey, 2010:1144). They concluded that discriminatory real estate practices restrict where minority groups reside and that these racist practices have a particularly pronounced effect on black households (more so than Hispanics)—a finding that also holds true for high-income blacks.

In sum, the literature consistently indicates that race is a powerful predictor of where hazardous waste facilities and environmental hazards are located. That is,

> the poor and especially the non-white poor bear a disproportionate burden of exposure to suboptimal, unhealthy environmental conditions in the United States. Moreover, the more researchers scrutinize environmental exposure and health data for racial and income inequalities, the stronger the evidence becomes that grave and widespread environmental injustices have occurred throughout the United States (Evans and Kantrowitz, 2002:323).

We conclude that environmental racism is part of the everyday experience that an unjust proportion of African Americans encounter in their daily lived experiences.

The Health Effects of Environmental Racism

Scholars stipulate that the presence of negative environmental characteristics (such as industrial pollution, hazardous waste, and noise) and the absence of positive environmental characteristics (such as parks, trees, and open spaces) are detrimental to a person's physical and mental health. For instance, the research shows that exposure to environmental toxins such as polychlorinated biphenyl (or PCBs) is related to cancer (Environmental Protection Agency, 2010a) while exposure to other chemicals, such as lead, predicts cognitive impairment (Environmental Protection Agency, 2010b). Other researchers have found that residential proximity to industrial activity had a negative impact on mental health (e.g., depression and powerlessness) (Downey and Van Willigen, 2005). Notably, these scholars report that the relationship between poor mental health and exposure is greater for minorities (i.e., African Americans and Hispanics) and the poor than it is for whites and wealthier individuals.

Below we highlight the effect of lead on the African American community and whether it is related to their offending because it is a toxin that has been extensively studied. In fact, it is probably the most studied environmental toxicant for which developmental effects are the main concern (Rice, 1998). However, we contend that the research on lead as a cause of crime among African Americans is just the "tip of the iceberg." That is, we disconcertingly assert that the findings related to lead will be replicated for a wide array of other toxins, most of which have not, as of yet, been studied. For example, research shows that African Americans suffer much higher body-pesticide burdens (Evans and Kantrowitz, 2002).

The Deleterious Consequences of Exposure to Lead

Individuals are exposed to lead in numerous ways, including leaded gasoline, lead-contaminated soil, paint, lead solder from plumbing, and lead-soldered cans (Sanborn, Abelsohn, Campbell, and Weir, 2002). Some products including plastic window blinds, candle wicks, costume jewelry, children's toys, and some knapsacks also have been found to have high levels of lead. In addition, scholars have found "lead in deteriorating household paint, lead at the workplace, lead used in hobbies, lead in some 'folk' medicines and cosmetics, and lead in crystal or ceramic containers that leaches into food and water" (Pirkle, Kaufman, Brody, Hickman, Gunter, and Paschal, 1998:745). Moreover, lead can be found in water and communities near smeltering plants or other industries that emit lead into the air (Environmental Protection Agency, 2010b).

Lead exposure is related to a host of injurious consequences, especially to children. More specifically, heavy lead exposure has been linked to damage to the brain and nervous system, encephalopathy, impaired semen parameters, delay in the onset of puberty, essential hypertension, behavior and learning problems such as attention-deficit disorder (ADD), slowed growth, hearing problems, and headaches (El-Zohairy, Youssef, Abul-Nasr, Fahmy, Salem, Kahil, and Madkour, 1996; Environmental Protection Agency, 2010b; Gonick and Behari, 2002; Naicker, Norris, Mathee, Becker, and Richter, 2010; Needleman, 2008; Nigg, Knott-nerusn, Martel, Nikolas, Cavanagh, Karmaus, and Rappley, 2008; Tuthill, 1996). Recent research has also challenged conventional standards set by the CDC in 1991 for the threshold for dangerous blood lead levels. Previously, the acceptable blood lead level standard was set at 10 μg/dL[1] but studies are now finding that much lower lead levels are harmful (Bellinger, 2008; Jusko, Henderson, Lanphear, Cory-Slechta, Parsons, and Canfield, 2008); as a result, some scholars have recommended that the standard be reduced to 2 µg/dL because more children are likely being affected by lead poisoning than is currently known (Gilbert and Weiss, 2006; Lanphear, Hornung, Khoury, Yolton, Baghurst, Bellinger, et al., 2005).

Research has consistently revealed racial disparities in the exposure to lead poisoning.[2] Data from the 1970s revealed that 9.1 percent of preschool children had elevated blood lead levels in comparison with nearly 25 percent of black children (Mott, 1995). Evans and Kantrowitz (2002:305) report that: "68% of urban black children in families with incomes below $6000 had blood lead levels that exceeded safe limits in comparison to 15% of the same population with incomes above $15,000. For white children, the comparable data were 36% and 12%." Sanborn et al. (2002:1288) report that: "Black children living in older housing, children living in metropolitan areas with populations of 1 million or more and poor children living in older housing were at the highest risk of exposure."

Because of aggressive government efforts to reduce lead exposure, there have been marked reductions in elevated lead levels among children from the 1970s to the present. Despite these dramatic reductions, in 2005 the CDC reported that 3.1 percent of African Americans between the ages of 1 and 5 had lead poisoning—a figure that was "higher than for the whole population of children in that age group" (AFHH, 2005:1). Notably, the research also reports that African American children are less likely than whites to be screened for lead poisoning (Narag, Pizarro, and Gibbs, 2009). Together, these studies clearly indicate that African Americans have a higher risk of being affected by the toxic consequences of lead exposure.

Lead Exposure and Cognitive Impairment

One of the most well-established consequences of exposure to lead is cognitive impairment (Byers and Lord, 1943; Lanphear et al., 2005). Braun, Kahn, Froehlich, Auinger, and Lanphear (2006) used data from the National Health and Nutrition Examination Survey to determine if there was a relationship between prenatal environmental tobacco smoke, environmental lead exposure, and ADHD. The results revealed that lead exposure and prenatal tobacco smoke exposure were significant predictors of ADHD. Using a sample of 500 black youth from Detroit, Chiodo, Covington, Sokol, Hannigan, Jannise, et al. (2007) examined, with a series of tests, the relationship between lead level exposure and intelligence (several domains), reaction time, inattentive behavior, and hyperactivity. The researchers found that "mean blood lead levels were related to poorer IQ scores, slower reaction times and inattentive behavior. In addition, increased hyperactivity, poorer central processing, and increased social and delinquent behavior problems were identified in relation to higher blood lead levels" (Chiodo et al., 2007:544). In short, researchers consistently find that children that experience short- or long-term exposure to lead "tend to have irreversible effects on the central nervous system" (Chandramouli, Steer, Ellis, and Emond, 2009:844).

Lead Exposure and Education

Given that lead exposure causes cognitive impairments, it is not surprising that it has been found to be negatively related to educational achievements. Bellinger, Stiles, and Needleman (1992) report, in a prospective study, that low levels of lead exposure at age of 24 months were associated with intellectual and academic performance deficits at age 10. Fergusson, Horwood, and Lynskey (1997) investigated the relationship between dentine lead levels measured at the age of 6–8 and educational outcomes measured at 18 in a birth cohort of 1,265 New Zealand children. They found at age 18 children with early elevated lead levels had poorer reading abilities, had more often left school without qualifications, and had lower levels of success in school examinations after controlling for a range of social and familial confounding factors. Lanphear, Dietrich, Auinger, and Cox (2000) found that low levels of exposure to lead were related to decreases in arithmetic, reading, nonverbal reasoning, and short-term memory scores after controlling for gender, race/ethnicity, poverty, region of the country, parent or caregiver's educational level, parent or caregiver's marital status, serum ferritin level, and serum cotinine level.

Min, Singer, Kirchner, Minnes, Short, et al. (2009) examined a sample of 283 inner-city (238 of them were black) children to determine the impact of early and low-level lead exposure on IQ and academic achievement at ages 4, 9, and 11. Their findings revealed a significant and consistent association between lead exposure and cognitive functioning in all three age groups. More specifically, the researchers found that "lower reading score was consistently associated with higher lead levels at 9 and 11 years, while math scores were not affected until 11 years of age" (Min et al., 2009:229). Most noteworthy, Fergusson, Boden, and Horwood (2008) studied a cohort of New Zealand-born children from birth to age 21 to assess whether dentine lead levels in childhood predicted criminal behavior in late adolescence and early adulthood (i.e., officially recorded violence/property convictions between the ages of 14 and 21). They found that low levels of lead exposure significantly predicted later criminal behavior but that these relationships were largely explained by linkages between lead exposures and diminished educational achievements.

Lead Exposure and Crime

Research indicates that lead poisoning is related to offending at both the aggregate and individual level. Nevin (2000) studied the aggregate relationship between lead exposure and violent crime using longitudinal data from the U.S. Geological Survey on American consumption of leaded gasoline and white lead (used in paints) and crime data from the U.S. Department of Justice. Nevin (2000:18) found that "the temporal relationship between murder rates back to 1900 and gasoline and white lead exposure rates back to 1876 suggests that lead exposure may have influenced crime rates throughout the century."

Nevin (2007) subsequently investigated whether there was a relationship between aggregate preschool lead exposure, arrest rates, and crime trends and whether these relationships generalized across offenses and crossnationally. His analyses revealed that blood lead levels significantly predicted arrest rates and crime trends in the United States, Britain, Italy, Canada, Australia, New Zealand, and West Germany while controlling for the unemployment rate in each country. Stretesky and Lynch (2001) report that aggregate rates of air lead concentration predicted homicide rates and Stretesky and Lynch (2004) found an interaction effect between aggregate lead exposure and county-level measures of deprivation. They report that "the most resource-deprived counties have the greatest amount of crime as a result of lead exposure" (Stretesky and Lynch, 2004:226).

Pihl and Ervin (1990) compared the lead and cadmium levels of violent and nonviolent offenders using a population of male inmates aged from 19 to 48. They found that lead and cadmium levels were related to hyperactivity, behavioral problems, and aggression in the subjects after controlling for age, father's socioeconomic status, months institutionalized, and home environment. Denno (1990) examined data from the Collaborative Perinatal Project and reports that over a 10-year period a large percentage of the sample exhibited lead toxicity and, among males, this exposure was one of the strongest correlates for delinquency and later adult criminality (based on official police records).

Needleman, Riess, Tobin, Biesecker, and Greenhouse (1996) examined a cohort from the Pittsburgh Youth Study (PYS). The researchers measured bone lead levels. Structured interview data were provided using the Self-reported Antisocial Behavior Scale (completed by parents and teachers to measure violent and nonviolent antisocial behaviors), the Child Behavior Checklist (to measure aggression, hyperactivity, bullying, conduct problems, defiance, violence), and the Self-reported Delinquency Scale (completed by subjects to measure delinquency). Needleman et al. (1996:367) found that "male children considered asymptomatic for lead toxicity with elevated bone lead levels at 11 years of age were judged by both parents and teachers to be more aggressive, have higher delinquency scores, and have more somatic complaints than their low–lead counterparts" while controlling for covariates including social and familial factors. The authors conclude that "altered social behavior might be among the earliest expressions of lead exposure" and that lead exposure should be considered along with other factors as a contributor to delinquent behavior (Needleman et al., 1996:369).

Dietrich, Douglas, Succop, Berger, and Bornschein (2001) investigated the effects of lead poisoning on delinquency using a largely black sample (92 percent of 195 respondents) drawn from the Cincinnati Lead Study. The mothers in the study were originally recruited in the 1970s and 1980s, but the researchers were able to track down some of their children that were 15 to 17 years of age at the time of contact with the researchers in the late 1990s. They reported that low levels of prenatal lead exposure were significantly associated with adolescent behavioral problems regardless of gender. This finding held true even when the researchers included controls for parental IQ, birth weight, and the home environment.

Needleman, McFarland, Ness, Fienberg, and Tobin (2002) conducted a case-control study of bone lead levels in adjudicated delinquents in the Pittsburgh area. The delinquent youth were located through the Allegheny Juvenile Court and the nondelinquent control group participants were recruited from the local high schools. In total, 195 youth were recruited for the study. There were 36 white delinquent adolescents and 95 whites in the control group and 158 African American delinquent adolescents and 51 blacks in the control group. The researchers found a strong association between lead bone levels and delinquency while controlling for race, parental education, parental occupation, number of parents in the home, number of children in the home, and neighborhood crime rate. They concluded that "the effect is substantial. With all the subjects in the model, bone lead level was the second strongest risk factor, exceeded only by race. In the stratified models, with race eliminated, bone lead levels was exceeded as a risk only by single parent status" (Needleman et al., 2002:715).

Wright, Dietrich, Ris, Hornung, Wessel, Lanphear, Ho, and Rae (2008) conducted a developmental analysis of the association between early and later lead exposure and criminal arrests. The study involved 250 subjects from the Cincinnati Lead Study. Ninety percent of the participants were African American. These researchers examined data on blood lead levels at three different time periods (prenatal, early child-hood, and 6 years of age). The data on criminal arrests were accessed through the criminal justice records for Hamilton County, Ohio. An analysis of the records identified 800 arrests related to the subjects. The researchers found an association between lead levels and adult crim-inality after controlling for covariates of crime including age, maternal IQ, marital status, socioeconomic status, and educational level. More specifically, the researchers report that prenatal blood lead levels were predictive of being arrested, while early childhood lead levels and blood lead levels at 6 years of age were associated with future arrests for a violent offense.

Lead Exposure and African American Offending

Nevin (2007) examined the relationship between crime trends and lead exposure within the U.S. with a specific focus on the racial disparities in crime. His analyses revealed that the blood-level rate of lead among African Americans from 1976 to 1980 was several times higher than the white rate. Nevin reports that this difference in exposure to toxic lead levels accounted for the racial differences in the juvenile burglary arrest rates and for the arrest rates for violent crime during the early 1990s. He concludes that racial differences in exposure to lead can partially explain black-white disparities in crime:

> Average black lead exposure might have changed little from the mid-1960s to the early-1970s as declining lead paint hazards offset the rise in ambient air lead, but severe poisoning prevalence likely rose among black children living near urban highways. A stronger association between severe lead poisoning and violence is also consistent with racial differences in the late 1970s blood lead levels and early-1990s juvenile arrest rates (Nevin, 2007:326).

In sum, the literature unequivocally shows that racial/ethnic minorities—especially African Americans—are unjustly exposed to environmental contaminants, such as lead, because they are more likely to reside near hazardous waste sites and other industrial plants that emit toxins. In addition, the research clearly reveals that African Americans are less likely than other races (e.g., whites) and ethnicities (e.g., Hispanics) to escape from polluted areas because of discriminatory practices in residential housing. Thus, the extant research indicates that environmental racism is a further cause of concentrated isolated racial segregation as whites are less likely to move into areas near environmental hazards (Stretesky and Lynch, 2004). The literature is also indisputable that exposure to environmental toxins has deleterious health consequences for the African Americans who live near environmental hazards. Furthermore, the research indicates that one of the injurious consequences of being exposed to environmental toxins is an increased risk of offending. Thus, studies clearly indicate that: (1) African Americans are disproportionately exposed to environmental toxins; and (2) this unparalleled exposure to environmental toxins increases their probability of offending.

Our Theory of African American Offending

Our basic thesis is that a theory of black offending has to be grounded in the peerless lived daily experiences of African Americans. At the core of these everyday experiences is the lived reality that African Americans are confronted by their racial subordination. In previous chapters, we have specified how racial discrimination, criminal justice injustices, and being pejoratively stereotyped increase the likelihood that blacks will offend. In this Epilogue, we add another dimension to their racial subordination—their lived experiences with environmental racism— that we stipulate further enhances the likelihood that African Americans will offend.

We consider environmental racism as another dimension of their racial subordination. That is, environmental racism is another form of racial discrimination. Scholars define environmental racism as the disproportionate exposure of African Americans to environmental stressors and toxins. It is beyond the scope of our theory to determine whether this unjust exposure is purposeful—intentionally racist—or a result of some other processes. Regardless, for us, the bottom line is that African Americans are being disproportionately exposed to environmental stressors and toxins.

We recognize that toxins and stressors do not discriminate. That is, being detrimentally exposed to environmental stressors and toxins will deleteriously harm everyone, regardless of the person's race, ethnicity, or socioeconomic status. However, the distressing reality is—and the data are unequivocal on this point—that African Americans are being discriminatorily exposed to these toxins and stressors and are less likely to be screened for whether they have been exposed.

We also recognize that our discussion of a biosocial cause of African American offending bumps up against a racist tradition in criminology of blaming black crime on a genetic cause. We want to be perfectly clear that our argument in no way is related to the thesis that there is a genetic cause to African American offending. Instead, we assert that environmental racism is an extraneous cause of African American offending. This is reinforced by our argument that everyone, regardless of their race, ethnicity, or social class, that is disproportionately exposed to environmental stressors and toxins will suffer deleterious consequences.

Environmental Racism and African American Offending

As stated above, we stipulate that there are four reasons why environmental racism—the disproportionate exposure of African Americans to environmental toxins and stressors—is related to black offending. We separately discuss each of these causes.

First, we consider environmental racism as a form of racial discrimination. Consequently, we stipulate that known environmental racist practices should trigger the same processes that we have previously outlined that increase the probability of African American offending. Please take a moment and imagine being black and living in an area that is dominated by a municipality's waste incinerator. This means that around the clock there will be garbage trucks entering and exiting your community, some of which contain hazardous waste material. There will never be a significant period of time of peaceful uninterrupted silence—just the incessant rumbling of massive garbage trucks. Your community will be constantly bombarded with the stench that emanates from rotting garbage. In addition, around the clock, the smokestacks from the incinerator will be polluting the air you breathe with thousands of chemicals, most of which have not been researched as to the level of their toxicity. This also means that your body will be contaminated with these chemicals. Most importantly, no one knows how your system simultaneously reacts to the chemical cocktail that invades your body. And, you are fully aware of exactly what is transpiring and perceive that the reason this is happening to you is because the owners of the incinerator do not care because you are an African American residing in a racially segregated area.

Our theory asserts that this lived experience is a chronic form of racial discrimination. Therefore, we hypothesize that some African Americans will react to this chronic form of racial discrimination with the same deleterious emotions as they would if they, for example, were exposed to chronic criminal justice injustices. That is, the chronic exposure to environmental racism will cause them to oscillate among a range of negative emotions including defiance, hostility, anger, powerlessness, and depression. We also stipulate that these negative emotions will directly and indirectly impact their probability of offending. These emotions will indirectly increase the chances of African American offending because they undermine the ability of blacks to create strong bonds with white-dominated institutions. They can directly cause offending when they overwhelm the person, depleting their emotional capital, which in turn increases their chances of acting impulsively by engaging in externalizing behaviors.

Second, we assert that the disproportionate exposure to environmental toxins and stressors can impair the cognitive developmental abilities of African Americans. This means that African Americans injured by their exposure do not have the same emotional capital as others. Consequently, we stipulate that these injured African Americans have an increased probability of reacting negatively (e.g., externalizing their reaction with impulsive aggression) when confronted by racial injustices—for example, a criminal justice injustice. We hypothesize that African Americans with impaired cognitive functioning will be less effective in fending off the toxic consequences of their racial subordination. In short, our theory asserts that chronic exposure to environmental racism substantively compromises the ability of African Americans to effectively cope with their racial subordination, which in turn increases their probability of offending.

Third, and relatedly, we contend that unequal exposure to environmental toxins and stressors negatively affects the ability of African American parents to effectively racially socialize their children. This occurs in two ways. First, injurious exposure will diminish the emotional capital that African American parents have in dealing with their children. Consequently, injured African American parents will be more likely to inappropriately respond to normal childhood development issues. For example, African American parents with diminished cognitive abilities may respond with impulsive anger when confronted by their children's "misbehavior." Second, we argue that injured African American children with cognitive deficits are more likely to be disruptive and are less likely to respond positively to effective parental socialization practices (including racial socialization practices). Consequently, in the worst case scenario, these diminished capabilities may cause a spiral downward as cognitively impaired African American children "act out" and cognitively compromised parents escalate their responses with increasingly negative reactions.

Fourth, we hypothesize that African Americans who are disproportionately exposed to environmental toxins and stressors will be less likely to bond, because of their cognitive impairments and lack of effective racial socialization, to white-dominated institutions, such as their schools and places of employment. The research is quite clear—detrimental exposure to environmental toxins and stressors diminishes the cognitive ability of African Americans and increases their likelihood of impulsively externalizing their negative emotions. The research is also unequivocal that these diminished attributes negatively impact the ability of African Americans to positively bond with white-dominated institutions such as their schools. Furthermore, the research is consistent that weak social bonds across the lifespan are powerful predictors of an increased probability of offending.

In closing, we recognize that the research on how environmental toxins and stressors impact offending—regardless of the race, ethnicity, or class of the person—at this point, is limited. At best, only one toxin—lead—out of thousands has been thoroughly researched. However, we argue that research on environmental toxins will continue to gain traction as more sophisticated technologies and methodologies are employed that expose the many substantive and nuanced ways these pollutants singularly, collectively, and cumulatively damage individuals. Indeed, we argue that in the near future the impact of environmental toxins and stressors will become a dominant research paradigm within criminology. The intent of this Epilogue is to ensure that researchers, as part of this emerging research paradigm, expose the multifaceted ways in which environmental racism has, for hundreds of years, disproportionately negatively impacted African Americans.

NOTES

Chapter 1: African American Offending

1 According to the 2006 Uniform Crime Reports (http://www.fbi.gov/ucr/cius2006), whites account for 55.8 percent of the robbery arrests and African Americans account for 40.3 percent in nonmetropolitan areas. African Americans and whites are as equally likely—49 percent—to be arrested for robbery in suburban areas. Thus, African Americans are disproportionately more likely to be arrested for robbery regardless of where they are likely to reside.

2 There is also a well-established body of research that has not found racial bias in police arrests (see D'Alessio and Stolzenberg, 2002; Hindelang, 1978; Smith, Fisher, and Davidson, 1984).

3 The following table presents the proportions (Puzzanchera, 2009).

Most Serious Offense	Black Proportion of Juvenile Arrests in 2008
Murder	58%
Forcible rape	37
Robbery	67
Aggravated assault	42
Simple assault	39
Burglary	35
Larceny-theft	31
Motor vehicle theft	45
Weapons	38
Drug abuse violations	27
Vandalism	19
Liquor laws	6

4 We acknowledge that Native Americans also have a particularly unique and brutal relationship with the United States. Consequently, we believe that a Native American theory is needed and that such a theory should include the impact of their colonization,

experiences with broken treaties and the impact the reservation system has had on their offending.

5 Athens (2010:341) argues that subordination has four components:

> (1) certain individuals or groups exhibit subservient attitudes while others exhibit superior attitudes; (2) super-ordinate roles are always differentiated from subordinate ones; (3) the individuals or groups who seek to perform the super-ordinate roles exhibit superior attitudes, whereas those who resign themselves to performing subordinate roles exhibit subservient attitudes; and (4) the individuals or groups performing the subordinate and super-ordinate roles consciously assume, however accurately, each other's superior and subservient attitudes, and their conscious assumption of these respective attitudes significantly affects the construction of the social act in which they are joint participants.

6 Until the use of the death penalty for the crime of rape was ruled unconstitutional by the Supreme Court in the 1977 case of *Coker v. Georgia*, blacks bore the brunt of the executions for this crime. Holden-Smith (1996) provides statistics showing that from the 1930s to the 1970s, 48 whites were executed for rape while 405 black men were executed for the same offense.

Chapter 2: An African American Worldview

1 Some scholars suggest that the racial dynamics of the case (black perpetrator and two white victims) contributed to the intense outrage expressed by whites (Russell-Brown, 2009).

2 Thus, the history of slavery is as similar to African Americans as "the internment of Japanese Americans during World War II, the removal of American Indians from their tribal lands, and refugee experiences. Aspects of oppression related historical events can be transmitted across generations through discussion, storytelling, and lessons taught to children, as well as observation of long-term effects" (Harrell, 2000:47).

3 Johnson (2007) found that there are some individual differences among African Americans in their support for punitive correctional policies. One demographic variable, income, predicted support. Johnson (2007) also found that African Americans who endorsed a dispositional attribution style (blame crime on the failings of individuals) and who feared crime were more punitive, whereas blacks who believed that their neighborhood was in disorder (had vacant houses) and those who perceived criminal justice injustices were less likely to embrace punitive attitudes.

Chapter 3: Perceptions of Criminal Justice Injustices and African American Offending

1 It is noteworthy that the research by Tyler and his colleagues (see, e.g., Sunshine and Tyler, 2003; Tyler, 1990) has found that African Americans and whites (and Hispanics) all essentially want the same thing from the criminal justice system; that is, to be treated fairly and with respect. We agree with this finding; that is, everyone wants to be treated fairly and with respect by people in authority. However, we question whether African Americans and whites share the same definitions of what it means to be treated fairly and respectfully. Research shows that whites living in disadvantaged neighborhoods bring into their interactions with the criminal justice system opinions that are both favorable and unfavorable, while African Americans similarly situated

only have the belief that the police are out to hassle or to "bully" them (Browning, Cullen, Cao, Kopache, and Stevenson, 1994; Brunson and Weitzer, 2009). Consequently, respect for African Americans may relate to their belief that the police did not instantly assume that they were a criminal (or a "scumbag"), whereas whites may judge the degree of respect that was afforded to them by the level of deference they perceived. It is also possible that African Americans may feel that they have to prove that they are not a "criminal" where whites may believe that they only have to talk the officer into believing that what they did in this specific instance was not wrong. That is, blacks may defiantly feel that they have to prove to the police that there is not something wrong with them; in contrast, whites may only have to prove, with deference, that, in this one isolated instance, they did nothing wrong.

2 Lee, Steinberg, and Piquero (2010) found that a select group of African American youths—those with a serious felony arrest record—were able to differentiate between procedural justice ("of the people you know who have had contact with the police in terms of crime accusation, how much of their story did the police let them tell?") and the legitimacy of the police ("people should support the police"). They argue that this differentiation can occur as African American youths have more contact—experience—with the criminal justice system and as the strength of their racial identity increases. They conclude that: "Thus, while adolescents held the perception, formed via personal and vicarious experiences, that police discriminate, they still held the view that the police and the laws they uphold were legitimate in theory and as an ideal, and this was especially the case as both age and experience increase" (Lee, Steinberg, and Piquero, 2010:787).

3 Note that Sherman (1993) does not identify the process by which people develop weak bonds with conventional institutions. In the next chapter, our theory posits that weak bonds are caused by perceiving criminal justice injustices, racial discrimination, and being prejoratively stereotyped.

4 We use this term with hesitation knowing full well that crime is largely intraracial and this term has been used to reify the notion that there is something special about crime committed by Blacks against other African Americans. Wilson (2005) presents an excellent discussion of the etiology of the term as well as the streotypical notions that have resulted from its use.

5 There is, however, research that indicates that middle-class African Americans may actually have a greater reaction to police misconduct. Schuck et al. (2008:513) argue: "Middle-class African-Americans, for example, may hold expectations for the police that are very similar to middle-class Whites. However, because middle-class African-Americans are more likely than middle-class Whites to live in or near disadvantaged areas which are known to be associated with more aggressive policing and complaints of police misconduct, their expectations for the police are less likely to be met. In other words, social class, particularly education, may be a big factor in shaping residents' expectations of the police, both those of Whites and African-Americans, but the latter are more likely to have their expectations violated."

6 See Sampson and Bartusch (1998) for an alternative perspective. Note, however, in their research, the equation that attenuated the black-white significant difference in satisfaction with the police included a control for the violent crime rate, which was not included in their model that attenuated the black-white difference in the prediction of legal cynicism.

Chapter 4: Racial Discrimination, Negative Stereotypes, Stereotype Threats, and African American Offending

1 African Americans also pejoratively stereotype white males. A free-listing technique revealed that African Americans stereotype white males as racist, privileged, uncoordinated, arrogant, intelligent, greedy, sexist, dishonest, ambitious, selfish, and drug users (Conley, Rabinowitz, and Rabow, 2010).

2 Research shows that racial tension, as measured by a self-reported item completed by school administrators, increased the level of reported crime in public schools (Maume, Kim-Godwin, and Clements, 2010). Unfortunately, this study did not examine whether the rates of crime increased specifically among African American students.

3 Stereotype threats can diminish the performance of any minority including women, Latinos and Latinas, and the economically disadvantaged (Brown and Pinel, 2003).

4 We argue that the same processes describe why African American adolescents may choose to develop weak ties with their schools also applies to why black adults may choose to be weakly commited to their occupation.

5 Research shows that "when workers expect their current employment to be of longer duration, they are less likely to engage in crime" (Crutchfield and Pitchford, 1997:93).

6 Ironically, it is likely that negative depictions of African Americans actually *decrease* the odds of whites engaging in crime. Haslam et al. (2008:3) assert that "if people are exposed to stereotypes about the inferiority of an out-group (those who are not part of the individual's in-group) in a given domain, then their performance is typically elevated—a phenomenon they refer to as stereotype lift. In this way, just as a sense of in-group inferiority can impair performance, an ideology of superiority can give members of high-status groups a performance boost" (see also Kellow and Jones, 2008).

7 Males (8 percent) were not significantly more likely than females (6 percent) to report that they "very often" received poorer service than other people at restaurants or stores. Note that other researchers report that they do not find any gender differences in perceived racial discrimination (Caldwell et al., 2004). However, Swim et al. (2003:63) contend that "the perception that men experience more prejudice than women may be based upon the types of incidents people consider when contemplating the frequency of women's and men's experiences with racism." We additionally assert that the research on the "street culture" omits from its analyses how everyday racism—that is, being routinely and chronically "dissed"—creates feelings among African Americans—especially disidentified youth—that cause them to negatively react to any further erosions to their sense of sense including their racial identity. Indeed, we hypothesize that the beliefs and behaviors that scholars attribute to the self-insular, self perpetuating street "culture"—such as overt aggression—would be vastly diminished if African Americans no longer had to deal with the microaggressions of everyday racism.

8 We could not find any research that examined whether there are gender differences in how African Americans emotionally respond to racial discrimination, stereotype threats, or pejorative stereotypes.

9 We base these conclusions on relatively scant research. Therefore, we argue that there is the need for future research that more substantially develops the precise and nuanced ways in which characteristics of institutions enhance the ability of African Americans to build strong bonds with schools and their places of employment, which should reduce their likelihood of offending.

Chapter 5: Racial Socialization and African American Offending

1 Our theory focuses on parental racial socialization experiences. However, there are other major racial socialization agents that can positively affect black youth development, including the black church, community-based mentoring programs, and other nonrelated individuals (see Brown, 2008; Nicolas et al., 2008; Noguera, 2003). Note that there are also other racial socialization experiences that can negatively impact the development of black youth, such as those acquired on the "street," which we do discuss. Further elaborations of our theory may find it profitable to explore how religion-spirituality positively impacts the racial socialization of African Americans (Keyes, 2009).

2 For two excellent reviews of the literature on racial socialization see Lesane-Brown (2006) and Hughes et al. (2006).

3 This is not to say that ethnic socialization is unrelated to offending among minorities other than African Americans. For a discussion of ethnic socialization see Hughes et al. (2006).

4 Constantine and Blackmon (2002:323) define self-esteem as "internalized feelings of mastery, value, and self-acceptance that are derived from individuals' assessment of their personal value based on implicit and explicit messages provided by significant others."

5 For a review on the literature on African American racial identity development, particularly as it applies to the education setting, see DeCuir-Gunby (2009).

6 Throughout the rest of the book, we interchangeably use the concepts of "positive racial socialization experiences" and having a "positive racial identity." We assume that African American parents who engage in positive cultural socialization experiences will inculcate their children with a positive racial identity. We recognize that the content of a positive racial identity developmentally changes across the lifespan. We also recognize that a racial identity is multifaceted, which means that the three most often measured aspects of a racial identity—race centrality, private regard, and public regard—may not align perfectly even though the individual has an overall positive racial identity. Thus, it is possible for African American youth to have a positive racial identity but still believe that whites devalue the black experience (be low in public regard but high in private regard and race centrality). Further elaborations of our theory may wish to explore how each of the aspects of a racial identity separately and combined impact African American offending. It may also examine the multitude of indices that are used to assess racial identity and whether they relate to offending.

7 Oliver (2006) suggests that individuals socialized on the streets can become immersed in the "code of the streets" (Anderson, 1999; Brezina, Agnew, Cullen, and Wright, 2004; Kubrin, 2005; Sharkey, 2006; Stewart and Simons, 2006, 2010). We do not dispute this insight. However, we argue that the "code of the street" is not the cause of African American inner-city offending. Rather, we argue that the "code of the street" that is applicable to African Americans has emerged and is sustained because blacks have been persistently and chronically exposed to the racial injustices that we have outlined here. We additionally assert that the research on the "street culture" omits from its analyses how everyday racism—that is, being routinely and chronically "dissed"—creates feelings among African Americans—especially disidentified youth—that cause them to negatively react to any further erosions to their sense of sense including their racial identity. Indeed, we hypothesize that the beliefs and behaviors that scholars attribute to the self-insular, self perpetuating street "culture"—such as overt aggression—would be vastly diminished if African Americans no longer had to deal with the microaggressions of everyday racism. Of note, scholars have identified

how African American girls negotiate schools and neighborhoods governed by the "code of the street" (Jones, 2010).

8 Link and Phelan (2001:367) argue that stigma exists when the following occurs: "In the first component, people distinguish and label human differences. In the second, dominant cultural beliefs link labeled persons to undesirable characteristics—to negative stereotypes. In the third, labeled persons are placed in distinct categories so as to accomplish some degree of separation of 'us' from 'them.' In the fourth, labeled persons experience status loss and discrimination that lead to unequal outcomes. Finally, stigmatization is entirely contingent on access to social, economic, and political power that allows the identification of differentness, the construction of stereotypes, the separation of labeled persons into distinct categories, and the full execution of disapproval, rejection, exclusion, and discrimination. Thus, we apply the term stigma when elements of labeling, stereotyping, separation, status loss, and discrimination co-occur in a power situation that allows the components of stigma to unfold."

9 There are excellent reviews of the research on the sociological and psychological consequences of being stigmatized, for example, see Link and Phelan (2001) and Major and O'Brien (2005).

10 We are not arguing that anger is an inappropriate response to racial injustices. However, anger can be debilitating if it is not positively expressed or it is repressed and internalized (see Stevenson et al., 1997).

11 For contradictory evidence see Caughy et al. (2002). They found no gendered differences in the cultural socialization of the very young—preschoolers. Relatedly, the research notes that the content of racial socialization may parallel the development of the child with parents being more cautious in how they racially socialize their younger than older children (Hughes et al., 2006).

12 Nicolas et al. (2008:271) define critical race consciousness as: "The capacity to critically evaluate various situations for racial power imbalances, to weigh one's options for coping with such situations, and to engage in personal and collective agency as necessary."

13 For a review of the literature on marital processes and parental socialization practices among African Americans see McLoyd, Cauce, Takeuchi, and Wilson (2000).

14 Schroeder et al. (2010) argue that differential effects by race are likely due to the broader social contexts within which parenting and child development takes place. They suggest "that Blacks experience more anger compared to Whites, primarily as a function of factors such as economic disadvantage, racial discrimination, and additional stressors related to their minority status. Parenting is, therefore, a challenging task for parents in minority communities, but the current study is consistent with the prior research that suggests parenting is an essential buffer to the negative effects of racial discrimination among Black adolescents, including anger and violent behavior [Simons et al., 2006]. Taken together, our results support a continued emphasis on the significance of parental control and supervision of adolescent children in protecting children from internalizing an angry identity and developing long-term patterns of criminal behavior, especially within African American communities" (Schroeder et al., 2010:88).

Chapter 6: A Theoretical Model of African American Offending

1 Smith et al. (2007) argue that African American males experience the following emotions as a result of being chronically exposed to racial microaggressions associated

with everyday racism: frustration, shock, avoidance or withdrawal, disbelief, anger, aggressiveness, uncertainty or confusion, resentment, anxiety, helplessness, hopelessness, and fear.

2 The experience of discrimination is particularly acute among African Americans who are ex-offenders; that is, those who have been either arrested or convicted of a crime, especially a felony. Pager (2003) found that employers would rather hire a white with a prior criminal record than a black who has never been arrested. Thus, Alexander (2010:148) argues that: "Not only are African Americans far more likely to be labeled criminals, they are also more strongly affected by the stigma of a criminal record. Black men convicted of felonies are the least likely to receive job offers of any demographic group, and suburban employers are the most unwilling to hire them." Alexander (2010) concludes that the African American ex-felon is the prototype of the "*criminal-blackman*" who justifies the "New Jim Crow" regime of racial oppression.

3 Eighteen of the 53 delegates in attendance at the Constitutional Convention of 1787 beyond the second week were slave owners at some point in their lives (McGuire and Ohsfeldt, 1986). Most notably, 12 presidents of the United States owned slaves and eight of them owned slaves while serving as president: George Washington, Thomas Jefferson, James Madison, James Monroe, Andrew Jackson, Martin Van Buren, William Henry Harrison, John Tyler, James Polk, Zachary Taylor, Andrew Johnson, and Ulysses S. Grant (Lopresti, 2010).

4 It is also possible that in the absence of parents who efficaciously racially socialize their children, adolescents may encounter other adults—"old heads" or "community mothers"—who provide these socialization experiences, thus inhibiting the likelihood of offending (Anderson, 1999).

5 Essed's (2002) research indicates that stigma consciousness does not equal African Americans being oversensitive and resorting too quickly to charging racism where it objectively did not occur. In fact, her research indicates that African Americans are deliberate in their evaluations of their encounters with everyday racism. Their deliberations include data related to "*context* (where did it happen, when, who were involved?); *complication* (what went wrong?); *evaluation* (was it racism?); and *reaction* (what did you do about it?)" (Essed, 2002:212). In addition, Sellers, Copeland-Linder, Martin, and Lewis (2006:207) report "that African Americans are quite accurate in estimating the racial bias of Whites through their nonverbal behavior."

6 Noble (2006) further argues that the "rage" that African Americans experience as a result of systematic racial oppression causes black offenders to seek out white victims, especially in the context of prisons. Thus, Noble (2006:117) states that "certain crimes have an ideological component, which represents an explosion of hatred by Black males against their oppressor."

7 Smith et al. (2007) refer to this need to be hypervigilant as being constantly "switched on." Thus, "African Americans are constantly dedicating time and energy to determining if there was a stressor, whether that stressor was motivated by a racist purpose, and how or if they should respond" (Smith et al., 2007:557). The end result of always being "switched on" is that African Americans—especially black males—develop a "racial battle fatigue." Smith et al. (2007:555) argue that "racial battle fatigue is the result of constant physiological, psychological, cultural, and emotional coping with racial microaggressions in less-than-ideal and racially hostile or unsupportive environments."

8 However, we do not agree with their premise that isolated residential segregation has created an "oppositional culture" (Massey and Denton, 1993).

9 Research shows that family stress is related to lower attendance and problems learning

at school and that it affects academic performance across the high school years. That is, higher levels of family stress and school problems at the start of high school are related to declining academic achievement at the end of 12th grade (Flook and Fuligni, 2008).

10 It is a compounding contradiction that areas of concentrated isolated disadvantage produce higher rates of African American offending, which in turn further diminish the well-being (e.g., academic success) of blacks residing in these areas as they either fear for their public safety or become victims of crimes themselves (Charles, 2003). It is also a compounding contradiction that ghettos reify the stereotype associating race with crime and crime with race, which further increases the likelihood that African Americans will experience criminal justice injustices, racial discrimination, and being pejoratively stereotyped, which in turn increases their probability of offending.

11 It is likely these admonitions may, in part, explain why "Afro-Caribbean blacks experience more favorable outcomes and see better returns to their human capital than African Americans do" (Charles, 2003:180).

Epilogue: Environmental Racism and African American Offending

1 The measurement refers to 10 micrograms of lead per deciliter (a tenth of a liter) of blood.

2 It should be noted that the literature on racial disparities in exposure to environmental toxins extends to air pollution, pesticides, and hazardous waste (Gwynn and Thurston, 2001; Mott, 1995). We focus on racial disparities in lead exposure because the scholarly literature in the area is more established.

References

Adeola, F. 1994. "Environmental hazards, health, and racial inequity in hazardous waste distribution." *Environment and Behavior* 26:99–126.

Agnew, R. 1992. "Foundation for a general strain theory of crime and delinquency." *Criminology* 30:47–88.

——. 2001. "Building on the foundation of general strain theory: Specifying the types of strain most likely to lead to crime and delinquency." *Journal of Research in Crime and Delinquency* 38:319–361.

Agnew, R., T. Brezina, J. P. Wright, and F. T. Cullen. 2002. "Strain, personality traits, and delinquency: Extending general strain theory." *Criminology* 40:43–71.

Akbar, N. 1991. "Mental disorder among African Americans." *Black Psychology* 3:339–352.

Akers, R. L. 2009. *Social learning and social structure: A general theory of crime and deviance.* New Brunswick, NJ: Transaction Publishers.

Akers, R. L., M. D. Krohn, L. Lanza-Kaduce, and M. Radosevich. 1979. "Social learning and deviant behavior: A specific test of a general theory." *American Sociological Review* 44:636–655.

Alexander, M. 2010. *The new Jim Crow: mass incarceration in the age of colorblindness.* New York: The New Press.

Alliance for Healthy Homes (AFHH). 2005. "Understanding new national data on lead poisoning." Retrieved on August 1, 2010, at http://www.afhh.org/hps/leaddocs/hps_lead_BLL_data_factsheet.htm.

Alliman-Brissett, A. E. and S. L. Turner. 2010. "Racism, parent support, and math-based career interests, efficacy, and outcome expectations among African American adolescents." *Journal of Black Psychology* 36:197–225.

Alter, A. L., J. Aronson, J. M. Darley, C. Rodriguez, and D. N. Ruble. 2010. "Rising to the threat: Reducing stereotype threat by reframing the threat as a challenge." *Journal of Experimental Social Psychology* 46:166–171.

Altschul, I., D. Oyserman, and D. Bybee. 2006. "Racial-ethnic identity in mid-adolescence: Content and change as predictors of academic achievement." *Child Development* 77:1155–1169.

Anderson, E. 1999. *Code of the street: Decency, violence, and the moral life of the inner city.* New York: W.W. Norton and Company.

Anna, S. 1987. "Poverty in America: What the data reveal." Retrieved on March 22, 2010, at http://www.heritage.org/Research/Reports/1985/12/Poverty-in-America-What-the-Data-Reveal.

Arbona, C., R. H. Jackson, A. McCoy, and C. Blakely. 1999. "Ethnic identity as a predictor of attitudes of adolescents toward fighting." *The Journal of Early Adolescence* 19:323–340.

Arbuthnot, K. 2009. "The effects of stereotype threat on standardized mathematics test performance and cognitive processing." *Harvard Educational Review* 79:448–473.

Arnett, J. J. and G. H. Brody. 2008. "A fraught passage: The identity challenges of African American emerging adults." *Human Development* 51:291–293.

Asante, M. K. 1980. *Afrocentricity: The theory of social change.* Koen Book Distributors.

———. 1988. *Afrocentricity.* Trenton, NJ: Africa World Press.

Aseltine, R. H. J., S. Gore, and J. Gordon. 2000. "Life stress, anger and anxiety, and delinquency: An empirical test of general strain theory." *Journal of Health and Social Behavior* 41:256–275.

Associated Press. 2006. "Surviving 'stressful process' of being black male: African-American men quietly combat negative stereotypes about them." Retrieved on July 22, 2010, at http://www.Msnbc.Msn.Com/id/13560066/.

Athens, L. 2010. "Human subordination from a radical interactionist's perspective." *Journal for the Theory of Social Behaviour.* 40:339–368.

Ayres, I. and P. Siegelman. 1995. "Race and gender discrimination in bargaining for a new car." *The American Economic Review* 85:304–321.

Ayres, I. and J. Borowsky. 2008. "A study of racially disparate outcomes in the Los Angeles police department." http://www.aclu-sc.org/documents/view/47. Retrieved, November 6, 2010.

Bandura, A. 1977. *Social learning theory.* Englewood Cliffs, NJ: Prentice Hall.

Banks, K. H., L. P. Kohn-Wood, and M. Spencer. 2006. "An examination of the African American experience of everyday discrimination and symptoms of psychological distress." *Community Mental Health Journal* 42:555–570.

Banner, S. 2006. "Traces of slavery: Race and the death penalty in a historical perspective." Pp. 96–113 in *Lynch mobs killing states*, edited by C.J. Ogletree, Jr. and A. Sarat. New York: New York University Press.

Barkan, S. E. and S. F. Cohn. 1994. "Racial prejudice and support for the death penalty by whites." *Journal of Research in Crime and Delinquency* 31:202–209.

Barnes, S. L. 2009. "Enter into his gates: An analysis of black church participation patterns." *Sociological Spectrum* 29:173–200.

Baron, S. W. 2008. "Street youth, unemployment, and crime: Is it that simple? Using general strain theory to untangle the relationship." *Canadian Journal of Criminology and Criminal Justice* 50:399–434.

Bass, S. 2001. "Policing space, policing race: Social control imperatives and police discretionary decisions." *Social Justice* 28:156–176.

Bassett, C. J. 1995. "House bill 591: Florida compensates Rosewood victims and their families for a seventy-one-year-old injury." *Florida State University Law Review* 503:503–525.

Beagan, B. L. 2003. "'Is this worth getting into a big fuss over?' Everyday racism in medical school." *Medical Education* 37:852–860.

Beckett, K., K. Nyrop, and L. Pfingst. 2006. "Race, drugs, and policing: Understanding disparities in drug delivery arrests." *Criminology* 44:105–137.

Beckett, K., K. Nyrop, L. Pfingst, and M. Bowen. 2005. "Drug use, drug possession arrests, and the question of race: Lessons from Seattle." *Social Problems* 52:419–441.

Beckett, K. and T. Sasson. 2003. *The politics of injustice: Crime and punishment in America.* New York: Sage Publications.

Belknap, J. 2007. *The invisible woman: Gender, crime and justice.* Belmont, CA: Wadsworth.

Bellinger, D., K. Stiles, and H. Needleman. 1992. "Low-level lead exposure, intelligence and academic achievement: A long-term follow-up study." *Pediatrics* 90:855–861.

Bellinger, D. C. 2008. "Very low lead exposures and children's neurodevelopment." *Current Opinion in Pediatrics* 20:172–177.

Belvedere, K., J. L. Worrall, and S. G. Tibbetts. 2005. "Explaining suspect resistance in police-citizen encounters." *Criminal Justice Review* 30:30–44.

Bendick, M. Jr., R. E. Rodriguez, and S. Jayaraman. 2010. "Employment discrimination in upscale restaurants: Evidence from matched pair testing." *The Social Science Journal* 47:802–818.

Bernard, T. J. 1984. "Control criticisms of strain theories: An assessment of theoretical and empirical adequacy." *Journal of Research in Crime and Delinquency* 21:353–372.

Biafora, F. A., D. L. Taylor, G. J. Warheit, R. S. Zimmerman, and W. A. Vega. 1993. "Cultural mistrust and racial awareness among ethnically diverse black adolescent boys." *Journal of Black Psychology* 19:266–281.

Bjornstrom, E. E. S., R. L. Kaufman, R. D. Peterson, and M. D. Slater. 2010. "Race and ethnic representations of lawbreakers and victims in crime news: A national study of television coverage." *Social Problems* 57:269–293.

Blistein, R. 2009. "Racism's hidden toll." *Miller-McCune* 2:48–57.

Blumer, H. 1965. "The future of the color line." Pp. 322–336 in *The South in continuity and change* by J. C. McKinney and E. T. Thompson. Durham, NC: Seeman.

Bobo, L. D. 2000. "Reclaiming a Du Boisian perspective on racial attitudes." *The ANNALS of the American Academy of Political and Social Science* 568:186–202.

Bobo, L. D. and C. Z. Charles. 2009. "Race in the American mind: From the Moynihan report to the Obama candidacy." *The ANNALS of the American Academy of Political and Social Science* 621:243–259.

Bobo, L. and D. Johnson. 2004. "A taste for punishment: Black and white Americans' views on the death penalty and the war on drugs." *Du Bois Review: Social Science Research on Race* 1:151–180.

Bonczar, T. P. and T. L. Snell. 2004. "Capital punishment, 2003." *Bureau of Justice Statistics Bulletin.*

Bonilla-Silva, E. 1997. "Rethinking racism: Toward a structural interpretation." *American Sociological Review* 62:465–480.

——. 2008. *Racism without racists: Color-blind racism and the persistence of racial inequality in the United States.* Princeton, NJ: Rowman and Littlefield.

Bonilla-Silva, E. and V. Ray. 2009. "When whites love a black leader: Race matters in Obama America." *Journal of African American Studies* 13:176–183.

Borrell, L., C. Kiefe, D. Williams, A. Diez-Roux, and P. Gordon-Larsen. 2006. "Self-reported health, perceived racial discrimination, and skin color in African Americans in the CARDIA study." *Social Science and Medicine* 63:1415–1427.

Borrell, L. N., D. R. Jacobs, Jr, D. R. Williams, M. J. Pletcher, T. K. Houston, and C. I. Kiefe. 2007. "Self-reported racial discrimination and substance use in the coronary artery risk development in adults study." *American Journal of Epidemiology* 166:1068–1079.

Bouffard, L. A. and N. L. Piquero. 2010. "Defiance theory and life course explanations of persistent offending." *Crime and Delinquency* 56:227–252.

Bowman, P. J. and C. Howard. 1985. "Race-related socialization, motivation, and academic achievement: A study of black youths in three-generation families." *Journal of the American Academy of Child Psychiatry* 24:134–141.

Braun, J., R. Kahn, T. Froehlich, P. Auinger, and B. Lanphear. 2006. "Exposures to environmental toxicants and attention deficit hyperactivity disorder in US children." *Environmental Health Perspectives* 114:1904–1909.

Brega, A. G. and L. M. Coleman. 1999. "Effects of religiosity and racial socialization on subjective stigmatization in African-American adolescents." *Journal of Adolescence* 22:223–242.

Brezina, T. 1996. "Adapting to strain: An examination of delinquent coping responses." *Criminology* 34:39–60.

——. 2010. "Anger, attitudes, and aggressive behavior: Exploring the affective and cognitive foundations of angry aggression." *Journal of Contemporary Criminal Justice* 86:547–559.

Brezina, T., R. Agnew, F. T. Cullen, and J. P. Wright. 2004. "The code of the street: A quantitative assessment of Elijah Anderson's subculture of violence thesis and its contribution to youth violence research." *Youth Violence and Juvenile Justice* 2:303–328.

Brody, G. H., Y. F. Chen, V. M. Murry, X. Ge, R. L. Simons, F. X. Gibbons, M. Gerrard, and C. E. Cutrona. 2006. "Perceived discrimination and the adjustment of African American youths: A five-year longitudinal analysis with contextual moderation effects." *Child Development* 77:1170–1189.

Broman, C., M. Torres, R. Canady, H. Neighbors, and J. Jackson. 2010. "Race and ethnic self-identification influences on physical and mental health statuses among blacks." *Race and Social Problems* 2:81–91.

Brondolo, E., N. Brady ver Halen, M. Pencille, D. Beatty, and R. Contrada. 2009. "Coping with racism: A selective review of the literature and a theoretical and methodological critique." *Journal of Behavioral Medicine* 32:64–88.

Brondolo, E., S. Thompson, N. Brady, R. Appel, A. Cassells, J. N. Tobin, and M. Sweeney. 2005. "The relationship of racism to appraisals and coping in a community sample." *Ethnicity and Disease* 15:14–19.

Brown, A., A. Abernethy, R. Gorsuch, and A. C. Dueck. 2010. "Sacred violations, perceptions of injustice, and anger in Muslims." *Journal of Applied Social Psychology* 40:1003–1027.

Brown, C. S. and R. S. Bigler. 2005. "Children's perceptions of discrimination: A developmental model." *Child Development* 76:533–553.

Brown, D. L. 2008. "African American resiliency: Examining racial socialization and social support as protective factors." *Journal of Black Psychology* 34:32–48.

Brown, R. P. and E. C. Pinel. 2003. "Stigma on my mind: Individual differences in the experience of stereotype threat." *Journal of Experimental Social Psychology* 39:626–633.

Brown, T. L., M. R. Linver, and M. Evans. 2010. "The role of gender in the racial and ethnic socialization of African American adolescents." *Youth and Society* 41:357–381.

Brown, T. N. and C. L. Lesane-Brown. 2006. "Race socialization messages across historical time." *Social Psychology Quarterly* 69:201–213.

Brownfield, D. 2005. "A defiance theory of sanctions and gang membership." *Journal of Gang Research* 13:31–43.

Browning, S., F. T. Cullen, L. Cao, R. Kopache, and T. J. Stevenson. 1994. "Race and getting hassled by the police: A research note." *Police Studies* 17:1–11.

Brunson, R. K. 2007. "Police don't like black people: African-American young men's accumulated police experiences." *Criminology & Public Policy* 6:71–101.

Brunson, R. K. and J. Miller. 2006. "Young black men and urban policing in the United States." *British Journal of Criminology* 46:613–640.

Brunson, R. K. and R. Weitzer. 2009. "Police relations with black and white youths in different urban neighborhoods." *Urban Affairs Review* 44:858–885.

Bryant, B. and P. Mohai. 1992. *Race and the incidence of environmental hazards: A time for discourse.* Boulder, CO: Westview Press.

Buckler, K., F. T. Cullen, and J. D. Unnever. 2007. "Citizen assessment of local criminal courts: Does fairness matter?" *Journal of Criminal Justice* 35:524–536.

Bullard, R. 1983. "Solid waste sites and the black Houston community." *Sociological Inquiry*, 53:273–288.

——. 1990. *Dumping in Dixie: Race, class, and environmental quality.* Boulder, CO: Westview Press.

——. 1993. *Confronting environmental racism: Voices from the grassroots.* Boston, MA: South End Press.

Bullard, R., P. Mohai, R. Saha, and B. Wright. 2007. *Toxic wastes and race at twenty: 1987– 2007.* United Church of Christ Justice and Witness Ministries.

Burgess, R. L. 1925. "The growth of the city: An introduction to a research project." Pp. 47–62, edited by R. Park, E. W. Burgess, and R. McKenzie. Chicago: University of Chicago Press.

Burgess, R. L. and R. L. Akers. 1966. "A differential association-reinforcement theory of criminal behavior." *Social Problems*: 128–147.

Burston, B. W., D. Jones, and P. Roberson-Saunders. 1995. "Drug use and African Americans: Myth versus reality." *Journal of Alcohol and Drug Education* 40:19–39.

Burt, C. H., R. L. Simons, and F. X. Gibbons. 2010. "Racial discrimination and crime: Ethnic-racial socialization matters." Paper presented at the American Society of Criminology. San Francisco, CA.

Burton, L. M., E. Bonilla-Silva, V. Ray, R. Buckelew, and E. H. Freeman. 2010. "Critical race theories, colorism, and the decade's research on families of color." *Journal of Marriage and Family* 72:440–459.

Butler, P. 2009. *Let's get free: A hip-hop theory of justice.* New York: The New Press.

Byers, R. and E. Lord. 1943. "Late effects of lead poisoning on mental development." *Archives of Pediatrics and Adolescent Medicine* 66:471–494.

Byrd, C. M. and T. M. Chavous. 2009. "Racial identity and academic achievement in the neighborhood context: A multilevel analysis." *Journal of Youth and Adolescence* 38:544–559.

Caldwell, C. H., L. P. Kohn-Wood, K. H. Schmeelk-Cone, T. M. Chavous, and M. A. Zimmerman. 2004. "Racial discrimination and racial identity as risk or protective factors for violent behaviors in African American young adults." *American Journal of Community Psychology* 33:91–107.

Caldwell, L. and H. T. Greene. 1980. "Implementing a black perspective in criminal justice." Pp. 143–156 in *Improving management in criminal justice*, edited by A. Cohn and B. Ward. Beverly Hills, CA: Sage.

Carr, P. J., L. Napolitano, and J. Keating. 2007. "We never call the cops and here is why: A qualitative examination of legal cynicism in three Philadelphia neighborhoods." *Criminology* 45:445–480.

Carson, R. 1962. *Silent spring.* New York: Houghton Mifflin.

Carswell, S. B. 2007. *Delinquency among African American youth: Parental attachment, socioeconomic status, and peer relationships.* New York: LFB Scholarly Publishing LLC.

Caspi, A., D. J. Bem, and H. E. Glen, Jr. 2006. "Continuities and consequences of interactional styles across the life course." *Journal of Personality* 57:375–406.

Caughy, M. O., S. M. Nettles, P. J. O'Campo, and K. F. Lohrfink. 2006. "Neighborhood matters: Racial socialization of African American children." *Child Development* 77:1220–1236.

Caughy, M., M. O'Brien, P. J. O'Campo, S. M. Randolph, and K. Nickerson. 2002. "The influence of racial socialization practices on the cognitive and behavioral competence of African American preschoolers." *Child Development* 73:1611–1625.

Cernkovich, S. A. and P. C. Giordano. 1992. "School bonding, race, and delinquency." *Criminology* 30:261–287.

Chandramouli, K., C. Steer, M. Ellis, and A. Emond. 2009. "Effects of early childhood lead exposure on academic performance and behaviour of school age children." *Archives of Disease in Childhood* 94:844–848.

Charles, C. Z. 2001. "Processes of residential segregation." Pp. 217–271 in *Urban inequality: Evidence from four cities*, edited by A. O'Connor, C. Tilly, and L. Bobo. New York: Russell Sage.

——. 2003. "The dynamics of racial residential segregation." *Annual Review of Sociology* 29:167–207.

Chavis, B. F. 1993. "Foreword." Pp. 3–5 in *Confronting environmental racism: Voices from the grassroots*, edited by R.D. Bullard. Boston: South End Press.

Chavous, T. M., D. H. Bernat, K. Schmeelk-Cone, C. H. Caldwell, L. Kohn-Wood, and M. A. Zimmerman. 2003. "Racial identity and academic attainment among African American adolescents." *Child Development* 74:1076–1090.

Chavous, T. M., D. Rivas-Drake, C. Smalls, T. Griffin, and C. Cogburn. 2008. "Gender matters, too: The influences of school racial discrimination and racial identity on academic engagement outcomes among African American adolescents." *Developmental Psychology* 44:637–654.

Chesney-Lind, M. and L. Pasko. 2004. *The female offender: Girls, women, and crime.* Thousand Oaks, CA: Sage Publications, Inc.

Chiodo, L., C. Covington, R. Sokol, J. Hannigan, J. Jannise, J. Ager, M. Greenwald, and V. Delaney-Black. 2007. "Blood lead levels and specific attention effects in young children." *Neurotoxicology and Teratology* 29:538–546.

Chiricos, T., K. Welch, and M. Gertz. 2004. "Racial typification of crime and support for punitive measures." *Criminology* 42:359–389.

Chu, D. C. and H. E. Sung. 2009. "Racial differences in desistance from substance abuse: The impact of religious involvement on recovery." *International Journal of Offender Therapy and Comparative Criminology* 53:696–716.

Clark, K. B. 1965. *Dark ghetto: Dilemmas of social power.* New York: Harper and Row.

Clark, R. 2003. "Subjective stress and coping resources interact to predict blood pressure reactivity in black college students." *Journal of Black Psychology* 29:445–462.

——. 2004. "Interethnic group and intraethnic group racism: Perceptions and coping in black university students." *Journal of Black Psychology* 30:506–526.

Clark, R., N. B. Anderson, V. R. Clark, and D. R. Williams. 1999. "Racism as a stressor for African Americans: A biopsychosocial model." *American Psychologist* 54:805–816.

Clarke, J. W. 1998. "Without fear or shame: Lynching, capital punishment and the subculture of violence in the American south." *British Journal of Political Science* 28:269–289.

Cloward, R. A. and L. E. Ohlin. 1960. *Delinquency and opportunity.* Glencoe, IL: Free Press.

Coll, C. G., G. Lamberty, R. Jenkins, H. P. McAdoo, K. Crnic, B. H. Wasik, and H. V. García. 1996. "An integrative model for the study of developmental competencies in minority children." *Child Development* 67:1891–1914.

Conley, T. D., J. L. Rabinowitz, and J. Rabow. 2010. "Gordon Gekkos, frat boys and nice guys: The content, dimensions, and structural determinants of multiple ethnic minority groups' stereotypes about white men." *Analyses of Social Issues and Public Policy* 10:forthcoming.

Constantine, M. G. and S. K. M. Blackmon. 2002. "Black adolescents' racial socialization experiences: Their relations to home, school, and peer self-esteem." *Journal of Black Studies* 32:322–335.

Costello, B. J. and P. R. Vowell. 1999. "Testing control theory and differential association: A reanalysis of the Richmond youth project data." *Criminology* 37:815–842.

Crime in the United States. Retrieved June 1, 2010, from www.Fbi.Gov/ucr/cius2008/data/table_43.Html.

Cross, W. E. and P. Fhagen-Smith. 2001. "Patterns of African American identity development: A life span perspective." Pp. 243–270 in *New perspectives on racial identity development: A theoretical and practical anthology*, edited by C.L. Wijeyesinghe and I. B.W. Jackson. New York: New York University Press.

Crowder, K. and L. Downey. 2010. "Interneighborhood migration, race, and environmental hazards: Modeling microlevel processes of environmental inequality." *American Journal of Sociology* 115:1110–1149.

Crutchfield, R. D. and S. R. Pitchford. 1997. "Work and crime: The effects of labor stratification." *Social Forces* 76:93–118.

Cutter, S. 1995. "Race, class and environmental justice." *Progress in Human Geography* 19:111–122.

D'Alessio, S. J. and L. Stolzenberg. 2002. "Race and the probability of arrest." *Social Forces* 81:1381–1397.

Daly, K. and M. Chesney-Lind. 1988. "Feminism and criminology." *Justice Quarterly* 5:497–538.

Deaux, K., N. Bikmen, A. Gilkes, A. Ventuneac, Y. Joseph, Y. A. Payne, and C. M. Steele. 2007. "Becoming American: Stereotype threat effects in Afro-Caribbean immigrant groups." *Social Psychology Quarterly* 70:384–404.

DeCuir-Gunby, J. T. 2009. "A review of the racial identity development of African American adolescents: The role of education." *Review of Educational Research* 79:103–124.

Deitch, E. A., A. Barsky, R. M. Butz, S. Chan, A. P. Brief, and J. C. Bradley. 2003. "Subtle yet significant: The existence and impact of everyday racial discrimination in the workplace." *Human Relations* 56:1299–1324.

Denno, D. W. 1990. *Biology and violence: From birth to adulthood*. Cambridge, UK: Cambridge University Press.

Devine, P. G. 1989. "Stereotypes and prejudice: Their automatic and controlled components." *Journal of Personality and Social Psychology* 56:5–18.

Devine, P. G. and A. J. Elliot. 1995. "Are racial stereotypes really fading? The Princeton trilogy revisited." *Personality and Social Psychology Bulletin* 21:1139–1150.

Dietrich, K., R. Douglas, P. Succop, O. Berger, and R. Bornschein. 2001. "Early exposure to lead and juvenile delinquency." *Neurotoxicology and Teratology* 23:511–518.

DiIulio, J. J. Jr. 1994. "The question of black crime." *The Public Interest* 117:3–32.

Dixon, T. L. 2000. "A social cognitive approach to studying racial stereotyping in the mass media." *African American Research Perspectives* 6:60–68.

——. 2007. "Black criminals and white officers: The effects of racially misrepresenting law breakers and law defenders on television news." *Media Psychology* 10:270–291.

——. 2008. "Network news and racial beliefs: Exploring the connection between national television news exposure and stereotypical perceptions of African Americans." *Journal of Communication* 58:321–337.

Dixon, T. L. and D. Linz. 2000. "Race and the misrepresentation of victimization on local television news." *Communication Research* 27:547–573.

——— . 2006. "Overrepresentation and underrepresentation of African Americans and Latinos as lawbreakers on television news." *Journal of Communication* 50:131–154.

Dixon, T. L. and K. B. Maddox. 2005. "Skin tone, crime news, and social reality judgments: Priming the stereotype of the dark and dangerous black criminal." *Journal of Applied Social Psychology* 35:1555–1570.

Dodge, K. A. and N. R. Crick. 1990. "Social information-processing bases of aggressive behavior in children." *Personality and Social Psychology Bulletin* 16:8–22.

Dodge, K. A., J. M. Price, J. A. Bachorowski, and J. P. Newman. 1990. "Hostile attributional biases in severely aggressive adolescents." *Journal of Abnormal Psychology* 99:385–392.

Dodge, K. A. and D. R. Somberg. 1987. "Hostile attributional biases among aggressive boys are exacerbated under conditions of threats to the self." *Child Development* 58:213–224.

Donaldson, K. 1996. *Through students' eyes: Combating racism in United States schools.* Greenwood Publishing Group.

Donziger, S. R. 1996. *The real war on crime: The report of the National Criminal Justice Commission.* New York: Harper Perennial.

Dotterer, A. M., S. M. McHale, and A. C. Crouter. 2009. "Sociocultural factors and school engagement among African American youth: The roles of racial discrimination, racial socialization, and ethnic identity." *Applied Developmental Science* 13:61–73.

Downey, L. 1998. "Environmental injustice: Is race or income a better predictor?" *Social Science Quarterly* 79:766–778.

Downey, L. and M. Van Willigen. 2005. "Environmental stressors: The mental health impacts of living near industrial activity." *Journal of Health and Social Behavior* 46:289–305.

Du Bois, W. E. B. 1898. "The study of the Negro problems." *The ANNALS of the American Academy of Political and Social Science* 11:1–23.

——— . 1899a. "The Negro and crime." *The Independent* 51:1355–1357.

——— . 1899b. *The Philadelphia Negro: A social study.* Philadelphia: University of Pennsylvania Press.

——— . 1901. "The relation of the negroes to the whites in the south." *The ANNALS of the American Academy of Political and Social Science* 18:121–140.

——— . 1903. *The souls of black folk.* Chicago: A. C. McClurg & Co.

——— . 1904. *Some notes on Negro crime, particularly in Georgia.* Atlanta: Atlanta University Press.

Du Bois, W. E. B. and A. Dill. 1913. *Morals and manners among Negro Americans: Report of a social study made by Atlanta University under the patronage of the trustees of the John F. Slater fund; with the proceedings of the 18th Annual Conference for the Study of the Negro Problems.* Atlanta: Atlanta University Press.

Dye, R. T. 1996. "Rosewood, Florida: The destruction of an African American community." *The Historian* 58:605–622.

Eberhardt, J. L., P. G. Davies, V. J. Purdie-Vaughns, and S. L. Johnson. 2006. "Looking deathworthy." *Psychological Science* 17:383–386.

Eberhardt, J. L., P. A. Goff, V. J. Purdie, and P. G. Davies. 2004. "Seeing black: Race, crime, and visual processing." *Journal of Personality and Social Psychology* 87:876–893.

Edwards, A. C., K. A. Dodge, S. J. Latendresse, J. E. Lansford, J. E. Bates, G. S. Pettit, J. P. Budde, A. M. Goate, and D. M. Dick. 2010. "MAOA-UVNTR and early physical discipline interact to influence delinquent behavior." *Journal of Child Psychology and Psychiatry* 51:679–687.

Eitle, D. and T. M. Eitle. 2010. "Public school segregation and juvenile violent crime arrests in metropolitan areas." *Sociological Quarterly* 51:436–459.

Eitle, D. and R. J. Turner. 2003. "Stress exposure, race, and young adult male crime." *Sociological Quarterly* 44:243–269.

Elliott, M. A. and F. E. Merrill. 1934. *Social disorganization*. New York: Harper and Brothers Publishers.

El-Zohairy, E. A., A. F. Youssef, S. M. Abul-Nasr, I. M. Fahmy, D. Salem, A. K. Kahil, and M. K. Madkour. 1996. "Reproductive hazards of lead exposure among urban Egyptian men." *Reproductive Toxicology* 10:145–151.

Entman, R. M. 1994. "Representation and reality in the portrayal of blacks on network television news." *Journalism Quarterly* 71:509–509.

Entman, R. M. and A. Rojecki. 2001. *The black image in the white mind: Media and race in America*. Chicago: University of Chicago Press.

——. 2010a. "Polychlorinated biphenyls (pcbs). Retrieved on July 31, 2010, at http://www. Epa.Gov/wastes/hazard/tsd/pcbs/pubs/about.Htm.

Environmental Protection Agency. 2010b. Lead. Retrieved on July 31, 2010, at http://www. epa.gov/lead/pubs/leadinfo.htm.

Essed, P. 1991. *Understanding everyday racism: An interdisciplinary theory*. Newbury Park, CA: Sage Publications, Inc.

——. 2002. "Everyday racism." Pp. 202–217 in *A companion to racial and ethnic studies*, edited by D.T. Goldberg and J. Solomos. Malden, MA: Wiley-Blackwell.

Evans, G. and E. Kantrowitz. 2002. "Socioeconomic status and health: The potential role of environmental risk exposure." *Annual Review of Public Health* 23:303–331.

Fagan, J. and T. R. Tyler. 2005. "Legal socialization of children and adolescents." *Social Justice Research* 18:217–241.

Fanon, F. 1967a. *Black skin, white masks*. New York: Grove Press.

——. 1967b. *A dying colonialism*. New York: Grove Press.

Farrington, D. P., B. Gallagher, L. Morley, R. J. St. Ledger, and D. J. West. 1986. "Unemployment, school leaving, and crime." *British Journal of Criminology* 26:335–356.

Farrington, D. P., R. J. Sampson, and P.O.H. Wikström. 1993. *Integrating individual and ecological aspects of crime*. Stockholm, Sweden: National Council for Crime Prevention.

Feagin, J. R. 1991. "The continuing significance of race: Antiblack discrimination in public places." *American Sociological Review* 56:101–116.

——. 2001. *Racist America: Roots, current realities, and future reparations*. New York: Routledge.

——. 2006. *Systemic racism: A theory of oppression*. New York: Routledge Press.

——. 2010. *Racist America (2nd edition)*. New York: Routledge.

Feagin, J. R. and C. B. Feagin. 2008. *Racial and ethnic relations (8th edition)*. Upper Saddle River, NJ: Pearson/Prentice-Hall.

Feagin, J. R. and M. P. Sikes. 1995. *Living with racism: The black middle-class experience*. Boston: Beacon Press.

Feagin, J. and H. A. Wingfield. 2009. *Yes we can?: White racial framing and the 2008 Presidential campaign*. New York: Routledge.

Feagin, J. R., H. Vera, and P. Batur. 2001. *White racism: The basics*. New York: Routledge Press.

Fearon, R. P., M. J. Bakermans-Kranenburg, M. H. van Ijzendoorn, A.-M. Lapsley, and G. I. Roisman. 2010. "The significance of insecure attachment and disorganization in the development of children's externalizing behavior: A meta-analytic study." *Child Development* 81:435–456.

Fellner, J. 2009. "Race, drugs, and law enforcement in the United States." *Human Rights Watch*. Retrieved on July 10, 2010, at http://www.hrw.org/en/news/2009/06/19/race-drugs-and-law-enforcement-united-states.

Fergusson, D., J. Boden, and L. Horwood. 2008. "Dentine lead levels in childhood and criminal behaviour in late adolescence and early adulthood." *Journal of Epidemiology and Community Health* 62:1045–1050.

Fergusson, D., L. Horwood, and M. Lynskey. 1997. "Early dentine lead levels and educational outcomes at 18 years." *Journal of Child Psychology and Psychiatry* 38:471–478.

Fine, M. and L. Weiss. 1998. "Crime stories: A critical look through race, ethnicity, and gender." *International Journal of Qualitative Studies in Education* 11:435–459.

Fischer, A. R. and C. M. Shaw. 1999. "African Americans' mental health and perceptions of racist discrimination: The moderating effects of racial socialization experiences and self-esteem." *Journal of Counseling Psychology* 46:395–407.

Fishman, L. T. 2006. "The black bogeyman and white self-righteousness." Pp. 197–211 in *Images of color, images of crime*, edited by C.R. Mann, M.S. Zatz, and N. Rodriguez. New York: Oxford University Press.

Flook, L. and A. J. Fuligni. 2008. "Family and school spillover in adolescents' daily lives." *Child Development* 79:776–787.

Frankenburg, E., C. Lee, and G. Orfield. 2003. *A multiracial society with segregated schools: Are we losing the dream?* Cambridge, MA: The Civil Right Project, Harvard University.

Franklin, J. H. and A. L. Higginbotham. 2010. *From slavery to freedom: A history of African Americans (9th edition)*. New York: McGraw-Hill.

Frantz, C. M., A. J. C. Cuddy, M. Burnett, H. Ray, and A. Hart. 2004. "A threat in the computer: The race implicit association test as a stereotype threat experience." *Personality and Social Psychology Bulletin* 30:1611–1624.

Frazier, E. F. 1949. *The Negro in the United States*. New York: Macmillan Company.

Gabbidon, S. L. 2000. "An early American crime poll by W.E.B. Du Bois." *Western Journal of Black Studies* 24:167–174.

——. 2007. *W.E.B. Du Bois on crime and justice: Laying the foundations of sociological criminology*. Aldershot, UK: Ashgate Publishing Company.

——. 2010. *Criminological perspectives on race and crime (2nd edition)*. New York: Routledge.

Gabbidon, S. L., R. Craig, N. Okafo, L. N. Marzette, and S. A. Peterson. 2008. "The consumer racial profiling experiences of black students at historically black colleges and universities: An exploratory study." *Journal of Criminal Justice* 36:354–361.

Gabbidon, S. L. and H. T. Greene. 2009. *Race and crime (2nd edition)*. Thousand Oaks, CA: Sage.

Gabbidon, S. L., H. T. Greene, and V. D. Young. 2002. *African American classics in criminology and criminal justice*. Thousand Oaks: Sage Publications, Inc.

Gabbidon, S. L. and G. E. Higgins. 2007. "Consumer racial profiling and perceived victimization: A phone survey of Philadelphia area residents." *American Journal of Criminal Justice* 32:1–11.

——. 2008. "Profiling white Americans: A research note on shopping while white." In *Racial divide: Race, ethnicity and criminal justice*, edited by M.J. Lynch, E.B. Patterson, and K. Childs. Monsey, NY: Criminal Justice Press.

——. 2009. "The role of race/ethnicity and race relations on public opinion related to the treatment of blacks by the police." *Police Quarterly* 12:102–115.

Gabbidon, S. L., G. E. Higgins, and H. Potter. 2011. "Race, gender, and the perception of recently experiencing unfair treatment by the police: Exploratory results from an all-black sample." *Criminal Justice Review* 36:5–21.

Gabbidon, S. L. and S. A. Peterson. 2006. "Living while black: A state-level analysis of the influence of select social stressors on the quality of life among black Americans." *Journal of Black Studies* 37:83–102.

Gado, M. 2010. "Lynching in America: Carnival of death." Retrieved on January 26, 2010, at http://www.trutv.com/library/crime/notorious_murders/mass/lynching/press_3.html.

Galster, G., D. Wissoker, and W. Zimmermann. 2001. "Testing for discrimination in home insurance: Results from New York City and Phoenix." *Urban Studies* 38:141–156.

Garland, D. 2005. "Penal excess and surplus meaning: Public torture lynchings in twentieth-century America." *Law and Society Review* 39:793–833.

Gates, H. L. and C. M. Steele. 2009. "A conversation with Claude Steele." *Du Bois Review: Social Science Research on Race* 6:251–271.

Gau, J. M. and R. K. Brunson. 2010. "Procedural justice and order maintenance policing: A study of inner-city young men's perceptions of police legitimacy." *Justice Quarterly* 27:255–279.

Gay, C. 2004. "Putting race in context: Identifying the environmental determinants of black racial attitudes." *The American Political Science Review* 98:547–562.

Geller, A. and J. Fagan. 2010. "Pot as pretext: Marijuana, race, and the new disorder in New York City street policing." *Journal of Empirical Legal Studies* 7:591–633.

Genovese, E. D. 1974. *Roll, Jordan, roll: The world the slaves made.* New York: Pantheon Books.

Geronimus, A. T., M. Hicken, D. Keene, and J. Bound. 2006. "'Weathering' and age patterns of allostatic load scores among blacks and whites in the United States." *American Journal of Public Health* 96:826–833.

Geronimus, A. T. and J. P. Thompson. 2004. "To denigrate, ignore, or disrupt: Racial inequality in health and the impact of a policy-induced breakdown of African American communities." *Du Bois Review: Social Science Research on Race* 1:247–279.

Gershoff, E. T., A. Grogan-Kaylor, J. E. Lansford, L. Chang, A. Zelli, K. Deater-Deckard, and K. A. Dodge. 2010. "Parent discipline practices in an international sample: Associations with child behaviors and moderation by perceived normativeness." *Child Development* 81:487–502.

Gibbons, F. X., P. E. Etcheverry, M. L. Stock, M. Gerrard, C.-Y. Weng, M. Kiviniemi, and R. E. O'Hara. 2010. "Exploring the link between racial discrimination and substance use: What mediates? What buffers?" *Journal of Personality and social Psychology* 99:forthcoming.

Gibbons, F. X., M. Gerrard, M. J. Cleveland, T. A. Wills, and G. Brody. 2004. "Perceived discrimination and substance use in African American parents and their children: A panel study." *Journal of Personality and Social Psychology* 86:517–529.

Gibbs, J. T. 1988. *Young, black, and male in America: An endangered species.* Dover, MA: Auburn House Publishing Company.

Gilbert, S. and B. Weiss. 2006. "A rationale for lowering the blood lead action level from 10 to 2 [mu] g/dl." *Neurotoxicology* 27:693–701.

Giordano, P. C., R. D. Schroeder, and S. A. Cernkovich. 2007. "Emotions and crime over the life course: A neo Meadian perspective on criminal continuity and change." *American Journal of Sociology* 112:1603–1661.

Glaeser, E. L., E. A. Hanushek, and J. M. Quigley. 2004. "Opportunities, race, and urban location: The influence of John Kain." *Journal of Urban Economics* 56:70–79.

Goffman, E. 1963. *Stigma: Notes on the management of spoiled identity.* Englewood Cliffs, NJ: Prentice Hall.

Goldsmith, P. A. 2004. "Schools' role in shaping race relations: Evidence on friendliness and conflict." *Social Problems* 51:587–612.

Gonick, H. C. and J. R. Behari. 2002. "Is lead exposure the principal cause of essential hypertension?" *Medical Hypotheses* 59:239–246.

Gottfredson, M. R. and T. Hirschi. 1990. *A general theory of crime*. Palo Alto, CA: Stanford University Press.

Government Accounting Office (GAO). 1983. *Siting of hazardous waste landfills and their correlation with racial and economic status of surrounding communities*. Washington, DC: US Government Accounting Office.

Greene, H. T. and S. L. Gabbidon. 2000. *African American criminological thought*. Albany, NY: State University of New York Press.

Greene, H. T. 1979. *A comprehensive bibliography of criminology and criminal justice literature by black authors from 1895–1978*. College Park, MD: Ummah Publications.

Gregory, A., R. J. Skiba, and P. A. Noguera. 2010. "The achievement gap and the discipline gap: Two sides of the same coin?" *Educational Researcher* 39:59–68.

Gregory, A. and R. S. Weinstein. 2008. "The discipline gap and African Americans: Defiance or cooperation in the high school classroom." *Journal of School Psychology* 46:455–475.

Grier, W. H. and P. M. Cobbs. 1996. *Black rage*. New York: Basic Books.

Gwynn, R. C. and G. D. Thurston. 2001. "The burden of air pollution: Impacts among racial minorities." *Environmental Health Perspectives* 109:501–505.

Hacker, A. 2003. *Two nations: Black and white, separate, hostile, unequal*. New York: Scribner.

Hagan, J. and H. Foster. 2003. "S/he's a rebel: Toward a sequential stress theory of delinquency and gendered pathways to disadvantage in emerging adulthood." *Social Forces* 82:53–86.

Hagan, J., C. Shedd, and M. R. Payne. 2005. "Race, ethnicity, and youth perceptions of criminal injustice." *American Sociological Review* 70:381–407.

Harrell, S. 2000. "A multidimensional conceptualization of racism-related stress: Implications for the well-being of people of color." *American Journal of Orthopsychiatry* 70:42–57.

Harris, A. M. G. 2003. "Shopping while black: Applying 42 u.S.C. § 1981 to cases of consumer racial profiling." *Boston College Third World Law Journal* 23:1–56.

Harris, A. M. G., G. R. Henderson, and J. D. Williams. 2005. "Courting customers: Assessing consumer racial profiling and other marketplace discrimination." *Journal of Public Policy and Marketing* 24:163–171.

Harris, D. A. 1999. "Driving while black: Racial profiling on our nation's highways." *American Civil Liberties Union Special Report*:1–30.

Harris-Britt, A., C. R. Valrie, B. Kurtz-Costes, and S. J. Rowley. 2007. "Perceived racial discrimination and self-esteem in African American youth: Racial socialization as a protective factor." *Journal of Research on Adolescence* 17:669–682.

Haslam, S. A., J. Salvatore, T. Kessler, and S. D. Reicher. 2008. "How stereotyping yourself contributes to your success (or failure)." *Scientific American* 3:1–6.

Hawkins, D. F. 1990. "Explaining the black homicide rate." *Journal of Interpersonal Violence* 5:151–163.

——— . 1995. "Ethnicity, race, and crime: A review of selected studies." Pp. 11–45 in *Ethnicity, race, and crime: Perspectives across time and place*. Albany, NY: State University of New York Press.

Heron, M. 2010. "Deaths: Leading causes for 2006." Hyattsville, MD: National Center for Health Statistics/Center for Disease Control and Prevention.

Higgins, G. E., S. L. Gabbidon, and G. Vito. 2010. "Exploring the influence of race relations and public safety concerns on public support for racial profiling during traffic stops." *International Journal of Police Science and Management* 12:12–22.

Higgins, G. E. (ed.) 2010. *Race, crime, and delinquency: A criminological theory approach*. Upper Saddle River, NJ: Pearson/Prentice-Hall.

Higgins, G. E. and M. L. Ricketts. 2005. "Self-control theory, race, and delinquency." *Journal of Ethnicity in Criminal Justice* 3:5–22.

Higgins, G. E., S. E. Wolfe, M. Mahoney, and N. M. Walters. 2009. "Race, ethnicity, and experience: Modeling the public's perceptions of justice, satisfaction, and attitude toward the courts." *Journal of Ethnicity in Criminal Justice* 7:293–310.

Hindelang, M. J. 1978. "Race and involvement in common law personal crimes." *American Sociological Review* 43:93–109.

Hipp, J. R. 2010. "A dynamic view of neighborhoods: The reciprocal relationship between crime and neighborhood structural characteristics." *Social Problems* 57:205–230.

——. 2010a. "Resident perceptions of crime and disorder: How much is 'bias,' and how much is social environment differences?" *Criminology* 48:475–508.

——. 2010b. "The role of crime in housing unit racial-ethnic transition." *Criminology* 48:683–723.

Hirschfield, P. J. and D. Simon. 2010. "Legitimating police violence: Newspaper narratives of deadly force." *Theoretical Criminology* 14:155–182.

Hirschi, T. 1969. *Causes of delinquency.* Berkeley: University of California Press.

——. 2003. "A control theory of delinquency." Pp. 172–180 in *Deviant behavior: A text reader in the sociology of deviance*, edited by D. H. Kelly and E. J. Clarke. New York: Worth Publishers.

Hirsh, E. and C. J. Lyons. 2010. "Perceiving discrimination on the job: Legal consciousness, workplace context, and the construction of race discrimination." *Law and Society Review* 44:269–298.

Ho, A. K. and J. Sidanius. 2010. "Preserving positive identities: Public and private regard for one's ingroup and susceptibility to stereotype threat." *Group Processes and Intergroup Relations* 13:55–67.

Hochschild, J. L. and V. Weaver. 2007. "The skin color paradox and the American racial order." *Social Forces* 86:643–670.

Holden-Smith, B. 1996. "Inherently unequal justice: Interracial rape and the death penalty." *Journal of Criminal Law and Criminology* 86:1571–1583.

Holloway, S. R. 1998. "Exploring the neighborhood contingency of race discrimination in mortgage lending in Columbus, Ohio." *Annals of the Association of American Geographers* 88:252–276.

Holmes, M. D. and B. W. Smith. 2008. *Race and police brutality: Roots of an urban dilemma.* Albany, NY: State University of New York Press.

hooks, b. 2004. *We real cool: Black men and masculinity.* New York: Routledge.

Hughes, D. and L. Chen. 1997. "When and what parents tell children about race: An examination of race-related socialization among African American families." *Personality and Social Psychology Review* 1:200–214.

Hughes, D., C. Hagelskamp, N. Way, and M. D. Foust. 2009. "The role of mothers' and adolescents' perceptions of ethnic-racial socialization in shaping ethnic-racial identity among early adolescent boys and girls." *Journal of Youth and Adolescence* 38:605–626.

Hughes, D., J. Rodriguez, E. P. Smith, D. J. Johnson, H. C. Stevenson, and P. Spicer. 2006. "Parents' ethnic-racial socialization practices: A review of research and directions for future study." *Developmental Psychology* 42:747–769.

Hughes, D., D. Witherspoon, D. Rivas-Drake, and N. West-Bey. 2009. "Received ethnic racial socialization messages and youths' academic and behavioral outcomes: Examining the mediating role of ethnic identity and self-esteem." *Cultural Diversity and Ethnic Minority Psychology* 15:112–124.

Hurwitz, J. and M. Peffley. 1997. "Public perceptions of race and crime: The role of racial stereotypes." *American Journal of Political Science* 41:375–401.

Inzlicht, M. and S. Kang. 2010. "Stereotype threat spillover: How coping with threats to social identity affects aggression, eating, decision making, and attention." *Journal of Personality and Social Psychology*:forthcoming.

Inzlicht, M., L. McKay, and J. Aronson. 2006. "Stigma as ego depletion: How being the target of prejudice affects self-control." *Psychological Science* 17:262–269.

James, J. 2010. "Campaigns against 'blackness': Criminality, incivility, and election to executive office." *Critical Sociology* 36:25–44.

Jang, S. J. and B. R. Johnson. 2003. "Strain, negative emotions, and deviant coping among African Americans: A test of general strain theory." *Journal of Quantitative Criminology* 19:79–105.

——. 2005. "Gender, religiosity, and reactions to strain among African Americans." *Sociological Quarterly* 46:323–357.

Jang, S. J. and J. A. Lyons. 2006. "Strain, social support, and retreatism among African Americans." *Journal of Black Studies* 37:251–274.

Jean, Y. S. and J. R. Feagin. 1998. *Double burden: Black women and everyday racism*. Armonk, NY: ME Sharpe Inc.

Jefferson, T. 1785/1999. *Notes on the state of Virginia*. New York: Penguin Books.

Johansson, P. and K. Kempf-Leonard. 2009. "A gender-specific pathway to serious, violent, and chronic offending?" *Crime and Delinquency*: 216–240.

Johnson, B. R., S. J. Jang, S. D. Li, and D. Larson. 2000. "The 'invisible institution' and black youth crime: The church as an agency of local social control." *Journal of Youth and Adolescence* 29:479–498.

Johnson, B. R., D. B. Larson, S. De Li, and S. J. Jang. 2000. "Escaping from the crime of inner cities: Church attendance and religious salience among disadvantaged youth." *Justice Quarterly* 17:377–391.

Johnson, D. 2007. "Crime salience, perceived racial bias, and blacks' punitive attitudes." *Journal of Ethnicity in Criminal Justice* 4:1–18.

——. 2009. "Anger about crime and support for punitive criminal justice policies." *Punishment and Society* 11:51.

Johnson, D. and J. Kuhns. 2009. "Striking out: Race and support for police use of force." *Justice Quarterly* 26:592–623.

Jones, J. M. 1997. *Prejudice and racism*. New York: McGraw-Hill.

——. 2006. "Whites, blacks, Hispanics disagree about way minority groups treated: Whites diverge from blacks, Hispanics in their views of black-Hispanic relations." Retrieved July 10, 2010, at http://www.gallup.com/poll/23629/whites-blacks-hispanics-disagree-about-way-minority-groups-treated-aspx.

Jones, N. 2010. *Between good and ghetto: African American girls and inner city violence*. Piscataway, NJ: Rutgers University Press.

Jungmeen, K. and D. Cicchetti. 2010. "Longitudinal pathways linking child maltreatment, emotion regulation, peer relations, and psychopathology." *Journal of Child Psychology and Psychiatry* 51:706–716.

Jusko, T., C. Henderson Jr., B. Lanphear, D. Cory-Slechta, P. Parsons, and R. Canfield. 2008. "Blood lead concentrations < 10 g/dl and child intelligence at 6 years of age." *Environmental Health Perspectives* 116:243–248.

Karenga, M. 2002. *Introduction to black studies (3rd edition)*. Los Angeles, CA: University of Sankore Press.

Kaufman, J. M., C. J. Rebellon, S. Thaxton, and R. Agnew. 2008. "A general strain theory of racial differences in criminal offending." *The Australian and New Zealand Journal of Criminology* 41:421–437.

Keijsers, L., S. J. T. Branje, I. E. VanderValk, and W. Meeus. 2010. "Reciprocal effects between parental solicitation, parental control, adolescent disclosure, and adolescent delinquency." *Journal of Research on Adolescence* 20:88–113.

Keith, V. M. and C. Herring. 1991. "Skin tone and stratification in the black community." *American Journal of Sociology* 97:760–778.

Keith, V. M., K. D. Lincoln, R. J. Taylor, and J. S. Jackson. 2010. "Discriminatory experiences and depressive symptoms among African American women: Do skin tone and mastery matter?" *Sex Roles* 62:48–59.

Kellow, J. T. and B. D. Jones. 2008. "The effects of stereotypes on the achievement gap: Reexamining the academic performance of African American high school students." *Journal of Black Psychology* 34:94–120.

Kennedy, R. 1994. "The state, criminal law, and racial discrimination: A comment." *Harvard Law Review* 107:1255–1278.

Kerner, O. 1968. *The Kerner report: The 1968 report of the National Advisory Commission on Civil Disorders*. NY: Bantom Books.

Keyes, C. L. M. 2009. "The black–white paradox in health: Flourishing in the face of social inequality and discrimination." *Journal of Personality* 77:1677–1706.

Kim, K. C. 1999. *Koreans in the hood: Conflict with African Americans*. Johns Hopkins University Press.

Kinder, D. R. and L. M. Sanders. 1996. *Divided by color: Racial politics and democratic ideals*. Chicago: University of Chicago Press.

King, A. E. O. 1997. "Understanding violence among young African American males: An afrocentric perspective." *Journal of Black Studies* 28:79–96.

King, R. S. and M. Mauer. 2002. *Distorted priorities: Drug offenders in state prisons*. Washington, DC: Sentencing Project.

——. 2006. "The war on marijuana: The transformation of the war on drugs in the 1990s." *Harm Reduction Journal* 3:1477–7517.

Kirk, D. 2008. "The neighborhood context of racial and ethnic disparities in arrest." *Demography* 45:55–77.

Klonoff, E. A., H. Landrine, and J. B. Ullman. 1999. "Racial discrimination and psychiatric symptoms among blacks." *Cultural Diversity and Ethnic Minority Psychology* 5:329–339.

Kornhauser, R. R. 1978. *Social sources of delinquency: An appraisal of analytic models*. Chicago: University of Chicago Press.

Krysan, M. and R. Farley. 2002. "The residential preferences of blacks: Do they explain persistent segregation?" *Social Forces* 80:937–980.

Kubrin, C. E. 2005. "Gangstas, thugs, and hustlas: Identity and the code of the street in rap music." *Social Problems* 52:360–378.

Kunjufu, J. 2004. *Solutions for black America*. Chicago, IL: African American Images.

Lamont, M. and V. Molnár. 2001. "How blacks use consumption to shape their collective identity." *Journal of Consumer Culture* 1:31–45.

Lanphear, B., K. Dietrich, P. Auinger, and C. Cox. 2000. "Cognitive deficits associated with blood lead concentrations < 10 microg/dl in US children and adolescents." *Public Health Reports* 115:521–529.

Lanphear, B., R. Hornung, J. Khoury, K. Yolton, P. Baghurst, D. Bellinger, R. Canfield, K. Dietrich, R. Bornschein, and T. Greene. 2005. "Low-level environmental lead exposure and children's intellectual function: An international pooled analysis." *Environmental Health Perspectives* 113:894–899.

Laurin, K., G. Fitzsimons, and A. Kay. 2011. "Social disadvantage and the self-regulatory function of justice beliefs." *Journal of Personality and Social Psychology* 100:149–171.

Lee, J. M., L. Steinberg, and A. R. Piquero. 2010. "Ethnic identity and attitudes toward the police among African American juvenile offenders." *Journal of Criminal Justice* 38:781–789.

Leiber, M. J., K. Y. Mack, and R. A. Featherstone. 2009. "Family structure, family processes, economic factors, and delinquency: Similarities and differences by race and ethnicity." *Youth Violence and Juvenile Justice* 7:79–99.

Lemert, E. M. 1972. *Human deviance, social problems and social control (2nd edition)*. Englewood Cliffs, NJ: Prentice-Hall.

Lesane-Brown, C. L. 2006. "A review of race socialization within black families." *Developmental Review* 26:400–426.

Levin, J. S. and R. J. Taylor. 1993. "Gender and age differences in religiosity among black Americans." *The Gerontologist* 33:16–23.

Lincoln, C. E. 1999. *Race, religion, and the continuing American dilemma*. New York: Hill and Wang.

Lincoln, C. E. and L. H. Mamiya. 1990. *The black church in the African-American experience*. Durham, NC: Duke University Press.

Link, B. G. and J. C. Phelan. 2001. "Conceptualizing stigma." *Annual Review of Sociology* 27:363–385.

Lippmann, W. 1922. *Public opinion*. New York: Free Press.

Littwin, M. 1995. "The great divide black and white: O.J. Simpson trial once again exposes the deep racial divisions in America." *Baltimore Sun*, Retrieved on July 5, 2010, at http://articles.baltimoresun.com/1995–10–04/features/1995277011_1_cochran-white-cops-racist-cops.

Lopresti, R. 2010. "Which U.S. Presidents owned slaves?" Retrieved on July 2, 2010, at http://www.nas.com/~lopresti/ps.htm.

Loury, G. C. 2004. *Racial justice: The superficial morality of colour-blindness in the United States*. Durban: United Nations Research Institute for Social Development.

Lynch, M. 2006. "Stereotypes, prejudice, and life-and-death decision-making: Lessons from laypersons in an experimental setting." Pp. 182–210 in *Lynch mobs killing state race and the death penalty in America*, edited by C. J. Ogletree and A. Sarat. New York: New York University Press.

MacDonald, J., R. J. Stokes, G. Ridgeway, and K. J. Riley. 2007. "Race, neighborhood context and perceptions of injustice by the police in Cincinnati." *Urban Studies* 44:2567–2585.

Maher, T. 1998. "Environmental oppression: Who is targeted for toxic exposure?" *Journal of Black Studies* 28:357–367.

Major, B. and L. T. O'Brien. 2005. "The social psychology of stigma." *Annual Review of Psychology* 56:393–421.

Mandara, J., N. K. Gaylord-Harden, M. H. Richards, and B. L. Ragsdale. 2009. "The effects of changes in racial identity and self-esteem on changes in African American adolescents' mental health." *Child Development* 80:1660–1675.

Markowitz, F. E. 1998. "The effects of stigma on the psychological well-being and life satisfaction of persons with mental illness." *Journal of Health and Social Behavior* 39:335–347.

Martin, J. K., S. A. Tuch, and P. M. Roman. 2003. "Problem drinking patterns among African Americans: The impacts of reports of discrimination, perceptions of prejudice, and 'risky' coping strategies." *Journal of Health and Social Behavior* 44:408–425.

Martin, L. 2010. "Strategic assimilation or creation of symbolic blackness: Middle-class blacks in suburban contexts." *Journal of African American Studies* 14:234–246.

Marx, D. M., S. J. Ko, and R. A. Friedman. 2009. "The 'Obama effect': How a salient role model reduces race-based performance differences." *Journal of Experimental Social Psychology* 45:953–956.

Massey, D. S. 1990. "American apartheid: Segregation and the making of the underclass." *American Journal of Sociology* 96:329–357.

——. 2005. "Racial discrimination in housing: A moving target." *Social Problems* 52:148–151.

Massey, D. S. and N. A. Denton. 1993. *American apartheid: Segregation and the making of the underclass.* Cambridge, MA: Harvard University Press.

Massey, D. S. and L. Probasco. 2010. "Divergent streams." *Du Bois Review: Social Science Research on Race* 7:219–246.

Mattison, E. and M. Aber. 2007. "Closing the achievement gap: The association of racial climate with achievement and behavioral outcomes." *American Journal of Community Psychology* 40:1–12.

Maume, M. O., Y. S. Kim-Godwin, and C. M. Clements. 2010. "Racial tensions and school crime." *Journal of Contemporary Criminal Justice* 26:339–358.

Maykovich, M. K. 1972. "Reciprocity in racial stereotypes: White, black, and yellow." *American Journal of Sociology* 77:876–897.

Mazama, A. 2001. "The Afrocentric paradigm: Contours and definitions." *Journal of Black Studies* 31:387–405.

Mazerolle, P., V. S. Burton, F. T. Cullen, T. D. Evans, and G. L. Payne. 2000. "Strain, anger, and delinquent adaptations: Specifying general strain theory." *Journal of Criminal Justice* 28:89–101.

Mazerolle, P., A. R. Piquero, and G. E. Capowich. 2003. "Examining the links between strain, situational and dispositional anger, and crime: Further specifying and testing general strain theory." *Youth and Society* 35:131–157.

McGuire, R. A. and R. L. Ohsfeldt. 1986. "An economic model of voting behavior over specific issues at the Constitutional Convention of 1787." *The Journal of Economic History* 46:79–111.

McHale, S. M., A. C. Crouter, J. Y. Kim, L. M. Burton, K. D. Davis, A. M. Dotterer, and D. P. Swanson. 2006. "Mothers' and fathers' racial socialization in African American families: Implications for youth." *Child Development* 77:1387–1402.

McKown, C. and M. J. Strambler. 2009. "Developmental antecedents and social and academic consequences of stereotype-consciousness in middle childhood." *Child Development* 80:1643–1659.

McKown, C. and R. S. Weinstein. 2008. "Teacher expectations, classroom context, and the achievement gap." *Journal of School Psychology* 46:235–261.

McLoyd, V. C., A. M. Cauce, D. Takeuchi, and L. Wilson. 2000. "Marital processes and parental socialization in families of color: A decade review of research." *Journal of Marriage and the Family* 62:1070–1093.

McMahon, S. D. and R. J. Watts. 2002. "Ethnic identity in urban African American youth: Exploring links with self-worth, aggression, and other psychosocial variables." *Journal of Community Psychology* 30:411–431.

McRae, M. B., P. M. Carey, and R. Anderson-Scott. 1998. "Black churches as therapeutic systems: A group process perspective." *Health Education and Behavior* 25:778–789.

Mead, N. L., Roy F. Baumeister, Tyler F. Stillman, Catherine D. Rawn, and K. D. Vohs. 2011. "Social exclusion causes people to spend and consume strategically in the service of affiliation." *Journal of Consumer Research* 37:902–919.

Mendoza. 2010. "AP impact: US drug war has met none of its goals." Retrieved July 11, 2010, at http://abcnews.go.com/ws/wirestory?ip=10642775.

Merton, R. K. 1938. "Social structure and anomie." *American Sociological Review* 3:672–682.

Mikula, G. 2003. "Testing an attribution-of-blame model of judgments of injustice." *European Journal of Social Psychology* 33:793–811.

Mikula, G., K. R. Scherer, and U. Athenstaedt. 1998. "The role of injustice in the elicitation of differential emotional reactions." *Personality and Social Psychology Bulletin* 24:769–783.

Miller, C. T. and C. R. Kaiser. 2001. "A theoretical perspective on coping with stigma." *Journal of Social Issues* 57:73–92.

Miller, D. B. 1999. "Racial socialization and racial identity: Can they promote resiliency for African American adolescents?" *Adolescence* 34:493–501.

Miller, D. T. 2001. "Disrespect and the experience of injustice." *Annual Review of Psychology* 52:527–553.

Miller, J. and C. Mullins. 2006. "The status of feminist theories in criminology." Pp. 217–249 in *Taking stock: The status of criminological theory*, edited by F. T. Cullen, J. P. Wright, and K. R. Blevins. New Brunswick, NJ: Transaction Publishers.

Min, M., L. Singer, H. Kirchner, S. Minnes, E. Short, Z. Hussain, and S. Nelson. 2009. "Cognitive development and low-level lead exposure in poly-drug exposed children." *Neurotoxicology and Teratology* 31:225–231.

Minior, T., S. Galea, J. Stuber, J. Ahern, and D. Ompad. 2003. "Racial differences in discrimination experiences and responses among minority substance users." *Ethnicity and Disease* 13:521–527.

Mitchell, C. M. 1993. "Environmental racism: Race as a primary factor in the selection of hazardous waste sites." *National Black Law Journal* 12:176–188.

Morenoff, J. D., R. J. Sampson, and S. W. Raudenbush. 2001. "Neighborhood inequality, collective efficacy, and the spatial dynamics of urban violence." *Criminology* 39:517–558.

Morin, R. 2009. "What divides America? Immigration and income—not race—are seen as primary sources of social conflict." Pew Research Center. Retrieved on May 15, 2010, at http://pewresearch.org/pubs/1354/social-conflict-in-America.

Mott, L. 1995. "The disproportionate impact of environmental health threats on children of color." *Environmental Health Perspectives* 103:33–35.

Murry, V. M. B., C. Berkel, G. H. Brody, S. J. Miller, and Y. Chen. 2009. "Linking parental socialization to interpersonal protective processes, academic self-presentation, and expectations among rural African American youth." *Cultural Diversity and Ethnic Minority Psychology* 15:1–10.

Naicker, N., S. A. Norris, A. Mathee, P. Becker, and L. Richter. 2010. "Lead exposure is associated with a delay in the onset of puberty in South African adolescent females: Findings from the birth to twenty cohort." *Science of the Total Environment*: forthcoming.

Narag, R. E., J. Pizarro, and C. Gibbs. 2009. "Lead exposure and its implications for criminological theory." *Criminal Justice and Behavior* 36:954–973.

NBC News. 2004. "NBC News Poll: 10 years after Simpson verdict issue of race still figures prominently in public opinion." Retrieved on January 23, 2010, at http://www.msnbc.msn.com/id/5139346/.

Needleman, H. L. 2008. "Lead hazards and poisoning." Pp. 39–45 in *International encyclopedia of public health*, edited by H. Kris. Oxford: Academic Press.

Needleman, H. L., C. McFarland, R. B. Ness, S. E. Fienberg, and M. J. Tobin. 2002. "Bone lead levels in adjudicated delinquents: A case control study." *Neurotoxicology and Teratology* 24:711–717.

Needleman, H. L., J. A. Riess, M. J. Tobin, G. E. Biesecker, and J. B. Greenhouse. 1996.

"Bone lead levels and delinquent behavior." *Journal of American Medical Association* 275:363–369.

Nevin, R. 2000. "How lead exposure relates to temporal changes in violent crime, and unwed pregnancy." *Environmental Research* 83:1–22.

——. 2007. "Understanding international crime trends: The legacy of preschool lead exposure." *Environmental Research* 104:315–336.

Nicolas, G., J. E. Helms, M. M. Jernigan, T. Sass, A. Skrzypek, and A. M. DeSilva. 2008. "A conceptual framework for understanding the strengths of black youths." *Journal of Black Psychology* 34:261–280.

Niemann, Y. F. 2001. "Stereotypes about Chicanas and Chicanos: Implications for counseling." *The Counseling Psychologist* 29:55–90.

Nigg, J. T., G. M. Knottnerusn, M. M. Martel, M. Nikolas, K. Cavanagh, W. Karmaus, and M. D. Rappley. 2008. "Low blood lead levels associated with clinically diagnosed attention-deficit/hyperactivity disorder and mediated by weak cognitive control." *Biological Psychiatry* 63:1–17.

Noble, R. L. 2006. *Black rage in the American prison system*. New York: LFB Scholarly Publishing LLC.

Noguera, P. A. 2003. "The trouble with black boys: The role and influence of environmental and cultural factors on the academic performance of African American males." *Urban Education* 38:431–459.

Nunnally, S. C. 2010. "Learning race, socializing blackness." *Du Bois Review: Social Science Research on Race* 7:185–217.

O'Brien, L. T., C. S. Crandall, A. Horstman-Reser, R. Warner, A. Alsbrooks, and A. Blodorn. 2010. "But I'm no bigot: How prejudiced white Americans maintain unprejudiced self-images." *Journal of Applied Social Psychology* 40:917–946.

Odom, E. C. and L. Vernon-Feagans. 2010. "Buffers of racial discrimination: Links with depression among rural African American mothers." *Journal of Marriage and Family* 72:346–359.

Ogletree, C. J. Jr. 2002. "Black man's burden: Race and the death penalty in America." *Oregon Law Review* 81:15–38.

Ogletree, C. J., Jr. 2006. "Making race matter in death matters." Pp. 55–95 in *Lynch mobs killing states*, edited by C. J. Ogletree, Jr. and A. Sarat. New York: New York University Press.

Ogletree, J. C. Jr. 2010. *The presumption of guilt: The arrest of Henry Louis Gates, Jr. And race, class and crime in America*. New York, NY: Palgrave Macmillan.

Ogletree, C. J. Jr. and A. Sarat. 2006. *From lynch mobs to the killing state: Race and the death penalty in America*. New York: New York University Press.

Oliver, W. 1984. "Black males and the tough guy image: A dysfunctional compensatory adaptation." *Western Journal of Black Studies* 8:199–203.

——. 1989a. "Sexual conquest and patterns of black-on-black violence: A structural-cultural perspective." *Violence and Victims* 4:257–273.

——. 1989b. "Black males and social problems: Prevention through Afrocentric socialization." *Journal of Black Studies* 20:15–39.

——. 2003. "The structural cultural perspective: A theory of black male violence." Pp. 280–318 in *Violent crime: Assessing race and ethnic differences*, edited by D. F. Hawkins. New York: Cambridge University Press.

——. 2006. "'The streets': An alternative black male socialization institution." *Journal of Black Studies* 36:918–937.

Olzak, S., S. Shanahan, and E. H. McEneaney. 1996. "Poverty, segregation, and race riots: 1960 to 1993." *American Sociological Review* 61:590–613.

Onwudiwe, I. D. and M. J. Lynch. 2000. "Reopening the debate: A reexamination of the need for a black criminology." *Social Pathology: A Journal of Reviews* 6:182–198.

Osborne, J. W. 1997. "Race and academic disidentification." *Journal of Educational Psychology* 89:728–735.

Oshinsky, D. M. 1997. *Worse than slavery: Parchman farm and the ordeal of Jim Crow justice.* New York: Free Press.

Outten, H. R., B. Giguere, M. T. Schmitt, and R. N. Lalonde. 2010. "Racial identity, racial context, and ingroup status: Implications for attributions to discrimination among black Canadians." *Journal of Black Psychology* 36:172–196.

Owens-Sabir, M. C. 2007. *The effects of race and family attachment on self-esteem, self-control, and delinquency.* El Paso, TX: LFB Scholarly Publishing LLC.

Oyserman, D. and K.-I. Yoon. 2009. "Neighborhood effects on racial–ethnic identity: The undermining role of segregation." *Race and Social Problems* 1:67–76.

Pager, D. 2003. "The mark of a criminal record." *American Journal of Sociology* 108:937–75.

Pager, D. and H. Shepherd. 2008. "The sociology of discrimination: Racial discrimination in employment, housing, credit, and consumer markets." *Annual Review of Sociology* 34:181–209.

Park, R. 1925. "The city: Suggestions for the investigation of human behavior in the urban environment." Pp. 1–46 in *The city*, edited by R. E. Park, E. W. Burgess, and R. D. McKenzie. Chicago: University of Chicago Press.

Park, R. E., E. W. Burgess, and R. D. McKenzie. 1925. *The city.* Chicago: University of Chicago Press.

Pastor, M., J. Sadd, and J. Hipp. 2001. "Which came first? Toxic facilities, minority move-in, and environmental justice." *Journal of Urban Affairs* 23:1–21.

Paternoster, R., R. Brame, R. Bachman, and L. W. Sherman. 1997. "Do fair procedures matter? The effect of procedural justice on spouse assault." *Law and Society Review* 31:163–204.

Patterson, G. R., B. D. DeBaryshe, and E. Ramsey. 1989. "A developmental perspective on antisocial behavior." *American Psychologist* 44:329–335.

Pauker, K., N. Ambady, and E. P. Apfelbaum. 2010. "Race salience and essentialist thinking in racial stereotype development." *Child Development* 81:1799–1813.

Payne, A. A. 2008. "A multilevel analysis of the relationships among communal school organization, student bonding, and delinquency." *Journal of Research in Crime and Delinquency* 45:429–455.

Payne, A. and K. Welch. 2010. "Modeling the effects of racial threat on punitive and restorative school discipline practices." *Criminology* 48:1019–1062.

Peffley, M. and J. Hurwitz. 1998. "Whites' stereotypes of blacks: Sources and political consequences." Pp. 58–99 in *Perception and prejudice: Race and politics in the United States*, edited by J. Hurwitz and M. Peffley. New Haven: Yale University Press.

———. 2002. "The racial components of 'race-neutral' crime policy attitudes." *Political Psychology* 23:59–75.

Peffley, M., J. Hurwitz, and P. M. Sniderman. 1997. "Racial stereotypes and whites' political views of blacks in the context of welfare and crime." *American Journal of Political Science* 41:30–60.

Penn, E. B. 2003. "On black criminology: Past, present, and future." *Criminal Justice Studies* 16:317–327.

Perez, A. D., K. M. Berg, and D. J. Myers. 2003. "Police and riots, 1967–1969." *Journal of Black Studies* 34:153–182.

Peterson, R. D. and L. J. Krivo. 2010. *Divergent social worlds: Neighborhood crime and the racial-spatial divide.* New York: Russell Sage Foundation.

Pew Center on the States. 2009. *One in 100: Behind bars in America 2008*. Washington, D.C.: Pew Charitable Trusts.

Pew Research Center. 2003. "The 2004 political landscape." Retrieved on January 25, 2010, at http://people-press.org/report/?pageid=754.

———. 2005. "Two-in-three critical of Bush's relief efforts: Huge racial divide over Katrina and its consequences." Retrieved on January 24, 2010, at http://people-press.org/report/255/two-in-three-critical-of-bushs-relief-efforts.

———. 2007. "Optimism about black progress declines: Blacks see growing values gap between poor and middle class." Retrieved on January 30, 2010, at http://pewsocialtrends.org/assets/pdf/Race.pdf.

———. 2010. "Blacks upbeat about black progress, prospects: A year after Obama's election." Retrieved on January 30, 2010, at http://pewsocialtrends.org/pubs/749/blacks-upbeat-about-black-progress-obama-election.

Phillips, C. and B. Bowling. 2003. "Racism, ethnicity and criminology: Developing minority perspectives." *British Journal of Criminology* 43:269–290.

Phinney, J. S. and V. Chavira. 1995. "Parental ethnic socialization and adolescent coping with problems related to ethnicity." *Journal of Research on Adolescence* 5:31–53.

Phinney, J. S. and M. J. Rotheram. 1987. *Children's ethnic socialization: Pluralism and development*. Thousand Oaks: Sage Publications, Inc.

Pieterse, A. L. and R. T. Carter. 2010. "The role of racial identity in perceived racism and psychological stress among black American adults: Exploring traditional and alternative approaches." *Journal of Applied Social Psychology* 40:1028–1053.

Pihl, R. O. and F. Ervin. 1990. "Lead and cadmium levels in violent criminals." *Psychological Reports* 66:839–844.

Pinel, E. C. 1999. "Stigma consciousness: The psychological legacy of social stereotypes." *Journal of Personality and Social Psychology* 76:114–128.

Piquero, A. R., J. Fagan, E. P. Mulvey, and L. Steinberg. 2005. "Developmental trajectories of legal socialization among serious adolescent offenders." *Journal of Criminal Law and Criminology* 96:267–298.

Piquero, N. and M. Sealock. 2010. "Race, crime, and general strain theory." *Youth Violence and Juvenile Justice* 8:170–186.

Piquero, N. L. and L. A. Bouffard. 2003. "A preliminary and partial test of specific defiance." *Journal of Crime and Justice* 26:1–22.

Pirkle, J., R. Kaufmann, D. Brody, T. Hickman, E. Gunter, and D. Paschal. 1998. "Exposure of the US population to lead, 1991–1994." *Environmental Health Perspectives* 106:745–750.

Plant, E. A., P. G. Devine, W. T. L. Cox, C. Columb, S. L. Miller, J. Goplen, and B. M. Peruche. 2009. "The Obama effect: Decreasing implicit prejudice and stereotyping." *Journal of Experimental Social Psychology* 45:961–964.

Plummer, D. L. and S. Slane. 1996. "Patterns of coping in racially stressful situations." *Journal of Black Psychology* 22:302–315.

Population Studies Center. 2010. "Residential segregation: What it is and how we measure it. University of Michigan." Retrieved on March 23, 2010, at http://enceladus.isr.umich.edu/race/seg.html.

Poussaint, A. F. 1983. "Black-on-black homicide: A psychological-political perspective." *Victimology* 8:161–169.

Pratt, T. C. and F. T. Cullen. 2000. "The empirical status of Gottfredson and Hirschi's general theory of crime: A meta-analysis." *Criminology* 38:931–964.

Provine, D. M. 2007. *Unequal under law: Race in the war on drugs*. Chicago, IL: University of Chicago Press.

Puzzanchera, C. 2009. "Juvenile arrests 2008." U.S. Department of Justice: Office of
    Juvenile Justice and Delinquency Prevention.
Quillian, L. and D. Pager. 2001. "Black neighbors, higher crime? The role of racial stereo-
    types in evaluations of neighborhood crime." *The American Journal of Sociology*
    107:717–767.
Rand, M. R. 2009. "Criminal victimization, 2008." Washington, D.C.: Bureau of Justice
    Statistics.
Reese, L. A. and R. E. Brown. 1995. "The effects of religious messages on racial
    identity and system blame among African Americans." *The Journal of Politics*
    57:24–43.
Rice, D. C. 1998. "Developmental lead exposure: Neurobehavioral consequences." Pp.
    539–557 in *Handbook of developmental neurotoxicology*, edited by William Slikker Jr. and
    L.W. Chang. San Diego: Academic Press.
Ridley, S., J. A. Bayton, and J. H. Outtz. 1989. "Taxi service in the District of Columbia: Is
    it influenced by patrons' race and destination." Washington, DC: The Washington
    Lawyers' Committee for Civil Rights Under the Law. Mimeographed.
Rivas-Drake, D., D. Hughes, and N. Way. 2009. "A preliminary analysis of
    associations among ethnic-racial socialization, ethnic discrimination, and
    ethnic identity among urban sixth graders." *Journal of Research on Adolescence*
    19:558–584.
Robinson, C. D. 1981. "The production of black violence in Chicago." Pp. 366–404 in
    Crime and capitalism: Readings in Marxist criminology, edited by D. F. Greenberg.
    Philadelphia, PA: Temple University Press.
Roche, K. M., S. R. Ghazarian, T. D. Little, and T. Leventhal. 2010. "Understanding
    links between punitive parenting and adolescent adjustment: The relevance of context
    and reciprocal associations." *Journal of Research on Adolescence*:forthcoming.
Rosenbloom, S. R. and N. Way. 2004. "Experiences of discrimination among African
    American, Asian American, and Latino adolescents in an urban high school." *Youth
    and Society* 35:420–451.
Ross, L. E. 1998. *African American criminologists, 1970–1996: An annotated bibliography.*
    Westport, CT: Greenwood Press.
Ruck, M. D. and S. Wortley. 2002. "Racial and ethnic minority high school students'
    perceptions of school disciplinary practices: A look at some Canadian findings." *Journal
    of Youth and Adolescence* 31:185–195.
Rusche, S. E. and Z. W. Brewster. 2009. "Teaching and learning guide for: 'Because they
    tip for shit!': The social psychology of everyday racism in restaurants." *Sociology
    Compass* 3:513–521.
Russell, K. K. 1992. "Development of a black criminology and the role of the black crimi-
    nologist." *Justice Quarterly* 9:667–683.
Russell-Brown, K. K. 2009. *The color of crime: Racial hoaxes, white fear, black protectionism,
    police harassment, and other macroaggressions (2nd edition).* New York: New York
    University Press.
Saad, L. 2007. "Black-white educational opportunities widely seen as equal: Americans
    favor merit over racial diversity for college admittance." Retrieved July 10, 2010, at
    www.gallup.com/poll/28021/blackwhite-educational-opportunities-widely-seen-equal.
    aspx.
Sabol, W. J., H. C. West, and M. Cooper. 2009. "Prisoners in 2008." Washington, D.C.:
    Bureau of Justice Statistics.
Salisbury, E. J. and P. Van Voorhis. 2009. "Gendered pathways." *Criminal Justice and
    Behavior* 36:541–566.

Sampson, R. J. 1987. "Urban black violence: The effect of male joblessness and family disruption." *American Journal of Sociology* 93:348–382.

Sampson, R. J. and D. J. Bartusch. 1998. "Legal cynicism and (subcultural?) tolerance of deviance: The neighborhood context of racial differences." *Law and Society Review* 32:777–804.

Sampson, R. and C. Graif. 2009. "Neighborhood social capital as differential social organization." *American Behavioral Scientist* 52:1579–1605.

Sampson, R. J. and J. H. Laub. 1993. *Crime in the making: Pathways and turning points through life*. Cambridge, MA: Harvard University Press.

——— . 2004. "A life-course theory of cumulative disadvantage and the stability of delinquency." Pp. 133–161 in *Developmental theories of crime and delinquency*, edited by T. P. Thornberry. New Brunswick, NJ: Transaction Publishers.

Sampson, R. J., J. D. Morenoff, and S. Raudenbush. 2005. "Social anatomy of racial and ethnic disparities in violence." *American Journal of Public Health* 95:224–231.

Sampson, R. J. and S. W. Raudenbush. 2004. "Seeing disorder: Neighborhood stigma and the social construction of 'broken windows.'" *Social Psychology Quarterly* 67:319–342.

Sampson, R. J., S. W. Raudenbush, and F. Earls. 1997. "Neighborhoods and violent crime: A multilevel study of collective efficacy." *Science* 277:918–924.

Sampson, R. J. and P. Sharkey. 2008. "Neighborhood selection and the social reproduction of concentrated racial inequality." *Demography* 45:1–29.

Sanborn, M., A. Abelsohn, M. Campbell, and E. Weir. 2002. "Identifying and managing adverse environmental health effects: Lead exposure." *Canadian Medical Association Journal* 166:1287–1292.

Schaffer, R. T. 2011. *Racial and ethnic groups (12th edition)*. Upper Saddle River, NJ: Pearson/Prentice Hall.

Scher, S. J. 1997. "Measuring the consequences of injustice." *Personality and Social Psychology Bulletin* 23:482–497.

Schiele, J. 1996. "Afrocentricity: An emerging paradigm in social work practice." *Social Work* 41:284–295.

Schiele, J. H. 1997. "The contour and meaning of Afrocentric social work." *Journal of Black Studies* 27:800–819.

——— . 2000. *Human services and the Afrocentric paradigm*. Binghamton, NY: The Haworth Press.

Schlesinger, T. 2011. "The failure of race neutral policies: How mandatory terms and sentencing enhancements contribute to mass racialized incarceration." *Crime & Delinquency* 57:56–81.

Schmader, T., M. Johns, and C. Forbes. 2008. "An integrated process model of stereotype threat effects on performance." *Psychological Review* 115:336–356.

Schoenfeld, H. 2010. "Mass incarceration and the paradox of prison conditions litigation." *Law & Society Review* 44:731–768.

Schott Foundation for Public Education. 2010. "Yes we can: The Schott 50 state report on public education and black males 2010." *Schott Foundation for Public Education*.

Schreer, G. E., S. Smith, and K. Thomas. 2009. "'Shopping while black': Examining racial discrimination in a retail setting." *Journal of Applied Social Psychology* 39:1432–1444.

Schroeder, R. D., R. E. Bulanda, P. C. Giordano, and S. A. Cernkovich. 2010. "Parenting and adult criminality: An examination of direct and indirect effects by race." *Journal of Adolescent Research* 25:64–98.

Schroeder, R. D., P. C. Giordano, and S. A. Cernkovich. 2010. "Adult child-parent bonds and life course criminality." *Journal of Criminal Justice* 38:562–571.

Schuck, A. M., D. P. Rosenbaum, and D. F. Hawkins. 2008. "The influence of race/ ethnicity, social class, and neighborhood context on residents' attitudes toward the police." *Police Quarterly* 11:496–519.

Schulman, K. A., J. A. Berlin, W. Harless, J. F. Kerner, S. Sistrunk, B. J. Gersh, R. Dube, C. K. Taleghani, J. E. Burke, and S. Williams. 1999. "The effect of race and sex on physicians' recommendations for cardiac catheterization." *The New England Journal of Medicine* 340:618–626.

Schur, E. M. 1971. *Labeling deviant behavior: Its sociological implications*. New York: Harper and Row.

Scott, L. D. 2003. "The relation of racial identity and racial socialization to coping with discrimination among African American adolescents." *Journal of Black Studies* 33:520–538.

——. 2004. "Correlates of coping with perceived discriminatory experiences among African American adolescents." *Journal of Adolescence* 27:123–137.

Scott, L. D. and L. E. House. 2005. "Relationship of distress and perceived control to coping with perceived racial discrimination among black youth." *Journal of Black Psychology* 31:254–272.

Seaton, E. K. 2010. "The influence of cognitive development and perceived racial discrimination on the psychological well-being of African American youth." *Journal of Youth and Adolescence* 39:694–703.

Seaton, E. and T. Yip. 2009. "School and neighborhood contexts, perceptions of racial discrimination, and psychological well-being among African American adolescents." *Journal of Youth and Adolescence* 38:153–163.

Seaton, E. K., T. Yip, and R. M. Sellers. 2009. "A longitudinal examination of racial identity and racial discrimination among African American adolescents." *Child Development* 80:406–417.

Sellers, R. M., C. H. Caldwell, K. H. Schmeelk-Cone, and M. A. Zimmerman. 2003. "Racial identity, racial discrimination, perceived stress, and psychological distress among African American young adults." *Journal of Health and Social Behavior* 44:302–317.

Sellers, R. M., N. Copeland-Linder, P. P. Martin, and R. L. H. Lewis. 2006. "Racial identity matters: The relationship between racial discrimination and psychological functioning in African American adolescents." *Journal of Research on Adolescence* 16:187–216.

Sellers, S. L., V. Bonham, H. W. Neighbors, and J. W. Amell. 2009. "Effects of racial discrimination and health behaviors on mental and physical health of middle-class African American men." *Health Education and Behavior* 36:31–44.

Sentencing Project. 2010. "Fair Sentencing Act signed by President Obama." Retrieved on August 3, 2010, at http://www.sentencingproject.org/detail/news.cfm?news_id= 984&id=128.

Sentencing Times. 2009. "Crack equalization bill passes in house judiciary." Washington, D.C.: The Sentencing Project.

Sharkey, P. 2006. "Navigating dangerous streets: The sources and consequences of street efficacy." *American Sociological Review* 71:826–846.

——. 2008. "The intergenerational transmission of context." *American Journal of Sociology* 113:931–69.

——. 2010. "The acute effect of local homicides on children's cognitive performance." Proceedings of the National Academy of Sciences 101:11733–11738.

Shaw, C. R. and H. D. McKay. 1942. *Juvenile delinquency and urban areas: A study of rates of delinquency in relation to differential characteristics of local communities in American cities*. Chicago: University of Chicago Press.

Shelton, J. E. 2008. "The investment in blackness hypothesis." *Du Bois Review: Social Science Research on Race* 5:235–257.

Shelton, J. N. and J. A. Richeson. 2006. "Ethnic minorities' racial attitudes and contact experiences with white people." *Cultural Diversity and Ethnic Minority Psychology* 12:149–164.

Sherkat, D. E. and C. G. Ellison. 2009. "Religion and race in 21st century America: Introduction." *Sociological Spectrum* 29:141–143.

Sherman, L. W. 1993. "Defiance, deterrence, and irrelevance: A theory of the criminal sanction." *Journal of Research in Crime and Delinquency* 30:445–473.

Shorter-Gooden, K. 2004. "Multiple resistance strategies: How African American women cope with racism and sexism." *Journal of Black Psychology* 30:406–425.

Sigleman, L. E. E. and S. A. Tuch. 1997. "Metastereotypes: Blacks' perceptions of whites' stereotypes of blacks." *Public Opinion Quarterly* 61:87–101.

Silberman, C. E. 1978. *Criminal violence, criminal justice.* New York: Random House.

Simons, R. L., Y. F. Chen, E. A. Stewart, and G. H. Brody. 2003. "Incidents of discrimination and risk for delinquency: A longitudinal test of strain theory with an African American sample." *Justice Quarterly* 20:827–854.

Simons, R. L., V. Murry, V. McLoyd, K. H. Lin, C. Cutrona, and R. D. Conger. 2002. "Discrimination, crime, ethnic identity, and parenting as correlates of depressive symptoms among African American children: A multilevel analysis." *Development and Psychopathology* 14:371–393.

Simons, R. L., L. G. Simons, C. H. Burt, D. Drummund, E. Stewart, G. H. Brody, F. X. Gibbons, and C. Cutrona. 2006. "Supportive parenting moderates the effect of discrimination upon anger, hostile view of relationships, and violence among African American boys." *Journal of Health and Social Behavior* 47:373–389.

Smalls, C., R. White, T. Chavous, and R. Sellers. 2007. "Racial ideological beliefs and racial discrimination experiences as predictors of academic engagement among African American adolescents." *Journal of Black Psychology* 33:299–330.

Smith, D. A., C. A. Fisher, and L. A. Davidson. 1984. "Equity and discretionary justice: The influence of race on police arrest decisions." *Journal of Criminal Law and Criminology* 75:234–249.

Smith, E. P., J. Atkins, and C. M. Connell. 2003. "Family, school, and community factors and relationships to racial–ethnic attitudes and academic achievement." *American Journal of Community Psychology* 32:159–173.

Smith, E. P. and C. C. Brookings. 1997. "Toward the development of an ethnic identity measure for African American youth." *Journal of Black Psychology* 23:358–377.

Smith, W. A., W. R. Allen, and L. L. Danley. 2007. "'Assume the position . . . You fit the description': Psychosocial experiences and racial battle fatigue among African American male college students." *American Behavioral Scientist* 51:551–578.

Spencer, M. B., E. Noll, J. Stoltzfus, and V. Harpalani. 2001. "Identity and school adjustment: Revisiting the 'acting white' assumption." *Educational Psychologist* 36:21–30.

Steele, C. M. 1997. "A threat in the air: How stereotypes shape intellectual identity and performance." *American Psychologist* 52:613–629.

Steele, C. M. and J. Aronson. 1995. "Stereotype threat and the intellectual test performance of African Americans." *Journal of Personality and Social Psychology* 69:797–811.

Steffensmeier, D., J. T. Ulmer, B. E. N. Feldmeyer, and C. T. Harris. 2010. "Scope and conceptual issues in testing the race–crime invariance thesis: Black, white, and Hispanic comparisons." *Criminology* 48:1133–1169.

Steinhauser, P. 2009. "CNN poll: Did Obama act stupidly in Gates arrest comments?" http://politicalticker.blogs.cnn.com/2009/08/04/cnn-poll-did-obama-act-stupidly-in-gates-arrest-comments. Retrieved, November 6, 2010.

Stevenson, H. C. 1994. "Validation of the scale of racial socialization for African American adolescents: Steps toward multidimensionality." *Journal of Black Psychology* 20:445–468.

———. 1995. "Relationship of adolescent perceptions of racial socialization to racial identity." *Journal of Black Psychology* 21:49–70.

Stevenson, H. C., J. Reed, and P. Bodison. 1996. "Kinship social support and adolescent racial socialization beliefs: Extending the self to family." *Journal of Black Psychology* 22:498–508.

Stevenson, H. C., J. Reed, P. Bodison, and A. Bishop. 1997. "Racism stress management: Racial social beliefs and the experience of depression and anger in African American youth." *Youth and Society* 29:197–222.

Stewart, E. A., C. J. Schreck, and R. L. Simons. 2006. "'I ain't gonna let no one disrespect me': Does the code of the street reduce or increase violent victimization among African American adolescents?" *Journal of Research in Crime and Delinquency* 43:427–458.

Stewart, E. A. and R. L. Simons. 2006. "Structure and culture in African American adolescent violence: A partial test of the 'code of the street' thesis." *Justice Quarterly* 23:1–33.

———. 2010. "Race, code of the street, and violent delinquency: A multilevel investigation of neighborhood street culture and individual norms of violence." *Criminology* 48:569–605.

Stretesky, P. and M. J. Hogan, 1998. "Environmental justice: An analysis of superfund sites in Florida." *Social Problems* 45:268–287.

Stretesky, P. and M. Lynch. 2001. "The relationship between lead exposure and homicide." *Archives of Pediatrics and Adolescent Medicine* 155:579–582.

———. 2004. "The relationship between lead and crime." *Journal of Health and Social Behavior* 45:214–229.

Sullivan, M. 1989. (ed.) *"Getting paid": Youth crime and work in the inner city.* Ithaca, NY: Cornell University Press.

Sulton, A. T. 1994. (ed.) *African-American perspectives on crime causation, criminal justice administration and crime prevention.* Englewood, CO: Sulton Books.

Sunshine, J. and T. R. Tyler. 2003. "The role of procedural justice and legitimacy in shaping public support for policing." *Law and Society Review* 37:513–548.

Sutherland, E. 1947. *Principles of criminology (4th edition).* Philadelphia: JB Lippincott.

Swain, R. 2008. "'Standing on the promises that cannot fail': Evaluating the black church's ability to promote community activism among African-Americans in the present day context." *Journal of African American Studies* 12:401–413.

Swim, J. K., L. L. Hyers, L. L. Cohen, D. C. Fitzgerald, and W. H. Bylsma. 2003. "African American college students' experiences with everyday racism: Characteristics of and responses to these incidents." *Journal of Black Psychology* 29:38–67.

Szasz, A. and M. Meuser. 1997. "Environmental inequalities: Literature review and proposals for new directions in research and theory." *Current Sociology* 45:99–120.

Tatum, B. 1994. "The colonial model as a theoretical explanation of crime and delinquency." Pp. 33–52 in *African American classics in criminology and criminal justice*, edited by A. T. Sulton. Englewood, CO: Sulton Books.

Taylor, C. A., J. A. Manganello, S. J. Lee, and J. C. Rice. 2010. "Mothers' spanking of 3-year-old children and subsequent risk of children's aggressive behavior." *Pediatrics* 125:e1057–e1065.

Taylor, D. L., F. A. Biafora, Jr., and G. J. Warheit. 1994. "Racial mistrust and disposition to deviance among African American, Haitian, and other Caribbean island adolescent boys." *Law and Human Behavior* 18:291–303.

Taylor, M. C. 1998. "How white attitudes vary with the racial composition of local populations: Numbers count." *American Sociological Review* 63:512–535.

Taylor, R. J. 1988. "Correlates of religious non-involvement among black Americans." *Review of Religious Research* 30:126–139.

Taylor, R. J., L. M. Chatters, and J. S. Jackson. 2007. "Religious and spiritual involvement among older African Americans, Caribbean blacks, and non-Hispanic whites: Findings from the national survey of American life." *The Journals of Gerontology Series B: Psychological Sciences and Social Sciences* 62:S238–S250.

Taylor, R. J., M. C. Thornton, and L. M. Chatters. 1987. "Black Americans' perceptions of the sociohistorical role of the church." *Journal of Black Studies* 18:123–138.

Terrell, F., A. R. Miller, K. Foster, and C. E. Watkins Jr. 2006. "Racial discrimination induced anger and alcohol use among black adolescents." *Adolescence* 41:485–492.

Thomas, A. J. and S. L. Speight. 1999. "Racial identity and racial socialization attitudes of African American parents." *Journal of Black Psychology* 25:152–170.

Thomas, A. J., K. M. Witherspoon, and S. L. Speight. 2008. "Gendered racism, psychological distress, and coping styles of African American women." *Cultural Diversity and Ethnic Minority Psychology* 14:307–314.

Thomas, O. N., C. H. Caldwell, N. Faison, and J. S. Jackson. 2009. "Promoting academic achievement: The role of racial identity in buffering perceptions of teacher discrimination on academic achievement among African American and Caribbean black adolescents." *Journal of Educational Psychology* 101:420–431.

Thomas-Lester, A. 2005. "A Senate apology for history on lynching vote condemns past failure to act." *The Washington Post*. Retrieved on July 15, 2010, at http://www.londonwashingtonpost.com/wp-dyn/content/article/2005/06/13/AR2005061301720.html.

Thompson, K. and C. W. Thompson. 2009. "Officer tells his side of the story in Gates arrest." Retrieved on January 26, 2010, at http://www.washingtonpost.com/wp-dyn/content/article/2009/07/23/AR2009072301073.html.

Thornton, M. C., L. M. Chatters, R. J. Taylor, and W. R. Allen. 1990. "Sociodemographic and environmental correlates of racial socialization by black parents." *Child Development* 61:401–409.

Tolnay, S. E. and E. M. Beck. 1992. "Racial violence and black migration in the American south, 1910 to 1930." *American Sociological Review* 57:103–116.

Tolnay, S. E., G. Deane, and E. M. Beck. 1996. "Vicarious violence: Spatial effects on southern lynchings, 1890–1919." *American Journal of Sociology* 102:788–815.

Tonry, M. H. 1996. *Malign neglect: Race, crime, and punishment in America*. New York: Oxford University Press.

Trawalter, S., A. R. Todd, A. A. Baird, and J. A. Richeson. 2008. "Attending to threat: Race-based patterns of selective attention." *Journal of Experimental Social Psychology* 44:1322–1327.

Turner, M. A. and F. Skidmore. 2001. "Mortgage lending discrimination: A review of existing evidence." *Washington, DC: Urban Institute*.

Tuthill, R. 1996. "Hair lead levels related to children's classroom attention-deficit behavior." *Archives of Environmental Health* 51:214–220.

Tyler, T. R. 1990. *Why people obey the law*. New Haven: Yale University Press.

——. 2001. "Public trust and confidence in legal authorities: What do majority and minority group members want from the law and legal institutions?" *Behavioral Sciences and the Law* 19:215–235.

Uggen, C. 2000. "Work as a turning point in the life course of criminals: A duration model of age, employment, and recidivism." *American Sociological Review* 65:529–546.

United States Census Bureau. 2009. "Annual estimates of the population by sex, race, and Hispanic origin for the United States: April 1, 2000 to July 1, 2008." Retrieved on July 1, 2010, at /www.census.gov/popest/national/asrh/NC-EST2008/NC-EST2008-03.xls.

Unnever, J. D. 2005. "Bullies, aggressive victims, and victims: Are they distinct groups?" *Aggressive Behavior* 31:153–171.

———. 2008. "Two worlds far apart: Black-white differences in beliefs about why African American men are disproportionately imprisoned." *Criminology* 46:511–538.Unnever, J. D. and D. G. Cornell. 2003. "Bullying, self-control, and ADHD." *Journal of Interpersonal Violence* 18:129–147.

Unnever, J. D. and F. T. Cullen. 2007. "The racial divide in support for the death penalty: Does white racism matter?" *Social Forces* 85:1281–1301.

———. 2010. "The social sources of Americans' punitiveness: A test of three competing models." *Criminology* 48:99–129.

———. 2011. "White perceptions of whether African Americans and Hispanics are prone to violence and their desire to punish." Unpublished manuscript.

Unnever, J. D., F. T. Cullen, and R. Agnew. 2006. "Why is 'bad' parenting criminogenic? Implications from rival theories." *Youth Violence and Juvenile Justice* 4:3–33.

Unnever, J. D., F. T. Cullen, and J. D. Jones. 2008. "Public support for attacking the root causes of crime: The impact of egalitarian and racial beliefs." *Sociological Focus* 41:1–33.

Unnever, J. D., F. T. Cullen, and C. L. Jonson. 2008. "Race, racism, and support for capital punishment." *Crime and Justice* 37:45–96.

Unnever, J. D., F. T. Cullen, S. A. Mathers, T. E. McClure, and M. C. Allison. 2009. "Racial discrimination and Hirschi's criminological classic: A chapter in the sociology of knowledge." *Justice Quarterly* 26:377–409.

Unnever, J. D., F. T. Cullen, and T. C. Pratt. 2003. "Parental management, ADHD, and delinquent involvement: Reassessing Gottfredson and Hirschi's general theory." *Justice Quarterly* 20:471–500.

Unnever, J. D., S. L. Gabbidon, and G. E. Higgins. 2011. "The election of Barack Obama and perceptions of criminal injustice." *Justice Quarterly* 28:23–45.

Utsey, S. O., J. G. Ponterotto, A. L. Reynolds, and A. A. Cancelli. 2000. "Racial discrimination, coping, life satisfaction, and self-esteem among African Americans." *Journal of Counseling and Development* 78:72–80.

Vandiver, M. 2006. *Lethal punishment: Lynchings and legal executions in the south*. New Brunswick, NJ: Rutgers University Press.

Vandiver, M., D. Giacopassi, and W. Lofquist. 2007. "Slavery's enduring legacy—executions in modern America." *Journal of Ethnicity in Criminal Justice* 4:19–36.

Vazsonyi, A. T. and J. M. Crosswhite. 2004. "A test of Gottfredson and Hirschi's general theory of crime in African American adolescents." *Journal of Research in Crime and Delinquency* 41:407–432.

Venkatesh, S. A. 2006. *Off the books: The underground economy of the urban poor*. Cambridge, MA: Harvard University Press.

Vollum, S., D. R. Longmire, and J. Buffington-Vollum. 2004. "Confidence in the death penalty and support for its use: Exploring the value-expressive dimension of death penalty attitudes." *Justice Quarterly* 21:521–546.

Wacquant, L. 2001. "Deadly symbiosis: When ghetto and prison meet and mesh." *Punishment and Society* 3:95–134.

———. 2008. "Forum." Pp. 57–70 in *Race, incarceration, and American values*, edited by G. C. Loury. Cambridge, MA: The MIT Press.

Waldrep, C. 2006. *A history in documents: Lynching in America*. New York: New York University Press.

Walker, S., C. Spohn, and M. DeLone. 2007. *The color of justice: Race, ethnicity, and crime in America (4th edition)*. Belmont, CA: Wadsworth.

Wang, F., H. Hu, J. Schwartz, J. Weuve, A. Spiro III, D. Sparrow, H. Nie, E. Silverman, S. Weiss, and R. Wright. 2007. "Modifying effects of the HFE polymorphisms on the association between lead burden and cognitive decline." *Environmental Health Perspectives* 115:1210–1215.

Ward, J. V. 1996. "Raising resisters: The role of truth telling in the psychological development of African American girls." Pp. 85–99 in *Urban girls resisting stereotypes, creating identities*, edited by B. J. Leadbeater and N. Way. New York: New York University Press.

Weitzer, R. 1999. "Citizens' perceptions of police misconduct: Race and neighborhood context." *Justice Quarterly* 16:819–846.

——. 2000. "Racialized policing: Residents' perceptions in three neighborhoods." *Law and Society Review* 34:129–155.

——. 2002. "Incidents of police misconduct and public opinion." *Journal of Criminal Justice* 30:397–408.

——. 2010. "Race and policing in different ecological contexts." Pp. 118–139 in *Race, ethnicity, and policing new and essential readings*, edited by S. K. Rice and M. D. White. New York: New York University Press.

Weitzer, R. and S. A. Tuch. 1999. "Race, class, and perceptions of discrimination by the police." *Crime and Delinquency* 45:494–507.

——. 2002. "Perceptions of racial profiling: Race, class, and personal experience." *Criminology* 40:435–456.

——. 2004. "Race and perceptions of police misconduct." *Social Problems* 51:305–325.

——. 2006. *Race and policing in America: Conflict and reform*. New York: Cambridge University Press.

Weitzer, R., S. A. Tuch, and W. G. Skogan. 2008. "Police-community relations in a majority-black city." *Journal of Research in Crime and Delinquency* 45:398–428.

Welch, K. 2007. "Black criminal stereotypes and racial profiling." *Journal of Contemporary Criminal Justice* 23:276–288.

Wells-Barnett, I. B. 1892/1969. *On lynchings: Southern horrors*. New York: Arno Press.

Williams, D. R., H. W. Neighbors, and J. S. Jackson. 2003. "Racial/ethnic discrimination and health: Findings from community studies." *American Journal of Public Health* 93:200–208.

——. 2008. "Racial/ethnic discrimination and health: Findings from community studies." *American Journal of Public Health* 98:S29–S37.

Williams, L. F. 2003. *The constraint of race: Legacies of white skin privilege in America*. College Stations, PA: Penn State University Press.

Wilson, A. N. 1990. *Black-on-black violence: The psychodynamics of black self-annihilation in service of white domination*. Brooklyn, New York: Afrikan World Infosystems.

——. 1992. *Understanding black adolescent male violence: Its remediation and prevention*. Brooklyn, NY: Afrikan World Infosystems.

——. 1993. *The falsification of Afrikan consciousness: Eurocentric history, psychiatry and the politics of white supremacy*. Brooklyn, NY: Afrikan World Infosystems.

——. 1998. *Blueprint for black power: A moral, political, and economic imperative for the twenty-first century*. New York: Afrikan World Infosystems.

——. 1999. *Afrikan-centered consciousness versus the new world order: Garveyism in the age of globalism*. Brooklyn, NY: Afrikan World Infosystems.

Wilson, D. (2005). *Inventing black-on-black violence: Discourse, space, and representation.* Syracuse, NY: Syracuse University Press.

Wilson, W. J. 1996. *When work disappears.* New York: A.A. Knopf.

Wingfield, A. H. 2010. "Are some emotions marked 'whites only'? Racialized feeling rules in professional workplaces." *Social Problems* 57:251–268.

Winnick, T. A. and M. Bodkin. 2008. "Anticipated stigma and stigma management among those to be labeled 'ex-con.'" *Deviant Behavior* 29:295–333.

——. 2009. "Stigma, secrecy and race: An empirical examination of black and white incarcerated men." *American Journal of Criminal Justice* 34:131–150.

Wong, C. A., J. S. Eccles, and A. Sameroff. 2003. "The influence of ethnic discrimination and ethnic identification on African American adolescents' school and socioemotional adjustment." *Journal of Personality* 71:1197–1232.

Wood, P. B. and M. Chesser. 1994. "Stereotype adherence in a university population." *Sociological Focus* 27:17–34.

Wortham, R. A. 2009. "W.E.B. Du Bois, the black church, and the sociological study of religion." *Sociological Spectrum* 29:144–172.

Wright, B. R. E. and C. W. Younts. 2009. "Reconsidering the relationship between race and crime: Positive and negative predictors of crime among African American youth." *Journal of Research in Crime and Delinquency* 46:327–352.

Wright, J., K. Dietrich, M. Ris, R. Hornung, S. Wessel, B. Lanphear, M. Ho, and M. Rae. 2008. "Association of prenatal and childhood blood lead concentrations with criminal arrests in early adulthood." *PLoS Med* 5:0732–0740.

Xie, M. 2010. "The effects of multiple dimensions of residential segregation on black and Hispanic homicide victimization." *Journal of Quantitative Criminology* 26:237–268.

Xie, M. I. N. and D. McDowall. 2010. "The reproduction of racial inequality: How crime affects housing turnover." *Criminology* 48:865–896.

Yinger, J. 1986. "Measuring racial discrimination with fair housing audits: Caught in the act." *The American Economic Review* 76:881–893.

Young, V. 1994. "The politics of disproportionality." Pp. 69–81 in *African American perspectives on crime causation, criminal justice administration, and crime prevention*, edited by A. T. Sulton. Boston: Butterworth-Heinemann.

Young, V. D. 2006. "Demythologizing the 'criminalblackman': The carnival mirror." Pp. 54–66 in *The many colors of crime: Inequalities of race, ethnicity, and crime in America*, edited by R. D. Peterson, L. P. Krivo, and J. Hagan. New York: New York University Press.

Young, V. D. and H. T. Greene. 1995. "Pedagogical reconstruction: Incorporating African-American perspectives into the curriculum." *Journal of Criminal Justice Education* 6:85–104.

Zadeh, Z. Y., J. Jenkins, and D. Pepler. 2010. "A transactional analysis of maternal negativity and child externalizing behavior." *International Journal of Behavioral Development* 34:218–228.

Zahn, M. A., R. Agnew, D. Fishbein, S. Miller, D.-M. Winn, G. Dakoff, C. Kruttschnitt, P. Giordano, D. C. Gottfredson, A. A. Payne, B. C. Feld, and M. Chesney-Lind. 2010. "Causes and correlates of girls' delinquency." *Office of Juvenile Justice and Delinquency Prevention.*

Zilney, L., D. McGurrin, and S. Zahran. 2006. "Environmental justice and the role of criminology: An analytical review of 33 years of environmental justice research." *Criminal Justice Review* 31:47–62.

Zimring, F. E. 2003. *The contradictions of American capital punishment.* New York: Oxford University Press.

INDEX

A General Theory of Crime 14

African American: coping with racism, 140–4; criminal justice injustices perceptions 52–72; environmental racism, 207–23; gender and crime 103–6; general well-being 76–8; heritage 4–7; lead exposure 218–19; negative stereotypes 73–112; offending 1–24, 52–73, 74–112, 79–88, 113–66; racial discrimination 76–112; racial socialization 113–66; shame, anger and defiance 57–61; stereotype threats 73–112; stereotypes 88–96; variations in offending 65–72; worldview 25–51, 167–9

Afrocentricity 21–3

Agnew's general strain theory 16–18

Aker's Social Learning Theory 19–20

alcohol drinking 158–60

American apartheid 5–6

anger-hostility-defiance-depression 176, 179, 180, 184

anomie 15

anti-self-expression 23

"apartheid schools" 83

Asante, M. K. 21

avoidance coping 143–4

"bad parenting" 116–18

Black Church 137–8

Black criminology 4–10; African American Heritage 4–7

Blumer, H. 110

Borders, K. 156–7

Brown Decision 4

Bullard, R. 209

capital punishment *see* death penalty

Carson, R. 208

Causes of Delinquency 13

Center for Epidemiological Studies Depression Scale (CES-D) 77

Child Behavior Checklist 216

"child–effects" 188

Children's Depression Inventory (CDI) 129

Cincinnati Lead Study 217–18

Civil Rights Movement 31

civil rights movement 208

cognitive impairment 213–15

Collaborative Perinatal Project 217

collective efficacy 12
collective memory 27–8
"collective spoiled identity" 112, 115, 178
"color blind" society 163, 199
color line 110
colorism 203–4
concentric zone approach 12
"confrontation coping" 143, 144
"Conspiracy" 93
control theory 79, 175
Convict laws 43
coping 140
"crack *versus* powdered cocaine" 38
crime: drugs, 158–60; gender 103–6, 158–60; lead exposure 212–19
Crime in the United States 2
criminal behavior 19
Criminal Justice Injustices: and defiance perceptions 57–61; perceptions of 52–7; shame, anger and defiance 57–61; variations in African American offending 65–72
Criminal Justice System: injustices 34–7, 169–73; perceptions of racial divide 32–47
Criminal Violence, Criminal Justice 169–70
criminalblackman 90, 91, 93, 104–6, 110, 153, 156–7, 178, 193
criminological theories 10–23; Afrocentricity 20–3; Agnew's general strain theory 16–18; Aker's Social Learning Theory 19–20; Gottfredson and Hirschi's Social Control Theory 14; Hirschi's social Control Theory 13–14; Merton's strain theory 15–16; Social disorganization theory 11–13
cultural misorientation 23
Cultural Mistrust Inventory 123

cultural socialization 120–1, 139
"cumulative continuity" 62

DDT 212
death penalty 32–4
defiance 57–61; variations in 70
depression 138–40
Diagnostic Interview Schedule for Children 79
differential association-social learning theory 79, 175
differential association theory 19
"disidentification" 97–8
"Don't call me nigger" 152
drugs 158–60
Du Bois, W. E. B. 8–9, 66–7, 75, 89–90
"dual levels of anger" 173

education: and lead exposure 214–15
egalitarian values 124–5, 154, 163
environmental decade 208
environmental racism: African American offending 207–23; crime 215–19; empirical research on 210–11; health effects of 211–12; lead exposure 213–19; lead exposure consequences 212–15; theory of African American offending 220–3
environmental toxins 210
ethnicity 201–3
Eurocentric 21
"everyday racism" 107

Fair Housing Act (1968) 6, 168
Family and Community Health Study 78, 79, 80, 138, 158

Gallup survey: civil rights movement 31; discrimination 50; educational opportunities 30–1; race relations 32
Gang Starr 80, 93

Gates, H. L. 45
gender: African American offending 70–2, 152–8; crime 103–6, 158–60; drugs 158–60; racial socialization 129–33
gendered racism 153
general strain theory 79, 175
"ghettos" 108, 110–11, 161, 195–8, 205
Gottfredson and Hirschi's Social Control Theory 14
Graduate Record Examination (GRE) 136

Hemmings, S. 177
Hirschi's Social Control Theory 13–14, 62–5
hostility 138–40
Hurricane Katrina 30
hypersegregation 195–8

immigration status 201–3
individual offending 182–6; variations in racial socialization 183–6; variations with racial injustices 182
injustice 34–7, 144, 169–73; rule of law restraints weakening, 171–3; see also Criminal Justice Injustices
innovators 15
internalizing see avoidance coping
intragroup racism 204
Irish Americans 7
isolated racial segregation 69, 163

Jackson and Williams discrimination stress scale 78
Jefferson, T. 177
Jim Crow law 4, 7, 36, 168

Kerner Commission 6, 168
King, R. 61, 169, 170, 191
Ku Klux Klan 5

law 54
lead 212, 223; deleterious consequences of 212–15
lead exposure: African American offending 218–19; cognitive impairment 213–14; crime 215–19; education 214–15
lead poisoning 213
"legal cynicism" 56, 66–70, 124
legal lynchings see state executions
legal socialization 55–7
legitimacy of the law 53
Let's Get Free: A Hip-Hop Theory of Justice 44
lynching 41

Maryland 135
mass incarceration 36, 44
Mater, P. 152
McDuffie, A. 169
Merton's strain theory 15–16
modes of adaptation 15
Multi-Group Ethnic Identity Scale 129

National Crime Victimization Survey 2
National Election Study 33
National Health and Nutrition Examination Survey 214
National Survey of American Life 76
National Survey of Black Workers 159
"Need for Change subscale" 84
negative stereotypes see stereotypes
"New Jim Crow" 90
Notes on the State of Virginia 177
noxious stimuli 17

Obama, B. 46–7
offending 1–24, 73–112; basic premise 26–32; Black criminology 4–10; criminal justice injustices 169–73;

criminal justice system 1–4; depression 138–40; environmental racism 207–23, 220–3; ethnic differences 201–4; gender 152–60, 190–5; general criminological theories 10–23; heuristic model of 186–90; hostility 138–40; individual offending 182–6; lead exposure 215–19; perceptions of 52–72; racial discrimination 138–40, 173–82; racial divide 26–9; racial identity 129; racial socialization 113–66, 138–40; and residence location 195–201; significance of place 106–11; stereotypes 94; theoretical model of 167–206; variations by gender 70–2; variations in 65–72; variations in criminal justice injustices perception 65–72; variations in defiance 70; variations in place 66–70
Oliver, W. 21–2
operant behavior 19

People of Color Environmental Groups Directory 210
perceived racial discrimination 47–51
Pew Research survey 30, 50–1
Philadelphia Birth Cohort (1945) 62
Pittsburgh Youth Study (PYS) 216
polychlorinated biphenyl (PCB) 211
preparation for social bias 121–2, 139–40, 149, 185
private regard 127, 136
problem-solving coping 143, 144
procedural justice 54–6
promotion of mistrust 122–4
public regard 127, 136

race 30–1
Race, Crime and Public Opinion Study 33, 38

Race-Based Rejection Sensitivity Scale 149
race centrality 127, 128, 135
race relations 31–2
race riots 6, 59–60, 168
Racial Attitudes Survey 31
racial discrimination 40, 47–51, 52, 73–112, 138–40, 173–82; and African American offending 78–88; and African Americans general well-being 76–8; gender and crime 103–6; significance of place 106–11; and weak school bonds 80–7
racial disparity 3
racial divide: evidence 29–30; Hurricane Katrina 30; perceptions of the criminal justice system 32–47
racial fairness 85
racial identity 126–9, 145; and offending 128–9
Racial Identity Attitude Scale (RIAS) 126
racial injustices 144, 163–5, 182–3
racial oppression 52
racial pride see race centrality
racial profiling 35
racial resentment 33, 39
racial segregation 66
racial socialization 113–66, 183–6; Black Church 137–8; coping with racism 140–4; cultural socialization 120–1; depression 138–40; different dimensions of 119–25; drugs, gender and crime 158–60; egalitarian values 124–5; gender 129–33; hostility 138–40; offending 138–40; place and offending 160–1; preparation for social bias 121–2, 184; promotion of mistrust 122–4; racial discrimination 138–40; racial identity 125–9; residence location

161–6; social bonds 133–7; theory on 144–66; and weak bonds 151–2
racially segregated neighborhood 162
racism 85; coping with 140–4; *see also* racial discrimination
racist epithets 82, 176
reciprocal disidentification process 181
reparations 31–2
"reservoir of bad will" 56
residential segregation 198
"resistance theory" 86
retreatists 15
Revised Children's Manifest Anxiety Scale (RCMAS) 129
Rosenberg scale 77
rule of law 171–3
Russell-Brown, K.K. 90

Scale of Racial Socialization for African American Adolescents (SORS-A) 126
Schiele's theory 22–3
school bonding 84
school grades 84–5
school self-esteem 84
Schoolly, D. 152
"sea of hostility" 57
"secondary deviance" hypothesis 99
self-control 14
Self-reported Antisocial Behavior Scale 216
Self-reported Delinquency Scale 216
Silent Spring 208
Simpson, O.J. 25–6
social bonds 133–7; theory of, 81–2
social disorganization 11
Social Disorganization Theory 11–13
social learning theory 19
spiritual alienation 22
spoiled collective identity 112, 149

state executions 43
stereotype threats 73–112, 137, 177–80; and African American offending 96–8; and weak social bonds 94–103
stereotypes 73–112, 177–82; consciousness of 94, 178; and offending 94; pejorative 98–101
stigma consciousness 148
stigma sensitivity 148–9
strain theory 80
"street socialization" 145–6
structural inequalities 22
structural pressures 21
subordinate group 73
superordinate group 73
Sutherland, E. 19

The New Jim Crow: Mass Incarceration in the Age of Colorblindness 36
The Philadelphia Negro 8, 53, 89
The Washington Post 103
Thomas, T. 59–60, 169
Toxic Wastes and Race in the United States 209

Uniform Crime Reports 2

Voting Rights Act (1965) 6

war on drugs 37–9, 68, 90–1
weak bonds 151–2; school bonds 80–8; social bonds 94–103
Wilson, A. 53
worldview 25–51, 167–9; African American offending 26–9; perceptions of racial divide in criminal justice system 32–47; racial discrimination 47–51; racial divide 29–32